The Insider's Guide to
FINDING
THE PERFECT JOB

ROBERT ORNDORFF

Director of Career Services at Elon College in North Carolina,
and Bestselling Author of *The Strategic Job Search*

www.petersons.com

PETERSON'S

THOMSON LEARNING ™

Australia • Canada • Mexico • Singapore • Spain • United Kingdom • United States

An ARCO Book

ARCO is a registered trademark of Thomson Learning, Inc., and is used herein under license by Peterson's.

About Peterson's

Founded in 1966, Peterson's, a division of Thomson Learning, is the nation's largest and most respected provider of lifelong learning online resources, software, reference guides, and books. The Education Supersite^{SM} at petersons.com—the Web's most heavily traveled education resource—has searchable databases and interactive tools for contacting U.S.-accredited institutions and programs. CollegeQuest^{SM} (CollegeQuest.com) offers a complete solution for every step of the college decision-making process. GradAdvantage^{TM} (GradAdvantage.org), developed with Educational Testing Service, is the only electronic admissions service capable of sending official graduate test score reports with a candidate's online application. Peterson's serves more than 55 million education consumers annually.

Thomson Learning is among the world's leading providers of lifelong learning, serving the needs of individuals, learning institutions, and corporations with products and services for both traditional classrooms and for online learning. For more information about the products and services offered by Thomson Learning, please visit www.thomsonlearning.com. Headquartered in Stamford, Connecticut, with offices worldwide, Thomson Learning is part of The Thomson Corporation (www.thomson.com), a leading e-information and solutions company in the business, professional, and education marketplaces. The Corporation's common shares are listed on the Toronto and London stock exchanges.

For more information, contact Peterson's, 2000 Lenox Drive, Lawrenceville, NJ 08648; 800-338-3282; or find us on the World Wide Web at: www.petersons.com/about

Library of Congress Cataloging-in-Publication Data
Orndorff, Robert.
  Insider's guide to finding the perfect job / Robert Orndorff.
    p. cm
  Includes bibliographical references.
  ISBN 0-7689-0591-5
    1. Job hunting—United States. I. Title.
HF5382.75.U6 O76 2000
650.14—dc21   00-062352

Printed in Canada

10 9 8 7 6 5 4 3 2 1   02 01 00

Contents

Contents

Introduction

Why This Book?

INSIDE ADVICE FROM TOP RECRUITERS

No other job-hunting book—to my knowledge—has ever included the number of quotes and viewpoints from recruiters as this book does. In other job-hunting books, you get advice from one person—the author. And each author, including myself, has his or her own biases toward finding a job. It's best to receive advice and perspectives from more than one person. And who better to get perspectives from than those doing the hiring—the recruiters?

Recruiters from eleven of the top organizations in America have offered their advice on every major job-hunting topic. The recruiters give you the inside scoop on how to write the strongest resumes and cover letters, how to win interviews, and how to find the best jobs. These inside quotes are found in every chapter of the book.

The companies offering quotes are as follows:

- Andersen Consulting
- Arthur Andersen
- Bell Atlantic
- Enterprise Rent-A-Car
- Glaxo Wellcome
- Jefferson Pilot
- John Hancock
- Johnson & Johnson
- Lab Corp
- Peace Corps
- Research Triangle Institute

ALL JOB-SEARCH TOPICS ARE THOROUGHLY COVERED

Due to the complexity of job hunting today, there's so much you need to know about finding the job that's perfect for you. Most job-hunting books cover some areas of job hunting thoroughly and other areas not so thoroughly. Authors tend to have strengths in certain parts of job hunting more so than in other parts. So, you'll get, for example, five chapters on interviewing and only one chapter on resume writing, or vice versa. In the *Insider's Guide to Findng the Perfect Job,* you'll receive detailed information on all stages of the job search—from choosing the perfect job to landing the perfect job. There's even a chapter that reveals strategies for succeeding *on the job*. I won't refer you to other books on resumes or interviewing to help fill gaps; each topic is completely covered.

YOUR OWN PERSONAL JOB-SEARCH TRAINER

As you move along through the chapters, you'll have the opportunity to build your own job-search plan that will serve as your roadmap to finding the perfect job. Your Personal Job Search Trainer outlines the specific strategies and tasks needed to conduct a successful job search. Within this outline, you'll fill in the strategies and resources that you want to use, based on the author's recommendations and referrals. Once you've completed your plan with the help of your Personal Job Search Trainer, you'll be ready to start searching for that perfect job!

HOW THIS BOOK IS ORGANIZED

This book is divided into six parts, each one covering a different topic of job hunting.

Part I

"Targeting the Perfect Job in the 21st Century" begins by providing you with an overview of the current trends in the 21st-century workforce. You'll then learn about and participate in self-assessment exercises to help you identify your skills, interests, personal qualities, and values related to the world of work. Finally, you'll learn how to explore careers and jobs to help you narrow down your options and identify the perfect job to pursue.

Part II

"Developing Your Self-Marketing Package" teaches you how to craft a perfect resume and write powerful cover letters. You'll be introduced to a new, cutting-edge resume style. You'll also learn how to generate references and develop portfolios.

Part III

"Finding the Perfect Job" describes all the best job-search strategies and how to use them in finding your perfect job. A 7-step networking plan is featured. You'll also learn about the "3 Ps to Success" in Chapter 8, which presents the three keys to a successful job search.

Part IV

"Landing the Perfect Job" presents inside information on how to prepare for and win interviews. "The Perfect 10" outlines the ten best interviewing strategies to use on your big day. You'll also learn how to evaluate and negotiate job offers.

Part V

"Succeeding on the Job" presents the 10 Career Commandments for realizing success on your new job and throughout your career.

Part VI

The appendices provide you with recommendations of the best Internet sites and printed resources out on the market today. Also provided in the appendices is a long list of the most common interview questions as well as the best questions to ask your networking contacts.

Special Features

Sidebars

To help you quickly and easily get the most out of this book, the text is enhanced with the following special sidebars:

FYI: Strategies that offer an easier or smarter way to do something
           Cautions and warnings about pitfalls to avoid
           An insider's fact or anecdote

Guidance: Statements from recruiters who can give you valuable
           insights

Your Personal Job Search Trainer

"Your Personal Job Search Trainer" is included in the back of the book for you to tear out and use as you move through the book. Your Personal Job Search Trainer is intended to help you structure your job search by developing a detailed action plan. Complete each of the goals that your trainer outlines when prompted by the author or move at your own pace.

ABOUT THE AUTHOR

Robert M. Orndorff holds a doctoral degree from Penn State University, specializing in career development, and is the Director of Career Services and Assistant Professor at Elon College near Burlington, North Carolina. He has worked at four other college career centers: Georgetown University, Indiana University of Pennsylvania, Penn State University, and Moravian College. While at Georgetown, Bob created *The Strategic Job Search,* which won a national award for "the best educational program related to career services in the nation."(Awarded by the National Association of Colleges and Employers)

Bob has authored articles on career planning and job searching and has been featured in such national journals as the *Journal of Counseling and Development.* He also has conducted book reviews related to job hunting for the National Association of Colleges and Employers. In addition to working in higher education, Bob is a career consultant in the education and business industries. Currently, Bob is consulting with the Alamance-Burlington NC Area Schools on developing a comprehensive career guidance program (K-16). He also has experience in private industry as a career and outplacement consultant, working with adults who are seeking employment or changing careers. Bob and his wife, Chris, and daughter, Jessica, reside in Burlington, North Carolina.

ACKNOWLEDGEMENTS

It would have been impossible to author a book and hold down a full-time job without the support and encouragement from my family, friends, and colleagues. The love and joy that I receive every day from my wife, Chris, and two-year old daughter, Jessica, provide me with a constant source of inspiration. You're the reason I smile so much! The greatest mother and father in the world—my parents—have given me so much, I'd have to write another book. My brother and sister, Erik and Kelly, who are my two best friends and biggest fans: what can I say? How lucky was I to be sandwiched in between the two of you growing up? Rocky, Julie, and Bo—my extra-special nephews and niece: I'll now have more time to make our commercials! Grandma O and Pop: Thanks for starting an incredible family. Nan and Pap, I know you're looking down and smiling; this book's for you! Thanks to my special uncles, aunts, and cousins in the Orndorff and Bair families. Thanks to my other sisters and brothers: Missy, Alicia, Peteman, Greg, Jeff, and Steve. Thanks to my mother- and father-in-law, Jean and Gene, and to the rest of the Logan Clan! And a special thanks to my three childhood, adolescent, and adult best friends: Pat, Todd, and John; thanks guys, for being there all those years! Thanks to all of my friends I've been blessed with—you know who you are!

A special thanks to my two professional mentors, Dr. Jack Rayman and Dr. Edwin Herr. I was blessed to be tutored by two of the most insightful and knowledgeable career development specialists in the world. I literally couldn't have completed this book without the support from my colleagues at Elon College—higher education's best-kept secret in America. Thanks to our Career Center staff, Pam, Steven, Debby, Kathy, and Jonathan, for "holding down the fort" while I was writing. Thanks to Lela Faye Rich, my boss and friend, for encouraging me along the way. To my exceptional former bosses, Ruth Riesenman, Jane Carey, and Bev Kochard: thanks for your patience and wisdom!

I was extremely fortunate to have such a talented and cool editor—Aaron Hartlett— work along side me during the writing of my first major book. Thanks, too, to Dave Henthorn for all of your positive encouragement along the way. A special thanks to my creative brother

Erik, for coming up with "The Whole in One" title used at the end of each chapter. Finally, I owe so much to my personal/professional mentors— Dr. Anthony Ceddia, president of my alma mater, Shippensburg University, and my Dad, Dr. Robert Orndorff, Retired Vice President of Shippensburg. I am very lucky to have two outstanding leaders in American higher education in my corner!

A special thanks also to the recruiters that contributed their viewpoints. You've added a lot to the book and offered great advice to our readers: Michelle Cacdac, David Reed (Andersen Consulting); Dana Ellis (Arthur Andersen); Kristin Dempsey, Donnie Edgemon, Kristin Murphy (Bell Atlantic); Mei Ling Ching, Al Pollard (Enterprise Rent-a-Car); Jane Hertel (Glaxo Wellcome); Al Capps (Jefferson Pilot); Roger Brooks (John Hancock); Kevin Renahan (Johnson & Johnson); Natalie Pierce (Lab Corp); Alexandra Stanat (Peace Corp); and Christine Carboni (Research Triangle Institute).

Part I

Targeting the Perfect Job in the 21st Century

Chapter 1

The New World of Work: Are You Ready for the 21st Century?

GET THE SCOOP ON . . .

- Major changes in the new world of work
- New sets of skills that employers want
- Personal qualities needed to succeed
- Hot careers and cities

MAJOR CHANGES IN THE NEW WORLD OF WORK

Remember the good old days of job stability and company loyalty? Maybe you don't. If you haven't had a career talk with your parents or grandparents yet, you should. Your grandfather or grandmother can tell you that in the good old days, people stayed in the same career field and were loyal to their company. Most workers back then climbed the corporate ladder to success by moving up within the same company. Work was work; it wasn't something they expected to enjoy. If you happened to like your job, it was a bonus. Work was also very streamlined and task oriented. People, for the most part, specialized in carrying out one job and using one main skill.

Times have changed. Before you get started looking for that perfect job, it's important for you to know the work environment that exists today. You must understand the new workforce culture and develop the skills and qualities needed to be successful in it. The major changes in the current and future workforce are outlined later. Additional Internet sites and printed resources can be found under "Career and Workforce Trends" in Appendix A and Appendix C, respectively.

Downsizing and the Emergence of Smaller Companies

As we all are too well aware, companies have been laying off many employees and eliminating numerous jobs, especially middle manage-

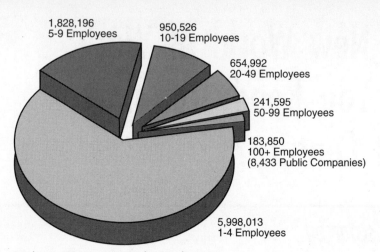

1,828,196
5-9 Employees

950,526
10-19 Employees

654,992
20-49 Employees

241,595
50-99 Employees

183,850
100+ Employees
(8,433 Public Companies)

5,998,013
1-4 Employees

Total U.S. Business Counts by Employee Size

ment jobs. In Fortune 500 companies alone, approximately 15 million jobs have been eliminated over the last twenty years. The elimination of jobs takes place due to market demand, organizational restructuring, building new business processes, incorporating new technology, and relocation of work. In the 1990s, close to 48 percent of companies eliminated jobs. Downsizing occurs when the number of jobs eliminated is greater than the number of jobs created. According to the American Management Association, in the 1990s, approximately 30 percent of companies downsized. (Source: Reprinted by permission from *1997 AMA Survey on Corporate Job Creation, Job Elimination, and Downsizing.* Copyright © 1997 American Management Association International, New York, NY. All rights reserved. http:www.amanet.org.)

At the same time, the number of small companies joining the workforce has grown considerably. In fact, almost all of last year's job growth occurred in small and medium-sized companies (under 500 employees). Look at the pie chart above and figures following reported by the American Business Information, a division of Info USA Inc., February, 1998.

A Service-Dominated Job Sector

In the 1970s, approximately 54 percent of the jobs were in the service sector, and 46 percent were in the manufacturing sector. Today, these percentages are closer to 80 percent and 20 percent, respectively. New jobs over the next five years are expected to be dominated even more by the service sector. The U.S. Bureau of Labor Statistics (BLS) estimates that by 2005, almost 93 percent of new jobs created will be in service-producing industries.

Job- and Company-Hopping and Job Security

Today's work environment is riddled with uncertainty and change, creating employees who tend to change jobs more frequently either out of desire or necessity. The challenge to the employer is to create an environment that effectively manages staffing fluctuations; changing skill mixes without losing opportunities to retain and maybe re-train talented workers.
—Glaxo Wellcome

Spending your entire career with one company is a thing of the past. Due to the downsizing and increase in small companies, there's less room to move up within the same company. Therefore, in order to move up, many times you'll need to move out. The average worker in the 21st century is projected to change jobs at least seven times in their lifetime.

Employees are Taking Control of Their Own Careers

With all this job-hopping and downsizing, employees are no longer expecting their company to take care of them for life. It's very important for today's workers to constantly be thinking and planning ahead, even when things at work seem great. In a recent Towers Perrin survey, 9 out of 10 people reported that they are taking personal responsibility for their career development. Specifically, 94 percent of the respondents reported that *they* are responsible for their careers, not their employers. (Source: Towers Perrin Workplace Index)

Globalization of the World of Work

With the Internet, air travel, and satellite communication, the economies of countries throughout the world are meshing. Just by looking at the cars on the road, it's obvious that other countries are affecting the workplace here in the states. Cars such as Hondas are made both in Japan and here in the U.S. Volkswagens are made in Germany and the U.S. The former Chrysler Corporation is now owned by Daimler/Chrysler, with headquarters in Germany.

Because of the strong economy and low unemployment, our job candidates now have more options than ever before. So the trends that we are seeing are directly related to them having a lot more options, being more picky, and looking at the career opportunity in more depth before making decisions.
—Jefferson Pilot

Think of some of the products you recently bought. Toys sold in the states are manufactured in China, Korea, and elsewhere. McDonald's hamburgers, Coke, and Pepsi are sold in countries all over the world.

Because of this globalization of economies, employers have greater expectations that their employees will be able to think and communicate with a global perspective. Geographical, cultural, and language proficiencies allow employees and job seekers to be more marketable in the new world of work.

Diversity in the Workplace

The workplace is becoming increasingly more diverse. Dominance by the white male in the workforce is gradually coming to an end. Women and racial and ethnic minorities are joining the work force at a much higher rate than white males. Take a look at the following information produced by the Bureau of Labor Statistics.

By the year 2006, women are expected to make up 47 percent of the labor force. From 1996 to 2006, Asian Americans and Hispanics are projected to have the largest net increases of employment growth, 41 and 36 percent, respectively. The rate of growth for African Americans is expected to be 14 percent.

The Emergence of Projects and Teams

In the past, when you were hired by a company, you were given a detailed job description that laid out all your daily responsibilities and duties in very detailed and very specific terms. You were evaluated yearly on the basis of how well *you* completed *your* responsibilities, and, with the exception of a few added responsibilities every year, your job stayed the same. Well, times have changed. In a service-dominated and technology-driven global market, organizational clients have many different needs that frequently change. Therefore, many companies must work with their clients on a project-to-project basis to most effectively fulfill their unique needs.

Since each project is different, a different number of people with different skill sets are required to successfully complete each project. Some projects are larger and require more people to complete them. Some projects are more technical in nature and require people with technical skills. Today, companies are trying to hire people with a wide variety of skills that can move from one team or project to another.

The consulting industry is the most obvious example of project-oriented work. In order to help a company become more efficient and productive, a consulting firm must assess existing technological systems, organizational procedures, personnel, and lines of communication. A team made up of only those members with technical skills lacks the expertise in organizational processes and staffing needed to make a complete evaluation.

To be successful in today's world of work, you must be able to adapt to new situations and projects and work within teams.

The Computer Age: High Tech, Low Touch

Perhaps the greatest influential force affecting the workplace today is technology. Computers are taking over the world—at least the world of work. Moving from face-to-face meetings to teleconferencing, to faxing proposals, to e-mailing and virtual chat sessions, the work world is increasingly moving to a high-tech, low-touch environment. Few would disagree that the incorporation of the computer and the Internet has saved companies lots of time and money. Few would also disagree that computers have changed the way we do business. For example, in the human resources industry, technology used to recruit job candidates has recently increased dramatically. In 1995, 40 percent of employers used electronic job sources to find job candidates. In 1997, this figure

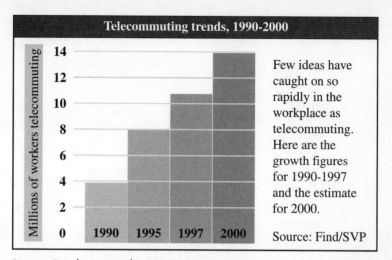

Source: Graph presented in *Career Opportunities News,* Ferguson Publishing, Chicago.

more than doubled, reaching 88 percent (Source: Lee Hecht Harrison). Regardless of what industry or career field you want to enter, the demand for computer skills among all workers and job seekers is at an all-time high.

More and More People are Working from Home

These emerging technologies have also led to the emergence of a new type of worker—the telecommuter. The widespread use of e-mail, fax machines, teleconferencing, and other technologies have made it possible for people to do their jobs as effectively at home as in the office. Approximately 10 million employees now work out of their homes, and the number is on the rise. Notice how this trend has consistently increased since 1990 in the graph above.

Telecommuting is very popular among high-tech companies. Close to 20 percent of employees working for IBM worldwide currently spend a minimum of two days out of the office. Take a look at some of the telecommuting-friendly employers in table 1.

A NEW TYPE OF WORKER IS EMERGING

All of these changes—downsizing, service-domination, diversity in the workplace, job-hopping, and globalization— have affected the workforce, and, as a result, a new type of worker is emerging. Not only are the skills of the emerging worker different, but their needs, expectations, and attitudes are different as well. In a recent study from Interim Services, Inc., six major differences between the "Traditional" worker and the "Emerging" worker were found. Take a look at these differences in table 2.

Table 1. Telecommuting-Friendly Employers

Employer	Percent of work force telecommuting
Arthur Andersen	20
AT&T	55
Cisco Systems	66
Hewlett-Packard	8
IBM	20
Leisure Company/America West	16
Merrill Lynch	5

Source: Reprinted from the October 12, 1998, issue of *Business Week* by special permission. © 1998 by McGraw-Hill Companies.

What Employers are Looking For

These changes in the new world of work drive the need for new skills and personal characteristics among employees and job candidates. Companies want people who can thrive in this new type of work environment, and they know that to do, so employees need certain skills. Following are the top 10 skills as well as the top 10 personal characteristics that employers want, based on a survey conducted by the National Association of Colleges and Employers (NACE).

Guidance

Our environments are team oriented, so skills that add to the effectiveness of teams are highly valued. Skills such as interpersonal skills, partnering skills, collaboration, and communication skills are highly desirable for our potential employees.
— Johnson & Johnson

Table 2. New Type of Emerging Workers

Traditional	Emerging
Demand long-term job security	Job security not a driver of commitment
Are less satisfied with their jobs	Are more satisfied with their jobs
Changing jobs damaging to careers	Changing jobs often part of growth
Defines loyalty as tenure	Defines loyalty as accomplishment
Work is opportunity for income	Work provides a chance to grow
Employer responsible for career	Individual is responsible for career

The Skills Employers Want

- Interpersonal
- Teamwork
- Analytical
- Oral communication
- Flexibility

- Computer
- Written communication
- Leadership
- Work experience
- Internship/Co-op experience

Top 10 Personal Characteristics Employers Seek in Job Candidates

- Honesty/Integrity
- Motivation/Initiative
- Communication skills
- Self-confidence
- Flexibility

- Interpersonal skills
- Strong work ethic
- Teamwork skills
- Leadership skills
- Enthusiasm

Source: *Job Outlook, 1998.* National Association of Colleges and Employers

Why These Skills and Qualities are Important

Notice that interpersonal, teamwork, communication, flexibility, and leadership were areas included in both skills and personal characteristics lists. Each of these are qualities that can be developed into useful skills in the workplace. It's important that you clearly understand why these skills and personal characteristics are valued in the new workplace. The best way to convince you of their importance is to show you how dependent they are on changes in the new world of work. These skills are closely related to and, in fact, have emerged because of how much the world of work has changed.

Interpersonal and Teamwork Skills

Notice that the top 2 skills employers want are *people skills:* interpersonal and teamwork. The increase of project work and diversity in the workplace have made these skills extremely valuable to companies. To be successful working in teams and with a wide variety of people from different cultures, you must have strong interpersonal and teamwork skills. Maintaining a positive attitude, handling conflicts tactfully, and having a sense of humor are just a few of the interpersonal skills needed to work well in teams and relate well with a wide variety of people.

Analytical Skills

You must have strong analytical skills to keep up with the ever-changing workplace and computer systems. New problems and situations arise daily and must be assessed and solved. Clients come from different backgrounds and have different perspectives. In order to meet their varying needs and values, workers must be able to think "outside the box."

Oral and Written Communication skills

With a service-dominated economy and emphasis on teams, you must be able to communicate well with clients and colleagues. Writing skills continue to be important. Today's worker is responsible for writing and producing memos, reports, business letters, and many other documents.

Technology has greatly impacted the way we communicate. Clients, co-workers, and supervisors expect to receive information immediately. Time is money! Faxing and e-mailing have become the preferred methods of communicating to someone in writing because they save so much time. Being able to send information quickly means you'll have to prepare it quickly. You must be able to write quickly without sacrificing quality or clarity.

Strong oral and written communication skills are also important in developing and maintaining relationships with clients in foreign markets. Communicating in more than one language is becoming increasingly important in order to do business in the global workforce.

Flexibility

The rise of small businesses and downsizing of larger corporations causes current professionals to wear more hats than ever before. One week you may find yourself minimally assisting a project team that's consulting with a small domestic company, while the next week you may be leading a large project team while working with a Fortune 500 international giant.

As the new workplace becomes more and more transient, the ability to adapt to new working relationships, new jobs, and different companies is more crucial than ever before.

Computer Skills

The importance of computer skills in high-tech occupations such as programming and information systems is obvious. But in our high-tech, low-touch environment, computer skills are important in almost *all* jobs. At the minimum, most jobs today require proficiency in word processing and using the Internet, especially e-mail. Many other jobs require knowledge and efficiency in using a field-specific or company-specific computer application. It could be a special type of database, spreadsheet, or custom-made application that you must learn.

Leadership Skills and Self-confidence

Companies are looking for candidates who are self-confident, outgoing, and self-starters, all of which are characteristics of a good leader. Organizations need to find people who are not afraid to lead others on various project teams and new initiatives. With fewer people doing more work, job seekers with the ability to take the initiative and lead are highly sought after.

Work Experience, Internships, and Co-op Experience

Because companies have become leaner, they have less time and personnel to devote to training and hand-holding for new employees. They're looking for candidates who have prior experience using the skills needed to perform the job at hand. For high school and college students, completing an internship is more important than ever.

Honesty/Integrity and Strong Work Ethic

There's no substitute for old-fashioned honesty and hard work. Regardless of how skilled and competent you are, the factor that separates most professionals is hard work. Putting in the extra hours, concentrating on tasks, and staying organized are not necessarily fun or exciting, but they add up to success. Being honest with co-workers and clients is the best way to maintain positive, long-lasting working relationships.

Motivation/Initiative and Enthusiasm

Recruiters know that a candidate's motivation and enthusiasm toward the job and company are critical factors of success and retention. If you can't prove to prospective employers that your heart is in the job and that you genuinely want to work for their company, then they'll find someone who can. Typically, the more enthusiastic you are about your job, the more productive you will be. The characteristics of the job and company that you choose should ideally be consistent with your personal interests and values.

> **Guidance**
>
> *Strong personal initiative: We are looking for people who proactively identify opportunities and issues, then persevere to achieve desired results.*
>
> —Arthur Andersen

HOT OCCUPATIONS AND CITIES

There are many factors to consider when deciding on the right career to pursue. In the next chapter, you'll learn about the importance of assessing your interests, skills, values, and personal qualities and determining how they relate to career options. It's also important to keep in mind those jobs and career fields that are currently in demand and those that are projected to be in demand in the future. As the workforce changes, different jobs become more or less in demand.

The types of occupations that are in demand in the 21st century world of work are presented later. The cities that will have the greatest employment growth are also presented. It's a good idea to keep an eye on these hot occupations and cities as you explore various career options.

Fastest Growing Occupations

The fastest growing occupations are occupations projected to add the highest percentage of jobs from 1996 to 2006. For example, in table 3, a 109 percent change for computer engineers means that the number of computer engineers needed in 2006 (451,000) is more than double the number needed ten years previously (215,700).

Hot Occupations by Educational Level

The following table identifies occupations projected to have the fastest rate of job growth in ten years, broken down by educational level. Find your appropriate educational level, and see what types of jobs that will be in demand.

High School Diploma Plus Up to One Year of Job Experience

- Home-care aides
- Retail salespersons
- Amusement attendants
- Truck drivers
- Cashiers
- Teacher's aides and educational assistants
- Medical assistants
- Dental assistants

Educational Level Open but Long-Term Work or Training Required

- Desktop-publishing specialists
- Musicians
- Flight attendants
- Police patrol officers
- Food service and lodging managers
- Carpenters
- Clerical supervisors
- Cooks, restaurant

Career School or Other Vocational Training

- Data-processing equipment repairers
- Manicurists
- Licensed Practical Nurses
- Surgical technologists
- Cosmetologists or barbers
- Medical secretaries
- Emergency Medical Technicians
- Automotive mechanics

Associate (Two-Year College) Degree

- Dental hygienists
- Registered Nurses
- Paralegals
- Radiologic technologists
- Respiratory therapists
- Health information technicians
- Cardiology technologists

Bachelor's Degree

- Database administrators
- Computer engineers
- Special education teachers
- Systems analysts
- Physical and corrective therapy assistants and aides

Master's Degree

- Physical and occupational therapists
- Speech pathologists
- Operations research analysts
- Librarians
- Psychologists
- Counselors
- Curators and archivists

TABLE 3. Top 25 Fastest Growing Occupations
(From 1996 to 2006)

Occupation	Employment		Percent Change*
	1996	2006	
Computer engineers	215,700	451,000	109
Systems analysts, electronic data processing	505,500	1,025,100	103
Personal and home-care aides	202,500	373,900	85
Physical and corrective	84,500	150,900	79
Therapy assistants and aides; Home-health aides	94,700	872,900	77
Electronic pagination	30,400	52,800	74
Medical assistants	224,800	391,200	74
Physical therapists	114,500	195,600	71
Occupational therapy assistants and aides	15,700	26,400	69
Paralegal personnel	112,900	189,300	68
Occupational therapists	57,400	95,300	66
Teachers, special education	407,000	647,700	59
Human services workers	177,800	276,300	55
Data processing equipment repairers	79,700	121,500	52
Medical records technicians	87,300	131,800	51
Speech-language pathologists and audiologists	87,300	131,500	51
Amusement and recreation attendants	288,100	426,100	48
Dental hygienists	132,800	196,800	48
Physician's assistants	63,800	93,500	47
Adjustment clerks	401,300	583,900	46
Respiratory therapists	81,800	119,300	46
Emergency medical technicians	149,700	217,100	45
Engineering, mathematical, and natural sciences managers	342,900	498,000	45
Manicurists	43,100	62,400	45
Bill and account collectors	268,600	381,100	42

* The national average percent change is between 10 and 20.
Source: Bureau of Labor Statistics, 1996

Doctorate
- Biological scientists
- Mathematicians and related fields
- College faculty member
- Medical scientists

Professional Degree
- Lawyers
- Veterinarians
- Physicians
- Chiropractors
- Clergy
- Dentists

Minichart developed by the Career Opportunity News, Ferguson Publishing, Chicago, based on data from the *Occupational Outlook Handbook*, 1998–99.

WHAT IT ALL MEANS TO YOU

Guidance

Other workforce trends include developing transferable skills in order to function in different business units. Employees that can understand processes, technology, and people will be an asset to the organization.

—Bell Atlantic

The days when the company took care of the career development of its workers are over. You must become self-sufficient when it comes to progressing through your career and job searching. Keep your resume updated and references current. Anticipate next steps by examining prospective jobs and companies, even when you are content in your current position. Remember that you're likely to change jobs close to seven times in your lifetime.

It's important to realize that most skills are transferable from one job to another and from one career field to another. It's critical that you constantly and consistently assess the skills that you enjoy utilizing and the parts of the job that are most rewarding. In doing this, you will have the capability of identifying that next perfect job and the one after that.

THE WHOLE IN ONE

- Smaller companies, diversity in the workplace, job-hopping employees, new technologies, global markets, and projects replacing jobs are some of the major concepts changing the way we do business.

- Interpersonal, analytical, computer, and communication skills, combined with teamwork, flexibility, leadership, motivation, self-confidence, honesty, and enthusiasm, are some of the top skills and qualities that current and future employers will be looking for in candidates.

- To succeed in the new world of work, you must be in control of your own destiny and examine your transferable skills on an ongoing basis.

Chapter 2

Self-Assessment: Establishing Your Professional Self-Profile

GET THE SCOOP ON . . .

- Identifying your perfect job target through self-assessment
- Being true to yourself
- Determining your skills
- Identifying your interests
- Prioritizing your values
- Knowing your personal characteristics
- Career-assessment instruments
- Career decision-making styles
- Your Professional Self-Profile

HOW SELF-ASSESSMENT HELPS YOU IDENTIFY YOUR PERFECT JOB TARGET

Before you can begin to search for the perfect job, you must have a good idea of what that perfect job looks like or what you are targeting. In other words, you need a "perfect job target" to shoot for. The perfect job target is not the same for everybody. Your perfect job is the job that is perfect for *you*! It's one that you're good at (skills), that you enjoy (interests), that makes you happy (values), and that allows you to be yourself (personality). So you don't need to look far to begin searching for the perfect job target. The first step is to take a good long look at yourself and assess your skills, interests, values, and personality.

Your top skills, interests, values, and personal qualities presented together is called your *Professional Self-Profile*. Your *Professional Self-Profile* will be used to eliminate career options that aren't a good match and to identify ones that are. In other words, your Professional Self-Profile will point you in the right direction as you begin to explore career options in Chapter 3. If you think of your job search as being similar to climbing a mountain, self-assessment is the first step toward the top. Take a look at the illustration "The 5-Step Climb To Your Perfect Job" on the next page.

As you can see, self-assessment lets you eliminate many career fields and occupations and will make your list of prospective jobs to explore much more manageable. Once you go through the exercises in this chapter, you will be able to build your Professional Self-Profile.

The 5-Step Climb To Your Perfect Job

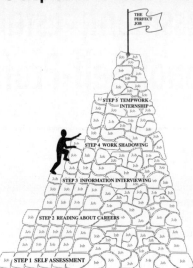

THE IMPORTANCE OF BEING TRUE TO YOURSELF

FYI

It may seem silly to you, but television and movies have proven to be strong external influences of career choices. When "LA Law" was big in the 1980s, the number of job seekers who chose law as their job target increased greatly. Today, shows like "E.R." and "Chicago Hope" are affecting the number of people entering medical and nursing schools.

Only *you* can truly determine what your perfect job looks like. However, for many job seekers, that perfect job has a tendency to stray off target due to external influences like societal norms, family and friends, television and movies, and significant others. Today, our American society's picture of success includes a huge house, overpriced sport-utility vehicles, and exotic vacations. Many job seekers choose a job target that will let them make enough money to reach *society's* level of success. This is fine if society's picture of success is consistent with yours or if you genuinely enjoy those jobs that make a lot of money. Just don't sacrifice your true interests and values.

Close friends and family will have the greatest impact on your job search. A large number of younger job seekers choose a job target that is closely related to a parent's or relative's position. Others are influenced by the type or level of jobs that their group of friends holds.

External influences will always exist. The question is how you handle them. Letting external influences manipulate your job search usually results in you working in a job that is less than perfect. You must be aware of these external influences and stay in control of making your own decisions. *You* are the final judge. You are the one who will get up each day and spend at least eight hours on the job. It's easy to fool ourselves into thinking a job is perfect for us when it really isn't. As you assess your skills, interests, values, personality, and decision-making style on the following pages, make sure you're honest with yourself.

HOW SELF-ASSESSMENT INSTRUMENTS WORK

Guidance

Self-assessment is an investment strategy. As a full-fledged member of the workforce, you're going to be spending at least eight hours a day, five days a week, 50 weeks a year, at work. Do yourself and the organization you work for a favor and determine what's enjoyable to you and will keep you "turned on."

—Andersen
Consulting

Self-assessment instruments and exercises provide a structured way for you to assess yourself. Through a lengthy series of questions, these instruments identify your strengths and weaknesses, your interests, and to some extent, even the career field that's right for you. Many self-assessment instruments require a trained, professional career counselor to administer the test and process the results. A certified career counselor is trained to interpret the results in an unbiased manner. The exercises presented in this book are ones that you can perform and score yourself. While these exercises are a great way to assess yourself, it doesn't hurt to complete some of the commercial assessment instruments as well. Some of these are explained later in this chapter. Refer to Appendix C, under "Self-Assessment," for a recommended list of self-assessment instruments.

As you complete the self-assessment exercises and instruments, be completely honest with yourself. It's tempting to answer in ways that make us look more like the people we wish we were, rather than the people we really are. You're only hurting yourself in the long run if you're not 100 percent honest.

THE IMPORTANCE OF DETERMINING YOUR SKILLS

There are many benefits to identifying your skills. First, knowing your skills will help you decide on a perfect job target. Second, in order to sell yourself to prospective employers, you must be able to express your skills on your resume and cover letter and during an interview. Third, it's helpful to know which skills you have that will be useful in conducting your job search. For example, if researching is one of your skills, you'll want to put that skill to work in researching companies and job prospects.

At this point, you simply want to *identify* all your skills. Later, when you have identified your perfect job target, you'll need to prioritize those skills that are most valued by the companies you're pursuing. The recruiters care only about those skills you have that are most important to performing well on the job.

Become "Skilled-Aware"

Job seekers fall into one of two categories: *skilled-aware* or *skilled-unaware*. Skilled-aware job seekers know what their skills are and can discuss them at length. Skilled-unaware job seekers also have skills, but they don't know what they are and, therefore, aren't able to talk about them. It's very important for you to be skilled-aware so that you can sell your skills to prospective employers. You may be an extremely skilled individual, but if you can't sell your skills to a recruiter, they do you no good. The goal of the following exercises is to make sure that you become, if you aren't already, "skilled-aware."

Skill Assessment Exercises
Exercise 2.1: Identifying Skill Families

Rank how strong you are in each skill below.

1–Very Weak   2–Weak   3–Average   4–Strong   5–Very Strong

____ Advising	____ Empowering	____ Presenting
____ Analyzing	people	____ Prioritizing
____ Articulating	____ Entertaining	____ Programming
____ Auditing	____ Evaluating	____ Projecting
____ Budgeting	____ Examining	____ Promoting
____ Building	____ Expressing	____ Providing
____ Calculating	____ Facilitating	therapy
____ Coaching	groups	____ Record keeping
____ Collaborating	____ Initiating	____ Repairing
____ Communicating	____ Inspecting	____ Reporting
____ Compiling	____ Instructing	____ Researching
____ Computing	____ Interpreting	____ Resolving
____ Conceptualizing	____ Interviewing	conflicts
____ Confronting	____ Inventing	____ Selling
____ Constructing	____ Investigating	____ Solving problems
____ Consulting	____ Leading people	____ Speaking
____ Coordinating	____ Lecturing	____ Strategic
____ Counseling	____ Listening	planning
____ Creating	____ Managing	____ Supervising
____ Critiquing	____ Marketing	____ Systems analysis
____ Debating	____ Mediating	____ Teaching
____ Decision making	____ Motivating	____ Teamwork
____ Delegating	____ Negotiating	____ Translating
____ Designing	____ Organizing	____ Visioning
____ Developing	____ Persuading	____ Working
____ Drafting	____ Planning	together
____ Editing	____ Preparing	____ Writing

On a piece of paper, list all of those skills that received a ranking of 5. (If there are fewer than five skills receiving a 5, list all skills receiving a 4 or 5.)

Identify Skill Families

Of your top skills, try to group similar skills together and form *skill families*. See the skill families that follow. If you have trouble identifying skill families, use these to identify those that best fit you.

Skill Families

1. Analyzing/Evaluating/Examining/Inspecting
2. Budgeting/Auditing/Recordkeeping/Calculating/Projecting
3. Computing/Programming/Analyzing systems
4. Conceptualizing/Visioning
5. Confronting/Critiquing/Debating/Negotiating
6. Constructing/Building/Repairing/Providing therapy
7. Coordinating/Planning/Preparing
8. Counseling/Advising/Mediating/Listening
9. Creating/Designing/Initiating/Inventing/Developing/Drafting
10. Decision making
11. Entertaining/Expressing
12. Facilitating groups
13. Interpreting/Translating
14. Managing/Supervising/Leading/Motivating/Empowering people
15. Organizing/Prioritizing/Delegating/Strategic Planning
16. Researching/Investigating/Reporting/Compiling/Interviewing
17. Selling/Persuading/Promoting/Marketing/Consulting
18. Solving problems/Resolving conflicts
19. Speaking/Lecturing/Presenting
20. Teaching/Coaching/Instructing
21. Teamwork/Collaborating/Working together
22. Writing/Editing/Communicating/Articulating

Exercise 2.2: Identifying Skills through Past Experiences

While ranking skills is very helpful, so is looking to your past experiences. In fact, one of the more effective ways to identify skills is to examine your past. It's usually easier to determine what you do well when you actually have tested your skills.

List your past experience (an activity, work experience, project, etc.), your key responsibilities, and the skills utilized to carry out those responsibilities. Then on a scale of 1–5 (5 being strongest), rank how well you performed each skill. The following sample illustrates how to complete this exercise.

Experience	Duties	Skills Used	Strength (1–5)
Chairperson, Business Club	Ran staff meetings	Delegating	4
		Speaking	5
		Motivating	3
		Organizing	2
	Coordinated banquet	Planning	3
		Delegating	4
		Organizing	3
		Negotiating	5

Identify the Skills Employers Want

In addition to the skills previously identified, you should determine what skills you have that are currently in high demand. As you read in Chapter 1, there's a general list of skills known as "hot" skills that most employers look for in candidates. Rank these skills based on your effectiveness. You may want to add your top two or three "hot" skills to your final list of skills you'll compile at the end of the chapter.

____ Interpersonal   ____ Flexibility

____ Teamwork   ____ Computer

____ Analytical   ____ Written communication

____ Oral communication   ____ Leadership

IDENTIFYING YOUR INTERESTS

Guidance

Just think, it's probably easier to find a career that fits your skills and interests than to fit yourself into a career that is not compatible with you. You want to grow with your chosen career— not grow out of it!
—Peace Corps

It's as important to identify your interests as it is your skills when you're looking for your perfect job target. What you *can* do is often very different from what you *like* to do. While I am fairly good at solving math problems, I don't particularly like doing them. When trying to identify your interests, it's helpful to break it down into *what* you're interested in doing and *where* you're interested in doing it. In other words, what skills do you want to use, and in which industry (where) do you want to use them? For example, you may be interested in utilizing your sales skills, but you still need to choose an industry of interest. You may be interested in the medical industry and choose to become a pharmaceutical salesperson. Or, you may enjoy the financial industry and become an investment banker or insurance salesperson.

Determining What Skills You Are Interested in Using

The two skill exercises you used before can be easily altered to assess your interests. Simply rank your scores based on your *interest* in using each skill rather than your *effectiveness* in using each.

Exercise 2.3: Identifying Your Interests

Rank how strong your interest is in each skill below.

1–Very Weak   2–Weak   3–Average   4–Strong   5–Very Strong

____ Advising	____ Empowering	____ Presenting
____ Analyzing	people	____ Prioritizing
____ Articulating	____ Entertaining	____ Programming
____ Auditing	____ Evaluating	____ Projecting
____ Budgeting	____ Examining	____ Promoting
____ Building	____ Expressing	____ Providing
____ Calculating	____ Facilitating	therapy
____ Coaching	groups	____ Record keeping
____ Collaborating	____ Initiating	____ Repairing
____ Communicating	____ Inspecting	____ Reporting
____ Compiling	____ Instructing	____ Researching
____ Computing	____ Interpreting	____ Resolving
____ Conceptualizing	____ Interviewing	conflicts
____ Confronting	____ Inventing	____ Selling
____ Constructing	____ Investigating	____ Solving problems
____ Consulting	____ Leading people	____ Speaking
____ Coordinating	____ Lecturing	____ Strategic
____ Counseling	____ Listening	planning
____ Creating	____ Managing	____ Supervising
____ Critiquing	____ Marketing	____ Systems analysis
____ Debating	____ Mediating	____ Teaching
____ Decision making	____ Motivating	____ Teamwork
____ Delegating	____ Negotiating	____ Translating
____ Designing	____ Organizing	____ Visioning
____ Developing	____ Persuading	____ Working
____ Drafting	____ Planning	together
____ Editing	____ Preparing	____ Writing

List all those skills that received a ranking of 5. (If there are fewer than five skills receiving a 5, list all skills receiving a 4 or 5.)

Exercise 2.4: Identifying Interests through Past Experiences

You can also easily alter Exercise 2.2 to add an interest component. Add another column that ranks the level of interest you had in using each skill. See the following example.

Experience	Duties	Skills Used	Strength (1–5)	Interest (1–5)
Chairperson, Business Club	Ran staff meetings	Delegating	4	3
		Speaking	5	3
		Motivating	3	4
		Organizing	2	2
	Coordinated banquet	Planning	3	2
		Delegating	4	5
		Organizing	3	5
		Negotiating	5	4

Determining Where You Are Interested in Using the Skills

Now that you've identified the skills you're interested in using, it's time to start focusing on where you want to use them. The industry or career field you choose should be one you enjoy and value. You may love what you do but hate the work environment. For example, Joe Jobhunter loves managing others but not in a large, financial corporation. He's not comfortable around the people with whom he works. Joe is much happier managing people who work in social service agencies, where he feels more at home.

Remember, at this point, you're only trying to identify a list of prospects—not find that one perfect industry.

Exercise 2.5: Identifying a List of Prospective Industries

The following list of industries was generated by the National Association of Colleges and Employers (NACE). On the line beside each industry, enter one of the following three options:

> NI = Not interested in pursuing
> I = Interested in pursuing
> ? = Don't know the industry well enough to decide

Service Employers

____ Accounting (Public)
____ Advertising
____ Architecture
____ Banking (Commercial)

____ Banking (Investment)
____ Communication Services
____ Computer Software
____ Development and Data-
Processing Services

Service Employers—*continued*

____ Consulting Services
____ Engineering/Surveying
____ Environmental/Waste
　　　Management
____ Financial Services
____ Hospitality (Amusements/
　　　Recreation/Fast-Food
　　　Restaurants)
____ Hospitality (Hotels/Motels/
　　　Full-Service Restaurants)
____ Insurance

____ Legal Services
____ Merchandising(Retail/
　　　Wholesale)
____ Personnel Supply Services
____ Protective/Security Services
____ Publishing
____ Real Estate
____ Research Organizations
____ Transportation
____ Utilities
____ Other Services Employers

Manufacturing Employers

____ Aerospace
____ Agriculture and Products
____ Automotive and Mechanical
　　　Equipment
____ Building Materials and
　　　Construction
____ Chemicals and Allied
　　　Products
____ Pharmaceuticals
____ Computers and Business
　　　Equipment
____ Electrical and Electronic
　　　Machinery and Equipment
　　　(including Communica-
　　　tions)
____ Food and Beverage
　　　Processing
____ Household and Personal Care
　　　Products

____ Metals and Metal Products
____ Mining
____ Packaging and Allied
　　　Products
____ Paper and Wood Products
____ Petroleum and Allied
　　　Products
____ Printing
____ Rubber Products
____ Scientific Equipment and
　　　Industrial Measuring
　　　Instruments (including
　　　Medical Supplies)
____ Stone, Clay, Glass and
　　　Concrete Products
____ Textiles and Apparel
____ Widely Diversified
____ Other Manufacturing
　　　Employers

Nonprofit Employers

____ Education
____ Government (Federal)
____ Government (State and
　　　Local)
____ Hospitals
____ Health Services (excluding
　　　Hospitals)
____ Membership Organizations

____ Museums and Cultural
　　　Organizations
____ Religious Organizations
____ Social Services/Private
　　　Agencies
____ Other Nonprofit Employers

From all the industries that received an "I," rank your top five industries at this time:

Top 5 Industry Prospects

1. _____

2. _____

3. _____

4. _____

5. _____

KNOW YOUR PERSONAL CHARACTERISTICS

Unlike your skills, which are acquired through experience, your personal characteristics tend to be qualities with which you are born. They are natural characteristics that simply make you who you are. Examples of personal characteristics are caring, thoughtfulness, friendliness, wisdom, enthusiasm, and sense of humor. Similar to skills, personal qualities are very important factors when deciding on a job target, searching for a job, and performing on the job.

Exercise 2.6: Determining Your Personal Characteristics

Use the following scale to rate yourself on each of the following personal characteristics.

1 = Definitely not a characteristic of mine
2 = Not really a characteristic of mine
3 = Somewhat of a characteristic of mine
4 = A strong characteristic of mine

____ Adaptable	____ Detail-oriented	____ Optimistic
____ Adventurous	____ Diplomatic	____ Outgoing
____ Affectionate	____ Enthusiastic	____ Patient
____ Ambitious	____ Flexible	____ Persistent
____ Artistic	____ Friendly	____ Poised
____ Assertive	____ Funny	____ Practical
____ Caring	____ Happy	____ Reliable
____ Clever	____ High energy	____ Resourceful
____ Competitive	____ Idealistic	____ Responsible
____ Confident	____ Independent	____ Self-critical
____ Conscientious	____ Intelligent	____ Sensitive
____ Conservative	____ Laid back	____ Serious
____ Creative	____ Likable	____ Shy
____ Critical	____ Open-minded	____ Strong-minded

____ Team player   ____ Uninhibited   ____ Verbal

____ Thoughtful   ____ Unselfish   ____ Versatile

____ Understanding

List those personal characteristics that received a score of 4. (If fewer than 5 characteristics received a score of 4, then add those that received a score of 3 also.)

Now rank your top five personal characteristics. The best way to do this is by asking the question, "If I was forced to keep only one characteristic about myself, which would I choose?" Keep asking that question until you have determined your top five. List your top five personal characteristics here:

Top 5 Personal Characteristics

1. _____

2. _____

3. _____

4. _____

5. _____

PRIORITIZING YOUR VALUES

By now, you've identified multiple skills, interests, and personal characteristics that have generated many job and industry prospects. There's more than one job target or industry out there that suits you and that ultimately could make you happy. The bottom line is finding the perfect job target that relates the best to you and makes you happiest overall. Prioritizing your values is a crucial step in the self-assessment process that lets you pinpoint that perfect job target. Prioritizing your values makes you answer the questions, "What is most important to me in a job? Is it the money? Location? The type of skills I am able to use? The level of enjoyment (interest) I have in my job? A caring work atmosphere (personal characteristic)? Or is it that I have my summers off?"

The following exercise provides a list of the most common values associated with work and asks you to assign a degree of importance for each value.

Exercise 2.7: Prioritizing Your Values

Using the following scale, assign a number to each of the following values. Then add the total number for each section and place it on the line provided.

1 = Not important at all
2 = Not very important
3 = Somewhat important
4 = Very important

Professional Outcomes

____ Prestige (status in society, positive recognition)
____ Advancement (opportunity to move up or get promoted)
____ Security (job stability and loyalty)
____ Success (achievement and accomplishment)
____ Professional development (benefits your long-term career)
____ Helping others (helping people or benefiting society)

____ TOTAL

Personal Lifestyle

____ Money (salary, benefits, perks)
____ Family (spending adequate time with family)
____ Location (urban or rural, near family or not, etc.)
____ Leisure (adequate personal time, vacations, weekends, etc.)
____ Health (impact job has on your mental and physical health)
____ Travel (the amount of travel involved)

____ TOTAL

Work Atmosphere

____ Flexibility (structured, punching the clock vs. flexible)
____ Teamwork/Cooperation (work together towards one
          common goal)
____ Competitive environment (work hard, produce, you'll be
          promoted)
____ Work pace (laid back vs. hectic)
____ Public contact (out and about vs. behind a desk most of
          the day)
____ Professional (formal, business-like vs. informal, family-like)

____ TOTAL

Individual Work Role

____ Variety (doing different things at work, changing frequently)
____ Adventure (work is exciting, creating new ideas)
____ Independence (freedom to do things your way on your time)
____ Power (to have authority and influence on what happens)
____ Enjoyment (the degree to which you enjoy your job)
____ Integrity (your behavior is consistent with your beliefs)

____ TOTAL

Determine the section of values that received the highest total score.
Overall, this section is most important to you in choosing that perfect

job target. Next, list all those individual values that received a score of 4. (If fewer than 5 values received a score of 4, then add those that received a score of 3 also.)

Now rank your top five values. The best way to do this is by asking the question, "If I was forced to keep only one value, which would I choose?" Keep asking that question until you have determined your top five. List your top five values here:

Top 5 Values

1. _____

2. _____

3. _____

4. _____

5. _____

CAREER ASSESSMENT INSTRUMENTS ON THE MARKET

Hopefully by now, you see how self-assessment exercises can help you determine your interests, skills, personal qualities, and values. If you'd like to experience self-assessment instruments that more directly relate to career options, there are many career assessment instruments out there. Most of these instruments must be scored and interpreted by a certified professional. Therefore, you should contact your local employment office or career center and schedule a meeting with a career counselor. Below are brief descriptions of some popular instruments on the market today. The contact information is provided in Appendix C.

The Career Assessments Based on Holland's Codes

John Holland is a career theorist who is famous for his six occupational types: realistic (R), artistic (A), conventional (C), investigative (I), social (S), and enterprising (E). When completing an instrument based on Holland's theory, you'll receive your Holland Code, consisting of the top three occupational types (in order). Therefore, if your highest interest is artistic, second highest is social, and third highest is enterprising, then your Holland Code is A–S–E. Holland maintains that occupations can be grouped by Holland Codes as well, and that a good career choice is one that matches your Holland Code with occupations that have the same code. Therefore, in the preceding example, you would want to explore occupations falling under the category of A–S–E.

Three of the better career assessment instruments that use Holland's theory are the Campbell Interests and Skills Survey (CISS), the Strong Interest Inventory (SII), and the Self-Directed Search (SDS). The CISS matches your interests and skills with those interests and skills of professionals in various occupations. If you score high in accounting on the CISS, for instance, that means that you have many similar interests and skills with professional accountants who have also taken the survey. The SII is very similar to the CISS. It, too, relates your interests with those professionals in a wide range of occupations. Both of these instruments can be administered and interpreted only by a professional.

The SDS is also based on Holland's theory, but unlike the SII and CISS, the instrument is self-scorable. Your Summary Code identified in the SDS can also be compared to occupations (using the *Occupations Finder*) that are categorized with that same code, thus matching your interests with occupations and eliminating ones that don't match. While you are able to buy the SDS and score it yourself, it's highly recommended that you meet with a career counselor who understands Holland's theory to interpret the results.

Computerized Career Guidance Systems

Sigi Plus and DISCOVER, two computerized career assessments, both contain a section that matches your self-assessment results with occupations. They also contain an additional section that allows you to read about those occupations that match. This is a great way to combine self-assessment with career exploration. Call your local employment office or career center to see if they have either system for you to use.

Other Career Assessment Instruments

There are many other career assessment instruments available today. Some exercises and instruments are offered on the Internet. See Appendix A, under "Self-Assessment," for a listing of sites offering online assessments. If you want to learn more about the numerous career assessment instruments, a great resource is *A Counselor's Guide to Career Assessment Instruments*. It's published by the National Career Development Association, and its most recent edition is from 1994. This guide thoroughly describes and evaluates a great number of the career assessment instruments.

IDENTIFYING YOUR CAREER DECISION-MAKING STYLE

As you begin to explore the world of work and decide on your perfect job target, it's important to gain an understanding regarding your style of decision making. When making decisions, do you tend to spend a lot of time exhausting all of the pros and cons, or are you closer to the other end of the spectrum—just going with what feels right or what your gut instinct is telling you? In the following section, you learn about the various career decision-making styles and identify the style or styles that you tend to gravitate toward. You may find that, due to the seriousness of choosing the perfect job target, you have to incorporate a style that you haven't had to use in the past.

The Procrastinating Decision Makers

Procrastinating decision makers have a tough time making a decision. The pressure of making a difficult decision gives them a sense of paralysis that leads to indecision. You'll hear the procrastinating decision maker saying things like, "I'll deal with it later," or, "I just can't decide." Many job seekers procrastinate their decision on a job target because of the amount of time it takes to explore all the options. Many other job seekers put off a decision due to their lack of exposure to career options. How can you choose if you don't know what's out there?

The Intuitive Decision Makers

Intuitive decision makers go with their gut feelings or instincts when making decisions. You'll hear these decision makers saying things like, "I made that decision because it felt like the right thing to do," or, "I just followed my heart in making this decision." Job seekers tend to use this style after being influenced by some external force, such as television, family, and friends. They see their cousin do well in accounting, so they feel like accounting would be good for them. There's not much thought put into the decision for the intuitive decision maker.

The Dependent Decision Makers

Dependent decision makers rely or depend heavily on the opinions of others. You'll hear the dependent decision makers asking, "What do *you* think I should do?" or "What would you do if you were me?" Many job seekers fall into this category, due again to the overwhelming feeling of trying to pick that one perfect job target out of the thousands of prospects. Job seekers rely on anyone and everyone to help them make this all-important decision.

The Educated Decision Makers

Educated decision makers identify all their options, research options of interest, ask numerous questions, and systematically engage in a process of elimination until that perfect option is found. These decision makers will say things like, "I need to explore more options before I'm able to make a decision," or, "I have gone over all the pros and cons and compared them to my other options." Educated career decision makers engage in a thorough self-assessment process, read about all the career options of interest, seek advice from career counselors and professionals in the workforce, and observe professionals at work (work shadowing). They keep logs of what they've learned and constantly analyze their options.

The Recommended Career Decision-Making Style: The Combination Style

The recommended career decision-making style is a combination of the preceding styles, with the exception of the procrastinating method. You should primarily use the *educated decision making* style, but along the way, rely on career counselors, professionals in careers of interest, and other people you respect to offer advice, guidance, and feedback (dependent decision-making). Then, once you have thoroughly completed the self-assessment and career exploration processes, incorporate the intuitive decision-making style to let your feelings and intuition in on the decision. Your intuition is always a pretty accurate gauge, but it's even more accurate after you have all the factors laid out on the table.

PUTTING IT ALL TOGETHER: YOUR PROFESSIONAL SELF-PROFILE

The complexity of the self-assessment process occurs when you put everything together: your skills, interests, personal characteristics, and values. In an ideal or perfect world, you would find the job that uses your top skills and personal characteristics, has everything you're interested in, and meets all your main values. In the realistic world, the perfect job will more likely utilize one or two of your top skills and characteristics and meet one or two of your interests and values. Therefore, it's important to rank your top skills, characteristics, interests, and values so you know which ones are more important in a job than others.

However, remember at this stage that the goal is to identify the perfect job *target*. The perfect job target will contain your top five skills, personal characteristics, interests, and values. Shooting for this perfect job target will head you in the direction of the perfect job. Therefore, using the results of the previous exercises, go to the end of your Personal Job Search Trainer and complete the Professional Self-Profile. You'll use this profile as you search for that perfect job target in the next chapter. You'll also use your Professional Self-Profile throughout the entire job search process, especially when you begin selling yourself to prospective employers through your resume, cover letters, interviews, and networking.

THE WHOLE IN ONE

- Self-assessment can help you eliminate jobs that aren't right for you and identify those for which you're more suited.

- Be honest with yourself as you assess your skills, interests, personal characteristics, and values.

- Prioritize your values to help you identify what is most important to you in a perfect job.

- Approach your career decision process by primarily using an educated decision-making style, with a splash of intuition at the end.

ASSIGNMENT

Complete Goal 1 of your Personal Job Search Trainer.

Chapter 3

Exploring the New World of Work to Identify Your Perfect Job

GET THE SCOOP ON . . .

- Why it's so important to explore your options
- The 5-Step Climb to Your Perfect Job Target
- Using "fit tests" to help identify the perfect job target
- The best Internet and printed resources

THE IMPORTANCE OF EXPLORING YOUR OPTIONS

Now that you've identified your skills, interests, values, and personality characteristics, can't you just jump right in and start looking for that perfect job? You can, but first you need to know what you're looking for. Knowing yourself is half the battle. Knowing what's out there in the ever-changing world of work is the critical next step. The majority of job seekers make the mistake of not spending enough time exploring their options as they identify their perfect job target. There are three main reasons why it's critical to explore your options in search for that perfect job target:

1. You need to broaden your exposure to career options of interest.
2. Recruiters hire candidates who know what they want.
3. Choosing your career is a major life decision.

Broaden Your Career Areas of Interest

Robert Frost (1874–1963) wrote, "Two roads diverged in a wood, and I . . . I chose the one less traveled, and that has made all the difference." Unfortunately, when choosing a career, most people aren't exposed to "the road less traveled," and are forced to choose the only one they know.

In other words, people make decisions based on options that are _familiar_ to them. If you're hungry for some doughnuts, for example, but only know about three types of doughnuts, you'll choose one of those three doughnuts. That perfect doughnut may be out there, but you don't even know it exists. The U.S. Department of Labor claims that there are

Insider's Guide to Finding the Perfect Job **33**

approximately 22,000 occupations in American society. However, most job seekers choose a career field or job based on a handful of options that are simply *familiar* to them. When asked why they chose their profession, the answers that most people give sound like this: *I chose accounting because my uncle is an accountant, and it seemed pretty neat.* Or, *my sister made a lot of money selling cellular phones, so I thought I would give it a try.*

As you begin to think about what that perfect job target may look like, don't limit yourself to only those career options that you're familiar with right now. Open yourself up to a whole new list of career options, for you never know where that perfect job is hiding. In this chapter, "The 5-Step Climb to Your Perfect Job Target" offers strategies and resources to help you expose yourself to a wider array of career options.

Recruiters Hire Candidates Who Know What They Want

The second reason to explore your options is to acquire the ability to demonstrate your interest and focus toward your career choice. In a time when workers are frequently changing jobs, recruiters are looking hard for candidates who show a genuine interest in the job. The more you explore career options, the more focused and knowledgable you'll become about your chosen job target. You'll have the opportunity to express your focused interest in your cover letter, resume, and, ultimately, in your interviews. The best way to express your interest is by describing how specific aspects of a job are consistent with your skills, values, and personality. You will see many examples of how to most effectively express your career focus to recruiters in the cover letter, resume, and interviewing chapters later in this book.

Choosing a Career Is a Major Life Decision

The fact that a career decision is one of the most important life decisions should be reason enough to explore. Think about the time and energy people spend on the exploration process when making any important decision—like buying a house. Many people take months to choose a home.

Identifying the perfect type of job is no easier—or less important—than finding the perfect home; you owe it to yourself to do the work and spend the time necessary to find the job that's right for you. Finding the perfect job means finding a job you can enjoy—one that offers the salary and opportunities for professional growth that will keep you motivated and challenged. You'll spend nearly one third of your life on the job. Don't waste that time waiting for the clock to hit 5:00 and for weekends.

What do you need to do to become one of the few job seekers who actually takes the time to explore their options and identify their perfect

Guidance

Unfortunately, most students do not realize that there are more than 22,000 different jobs available within U.S. society. In fact, the typical student knows very little about more than two or three jobs within this vast pool. The major obstacle to more broad consideration of occupational options is often lack of exposure.
—Jack Rayman, Ph.D., Director of Career Services, Penn State University

job target? First, you must whole-heartedly commit to the importance of exploring career options. Just like everything else in life, if you don't genuinely believe in something, you won't spend much time on it. Hopefully, the three main reasons previously outlined showed you the importance of exploring career options to find your perfect job target. Next, you must identify blocks of time that you can afford to spend on exploring career options. If you don't plan and organize the time you can spend exploring careers, chances are that nothing will get accomplished. Finally, you need to identify how to best utilize your time. "The 5-Step Climb to Your Perfect Job Target" presents many ways to use your time in exploring career options. It's important that you identify those strategies and resources that will work for you and list them in your Personal Job Search Trainer. Certain strategies will fit into your daily routine and lifestyle better than others. Likewise, the resources you choose will depend on their accessibility and cost.

THE 5-STEP CLIMB TO YOUR PERFECT JOB TARGET

FYI

Over the past ten years in career development, I've had the opportunity to ask hundreds of recruiters what they value most in candidates. Genuine interest and commitment to the field is almost always on the top of their list. Recruiters are looking for candidates who know what they want and who have a deep level of interest in their career field and job at hand.

"The 5-Step Climb to Your Perfect Job Target" teaches you the strategies and resources you need to explore career options and, ultimately, identify that perfect job target. Once the perfect job target is identified, you'll have the rare ability to conduct a focused and efficient job search. You'll know what the perfect job looks like when you come across it, and then you'll be able to demonstrate your genuine interest and commitment to it on your resume, cover letters, and interviews.

Searching for the perfect type of job is a lot like choosing a movie at the video store. When you come across a video that, on the surface, catches your eye, there are a number of ways you can thoroughly explore it. You can read about it on the back cover, you can talk to people who know something about it, you can preview it, and you can view it. What's most important to realize is that certain strategies provide you with a higher degree of exploration than others. Likewise, when exploring jobs and career fields, the higher degree of exploration you devote to each field, the easier it will be for you to see if this is the right job for you.

"The 5-Step Climb to Your Perfect Job Target" actually started when you completed the self-assessment exercises and developed your Professional Self-Profile. The first step in the 5-Step Climb is narrowing down your list of career prospects through self-assessment (*internal exploration*). The other four steps deal with exploring careers (*external exploration*). Specifically, the career exploration section identifies four progressional levels of exploring career options: reading about careers, talking to insiders (*information interviewing*), observing professionals (*work shadowing*), and experiencing it directly (*internships and tempo-*

The 5-Step Climb To Your Perfect Job Target

THE PERFECT JOB

STEP 5 TEMPWORK INTERNSHIP

STEP 4 WORK SHADOWING

STEP 3 INFORMATION INTERVIEWING

STEP 2 READING ABOUT CAREERS

STEP 1 SELF ASSESSMENT

rary work). Look at the *Job Mountain* (above) that illustrates the 5-Step Climb. The rocks represent all the jobs you must eliminate along the way. Each step eliminates more job options than the one before it, until you finally find that perfect job target. Also, as you go up each step, there will be fewer rocks to climb, but since you're that much higher, you'll need to examine each rock more closely. Likewise, there will be fewer careers to explore on each step you take. As you go up each step, the careers still in the running are ones in which you have the most interest. Therefore, you'll need to spend more time exploring them.

To identify the perfect job target, you must, at the very least, spend a considerable amount of time reading about career options and talking to professionals. Directly observing professionals and experiencing fields would further increase your ability to identify the perfect job target.

Step One: Narrow Down Your List of Career Prospects

First and foremost, you have to cut the fat. With 22,000 jobs out there, it's impossible to explore all of them. The easiest way to make this number more manageable is by cutting out jobs that you already know you won't like. If you don't like math, hundreds of jobs like engineering, accounting, and teaching math can easily be ruled out. Using what you know about yourself from your Professional Self-Profile and other career assessment instruments, you can eliminate numerous career fields and occupations. Your skills, interests, personal characteristics, and values presented on your Professional Self-Profile will lead you in the right direction.

Guidance

In a highly competitive employee market, top candidates have multiple options to consider. Thus, it is to their advantage to consider opportunities rather than taking the easiest or first job that comes along.

—Arthur Andersen

When you start to look at jobs that you're not sure about, be sure to use your Professional Self-Profile to help you eliminate even more undesirable career fields and occupations so that you can focus more on those that *are* of interest. It's helpful to eliminate both occupations (what you do) and career fields (where you do it).

Step 2: Read about Career Options (Level 1 Exploration)

Through self-assessment, you eliminated thousands of jobs and many career fields and identified a list of career prospects that seem to be a good match. The next step is to learn more about these prospects through reading about them. Reading about career options lets you explore a wide breadth of career fields, occupations, and companies of interest. On the flip side, reading is one-dimensional, general, and impersonal. It's a great first step to learning more about jobs, but by no means is it your final step. You'll need to follow up any reading you do with more detailed exploration of the fields that interest you. For now, though, read about those careers and jobs of interest to continue eliminating prospects and narrowing your search for that perfect job target.

Recommended Resources

There are hundreds of books, magazines, and journals available that let you explore careers and jobs. In addition, many Internet resources continue to grow rapidly. In fact, there are so many resources that it can be overwhelming to decide which ones to use. Therefore, I have labeled these resources "Exploring Career Fields and Occupations" in Appendix A and "Exploring Careers" in Appendix C. Appendix B contains Internet sites within particular career fields. These resources describe jobs and occupations across many career fields. Use these resources to read about your career prospects

As you read these resources, pay attention to the types of existing jobs, the nature of the work, the work atmosphere, the job outlook, and the qualifications required. Three "fit tests" are presented later in the chapter to help you more thoroughly research career prospects. Before you begin reading, you may want to read the section on "fit tests."

Following are two other types of resources that can be helpful to use in exploring your career prospects.

Employer Directories and Literature

Most employer directories are separated by career field or industry to give you a better understanding of the types of companies and organizations that exist in various career fields. There are generally four types of printed employer directories. The *mass listings* of nationwide or international employers are very inclusive and cover a wide range. However, the amount of information provided for each organization is minimal. *Industry-specific* employer directories are best to use once you have decided on a career field or career fields of interest. *Geographic-specific* employer directories are useful if you are relocating to or want to work in a certain region. Finally, *top-rated* employer directories provide you with listings of some of the best companies based on factors like advancement opportunities, work atmosphere, high salaries, strong benefits package, management style, family orientation, and flexible hours. See Appendix C under "Career-related Catalogs" and "Researching Organizations" to identify printed employer directories.

Many employer directories can be found on the Internet. In fact, more often today, companies are directing job seekers to their Web site rather than printed literature. Company Web sites are updated much more regularly than printed literature and are more entertaining to review. The Internet directories often link to the company Web pages. Use Appendix A under "Researching Organizations/Employer Profiles" to find Internet sites that allow you to research companies. Most of these *online career centers* contain an employer search section, where you can search by industry and geographical area. These Internet resources let you personalize your search, thus quickly finding appropriate lists of organizations.

While these directories and Internet sites are helpful in identifying prospective employers, you should use them only as the first step of your employer research, because the amount of information provided per organization is typically not very great. The second step is to conduct company-specific research. Company-specific literature and Web pages typically provide ample information about their respective organization, including the products or services provided, size (number of employees), branch and headquarter locations, management style, company culture, advancement opportunities, competitors, markets, and financial assets. Public organizations have annual reports that can be accessed (usually at your public library), while all companies typically have detailed company literature. Also, most organizations now have Web sites that help you learn more about them. Some even have job openings on their site.

Current Job Listings
Reviewing job listings can give you a clear picture of positions existing in your field(s) of interest. Reading the job responsibilities and duties in the job descriptions can help you identify the types of positions that interest you most. Completing your Position/Occupation-Fit Test for each listing will make it easier for you to identify appealing jobs (see "fit tests" later in this chapter). Job listings can be found in newspapers (want ads), professional/trade journals, college career centers, high school guidance offices, and local employment offices. If you have

access to the Internet, thousands and thousands of job listings are posted on numerous online career center sites. See Appendix A under "Job Openings" for sites that list job openings.

Take a look at the job opening below. This job description was listed in a local newspaper. When reviewing job descriptions, pay close attention to the skills and qualities the company is seeking and compare them with those on your Professional Self-Profile. When considering skills, it's helpful to identify the primary skills and the secondary skills. The primary skills in this job description appear to be written communication and editing skills, while the computer skills are more secondary. Also notice that personal qualities of teamwork ("cooperativeness") and reliability are "essential."

Copy Editor
XYZ News

Edit copy for spelling, grammar, and style; revise and condense stories; write headlines and photo captions; design pages; newspaper experience preferred; computer experience helpful; reliability and cooperativeness essential. Other requirements are excellent written communication skills; headline-writing skills; general editing, spelling, grammar, and compositional skills; ability to work with speed and precision under deadline pressure. Shifts include early mornings and weekend nights. Send resume, references, salary requirements, and any supporting materials (page designs, headlines, etc.) to Joe Recruiter, Managing Editor. No phone calls please.

Step 3: Interviewing People about Career Options of Interest (Level 2 Exploration)

Reading about career fields is a good place to start, but talking to people about career fields and occupations gives you a deeper, more personalized understanding. Specific questions you have regarding a certain profession can be addressed and answered. For the most part, there are two types of people that you can talk to for more information about your career fields of interest: career generalists and inside professionals. Career generalists consist of college career counselors, guidance counselors, and other professional career counselors. They tend to have a basic understanding of many career options. Inside professionals are people who actually work in your career fields of interest. They will be able to give you more in-depth information than the generalist can.

Talking to Career Generalists

Career generalists, consisting of professional career counselors, college career counselors, employment specialists, and other career experts, are trained to know a little bit about most professions. They've researched trends in employment, companies in various career fields, and the best ways to conduct a job search. The benefit of talking with these generalists is that they are unbiased and, therefore, will tell you both the good and the bad about each career field and occupation. They will also give you information based on a wider range of perspectives rather than from just one person. The downside is that these generalists are just that: generalists who have not experienced first hand what it's like to work in your career fields of interest.

The number of career generalists is increasing. For those of you who have attended college or are currently in college, you can meet with a career counselor on campus to discuss various career fields and occupations. If you're not associated with a college, you may try your local community. See if your local government has an employment office and a career adviser with whom you may speak. Most communities also have private, independent career counselors you can pay on a contractual basis. For high school students, make an appointment with your guidance counselor to talk about career options.

Talking to Inside Professionals

There's nothing like hearing it straight from the horse's mouth. While getting some unbiased advice from a career generalist is a good idea, you can gain an even greater understanding of your fields of interest by talking to professionals who have worked or are currently working in the field. This activity is known as *information interviewing* since you are interviewing people to obtain information. These professionals eat, drink, and sleep this stuff. They can tell you what they like and dislike, what is challenging and boring, and what the work atmosphere entails. The only real concern in talking to inside professionals is that you get just one perspective at a time. Don't generalize too much from this one perspective. The particular insider that you're talking to may have just been promoted or demoted or is currently feeling burnt out. Their feelings about their profession will most likely affect the information that they share with you. So it's advised that you talk to more than one professional from each field of interest.

Identify "Friendly Contacts" to Information Interview

No matter how hard you try, some professionals will not be willing to do an information interview with you. Some people will see it as a waste of time, some will just not care, and others will simply be too busy to help you. It's important, then, for you to find people who *will* talk to you about their jobs, bosses, and companies. The best people to conduct an information interview with are "friendly contacts." Friendly contacts include friends, family, neighbors, people in your hometown or city, people in your church or community organization, fellow high school or college alumni, friends of friends, and friends of family. These friendly contacts are usually more receptive to talking with you. Check with your college or alma mater career center to see if they've developed an alumni mentoring program. Many college career centers have a database of alumni and other friendly employers who have volunteered to serve as career mentors or advisers, and information interviewing is one of their main roles.

Setting Up the Information Interview

Information interviews come in many shapes and sizes. Some are conducted at the professional's workplace and last more than two hours, while others are conducted over the phone and last only 15 minutes. To set up an information interview, you can either call, write, or e-mail your friendly contacts. The method of correspondence depends on your comfort level toward each. Be considerate by emphasizing to your contacts that the date, time, and location of the information interview is at their convenience. If you're calling them for the first time, don't assume they have time right then and there to answer your questions.

Preparing for the Information Interview: Develop Questions

Preparing yourself for the actual interview is crucial. Conduct preliminary research on your contact's company and career field so that you can discuss more substantive issues than "how many people work at your organization." Develop a list of questions to ask your contact. Good questions to ask fall under the following categories: the contact's current job, career path, organization, industry, working conditions, and career preparation. See Appendix D, "Information Interview Questions," to help you develop your list of questions.

Information interviewing is frequently used in networking as well as exploring careers. Typically, there's much more at stake when networking for jobs than when exploring careers. Information interviewing is covered in much more depth later in Chapter 11's "The 7-Step Plan to Mastering Information Interviews." Topics include a long list of information interview questions and people to contact, a detailed description of setting up the information interview, and a recommended order of questions to enable you to generate rapport. You should review Chapter 11 to help you become better prepared for setting up and conducting information interviews. Even though you're just trying to gather more information about career options at this point, you never know who may turn into a good networking contact later on.

Immediately after you conduct an information interview, be sure to complete the appropriate "fit tests" to help you determine the position fit, industry fit, and organizational fit for each of the jobs, career fields, and organizations about which you learned. Also, make sure you promptly send a thank-you letter to your friendly contact. Chapter 14 includes a section on writing effective thank-you letters.

Step 4: Observe Professionals at Work (Level 3 Exploration)

To help you choose among those top occupations and career fields that interest you, you can observe professionals at work. Observing a professional at work is typically known as *work shadowing*. Work shadowing allows you to see first hand, over a substantial period of time, the types of duties, projects, challenges, co-workers, and meetings associated with a particular line of work. You can spend anywhere from 1 hour to two weeks, shadowing every move your chosen work-shadowing professional makes.

Here's how it works. First, identify a contact that is comfortable with you shadowing them at work. Then, once the arrangements have been made, go to work with your partner and observe them in their various roles and responsibilities.

The procedures for setting up and preparing for work-shadowing assignments are the same as they are for information interviewing. You must identify a friendly contact willing to let you shadow them and develop a list of questions to ask while you're there. The arrangements are more complex due to the longer period of time associated with work shadowing.

Following are some tips to help you get the most out of the work-shadowing experience:

1. Take notes on what you observe, using the following questions:

   - What were the main responsibilities and duties performed?
   - What were the primary and secondary skills used?
   - Which areas of work interested you, and which didn't?
   - Rate the duties based on their importance.
   - What were you feeling throughout the experience? When were you excited, bored, intrigued, disinterested, etc.?
   - What were your impressions of the work atmosphere?
   - How often did your work-shadowing partner interact with people?
   - What types of people did he or she interact with?
   - What were your impressions of the organization?

2. Set up an information interview with your work-shadowing partner sometime during the work-shadowing experience.

   - Ask the information interview questions outlined in Chapter 11 and presented in Appendix D.
   - Ask your partner questions based on what you observed, using the notes you took.

3. Ask your partner if he is willing to help you set up additional work-shadowing or information-interviewing sessions with his colleagues or friends. It's good to get more than one perspective. Plus, you'll add to your list of networking contacts if you conduct additional work-shadowing assignments.

4. Immediately following the work-shadowing assignment, perform your "fit tests," which are outlined later in the chapter.

5. Remember to promptly send a thank-you letter. Review Chapter 14 on writing effective thank-you letters.

Step 5: Directly Experience Occupations and Career Fields (Level 4 Exploration)

Directly experiencing jobs and career fields is the highest level of career exploration, but it's also the most time consuming. It's impossible to experience every career field and job that interests you. Therefore, it's important to significantly narrow down your prospects through Steps 1 to 4 prior to selecting an occupation or career field to directly experience. The most effective ways to experience jobs that interest you are through internships, co-ops, part-time work, or even volunteering.

Internships or Cooperative (Co-op) Education

If you're a high school student, college student, or graduate student, internships are the best way for you to directly experience an occupation. Most internships occur on a part-time basis during a semester or summer break, giving you three to four months of hands-on experience. Internships come in all shapes and sizes, though. Some student interns receive academic credit; others do not. Some interns get paid; others do not. Some interns work 10 hours per week at their internship site; others work up to 40 hours. The best thing to do is to talk with a career counselor or guidance counselor about internship opportunities that exist at your school.

Traditionally, cooperative education opportunities, or co-ops, were mainly available for science students, especially engineering students. Co-op students tend to spend larger chunks of time at their work site than interns do. Many co-op students will spend an entire semester at their work site, working full-time. During the next semester, they'll return to their campus to enlist in classes. The subsequent semester is once again spent at the co-op site.

Identify Prospective Internships

The first step to obtaining an internship or co-op is to identify organizations in your field of interest that offer them. Meeting with your career or guidance counselor is the best way to start. Discuss with them your Professional Self-Profile and occupations that you're considering.

Guidance

Getting a prior feel about a prospective employer is the most accurate way to assess an individual's long-term satisfaction with an employer. We recommend internship and co-op opportunities for college students when available, not only to gather skills and real work experience, but also to assess how well the prospective employee fits with the organization.
—Johnson & Johnson

Ask your counselor for a list or database of internship sites related to your chosen field. Also ask for their recommendations of companies appearing on this list. If you're a college student, it's a good idea to meet with your academic adviser. Sometimes your adviser will know about internship opportunities that are not publicly advertised.

Another strategy for identifying possible internship opportunities is to review internship resources. There are many national and regional printed resources and Internet resources that list and describe internships. These resources are typically broken down by career field and geographical region, so you can easily find appropriate internships. Appendix B has a section on internship sites that identifies some of the better Internet sites that list internships.

Many internships are also obtained through networking. Refer to Chapter 10 for detailed information on how to network for jobs. The same concepts apply for obtaining internships.

Pursue Internships of Interest

Most internship listings include contact information. Pay attention to the application procedures and deadlines, for they can greatly vary from one internship to another. Before spending hours writing cover letters and filling out applications, call the contact person to make sure the internship is still available. This call also gives you a chance to ask questions about the internship and build a rapport with the contact. Once you're given the green light, follow the application procedures. Most internships request a resume and cover letter, and some require a copy of your academic transcript. Others have a standard application form to be filled out. Refer to the chapters in this book that deal with resume and cover letter writing to help you produce these documents.

Volunteer Work

For some career fields, it's possible to gain experience on a volunteer basis. For example, if you are interested in working with children, there are many volunteer organizations in your community that work with children. You need to determine whether your career field(s) is conducive to volunteer work. The best way to obtain volunteer experience is to directly contact organizations in which you're interested. Most organizations are short staffed, trying to "do more with less." Therefore, many are usually very open to prospective volunteers.

Part-Time and Temporary Work

There are also part-time work opportunities to help you gain some experience. For example, if you're interested in the hotel/restaurant industry, you could work part-time as a waiter or hostess as a way to experience this industry first hand. Another method of finding part-time or short-term employment is by registering with a temporary employment agency. Most temporary agencies are paid by companies who need to hire temporary or part-time staff members. Temporary agencies can be found in your local phone book or on the Internet. Career counselors in the area can also help you determine appropriate temporary agencies. Look under the "Employment Services" sections in Appendix A and Appendix C to help you find temporary agencies.

When choosing temporary agencies, follow these guidelines:

1. Make sure that the company picks up the fee, not you.
2. The "positions commonly filled" should be consistent with your interests.
3. Meet with an agency representative to personally inform them of the types of jobs you're seeking.

USING "FIT TESTS" TO DETERMINE YOUR PERFECT JOB TARGET

As you go through "The 5-Step Climb to Your Perfect Job Target," you must learn what to look for when examining your career prospects. Your perfect job is dependent on three factors: position/occupation, industry, and organization. Therefore, to define your perfect job target, there are three "fit tests":

1. Position/Occupation Fit: How well a position or occupation fits your Professional Self-Profile
2. Industry Fit: How well an overall industry fits your Professional Self-Profile
3. Organizational Fit: How well a specific organization fits your Professional Self-Profile

Review the three "fit tests" below. Then, as you explore your career prospects, take the fit tests with you to help pinpoint that perfect job target

Position/Occupation "Fit Test"

The Position/Occupation "Fit Test" helps you determine whether or not a job or occupation prospect fits well with your Professional Self-Profile. Earlier in the chapter, you saw how exploring real job openings can be a good way to explore career prospects. The Position/Occupation "Fit Test" can be very helpful in evaluating these job openings.

The following is a list of questions you can use when reviewing a job description or occupation to test its fit. Refer to your Professional Self-Profile to help you answer the questions.

1. How well do the primary skills on this job/occupation description match my top skills, as identified in my Professional Self-Profile?

2. How well do the secondary skills on this job/occupation description match my top skills, as identified in my Professional Self-Profile?

3. How many of the job duties would I enjoy?

4. How important is this job/occupation in general?

5. Upon successfully completing the job duties, would I feel a sense of accomplishment?

6. Do the job/occupational responsibilities appear to be consistent with my top values, as listed on my Professional Self-Profile?

7. Are the duties and responsibilities too challenging or not challenging enough?

8. Will I be interacting too much with people or not enough?

Industry "Fit Test"

In addition to assessing what you would like to be doing (position fit), you also need to determine where you want to be doing it (industry fit). Your skills can be used in many different industries. For example, if you have management skills, you can manage a bank (banking industry), a hospital (health-care industry), or a car dealer (automotive industry). You need to decide where you would most enjoy using your management skills.

Following are some questions you can ask as you explore career field or industry prospects. Refer to your Professional Self-Profile as you examine each industry.

1. Does the industry I'm considering allow me to use my top skills in the way I want to use them?

2. Is the overall industry or career field interesting to me?

3. Do the types of people who work in this industry have similar values and interests as I do?*

4. Would I feel comfortable working with the types of people found in this industry?*

5. Is this industry consistent with the top few values, as listed on my Professional Self-Profile?

Organizational "Fit Test"

Organizations vary greatly in size, structure, philosophies, products and services, and culture. Some people fit in better with a larger corporation, while others prefer the small-company climate. Some prefer an open, team-oriented work atmosphere, while others would rather be working alone in their office.

---

* Note: As noted previously, when trying to assess how well you would fit in with people, the most effective strategy is to talk directly to professionals who work in those organizations you're considering.

Following are questions you can use to assess the level of organizational fit you have with the organizations you explore.

1. Are my top skills valued in this organization?

2. Is the size of this organization too large or too small for my liking?

3. Do I value the types of products or services that this organization offers?

4. Are the mission and philosophies consistent with my beliefs and values?

5. Would I feel comfortable in the type of work atmosphere that appears to exist in this type of organization?*

6. Do the employees seem to be people that I would enjoy being around?*

7. As I research this organization, do I have a good gut feeling about this organization?

Finally, too many job seekers just look at the position title alone in judging how well it fits. Don't judge a book by its cover. Your perfect job will have a strong position fit, industry fit, and organizational fit. Make sure to use all three tests as you explore your career prospects.

THE WHOLE IN ONE

- Take the time to explore career fields and occupations of interest.

- Follow "The 5-Step Climb to Your Perfect Job Target" to most effectively explore your prospects.

- Read about your career prospects, talk to professionals, observe professionals at work, and directly experience occupations, if at all possible.

- As you explore, test your fit with various positions or occupations, industries, and organizations.

ASSIGNMENT

Complete all of Goal 2 of your Personal Job Search Trainer.

---

* Note: As noted previously, when trying to assess how well you would fit in with people, the most effective strategy is to talk directly to professionals who work in those organizations you're considering.

Part II

Developing Your Self-Marketing Package

Chapter 4

The Resume Basics

GET THE SCOOP ON . . .

- The purpose and nature of a resume
- What's important enough to put on a resume
- Fundamental do's and don'ts
- Real resume bloopers

THE PURPOSE AND NATURE OF A RESUME

The resume is, by far, the most important job-search document. Make no mistake about it. The resume presents and introduces your most important experiences, skills, and academic training to prospective employers. The resume usually meets recruiters before you do. It's the first impression a recruiter gets of you. Your resume serves as your spokesperson, your advocate, and your personal advertisement. It's your ticket to an interview.

Your goal is to write a resume that strategically presents your major selling points to prospective employers and networking contacts. Too many job seekers haphazardly throw down their information on a piece of paper with no rhyme or reason. What makes a resume strong is identifying your major selling points and using a formatting style that intentionally accentuates them. Before you're able to do that, you must understand the common resume components and formatting styles. Then in Chapter 5, "Crafting the Perfect Resume," you learn how to strategically accentuate your selling points and build a perfect resume.

The nature of a resume is very subjective. There are thousands of recruiters out there. They come in all shapes and sizes, and no two recruiters perceive resumes exactly the same way. Therefore, a fundamental point to remember is that there are no absolute rights and wrongs to writing a resume. For example, during a recent conference between career services professionals and recruiters, the question was raised, "How important is an objective on a resume?" Close to half of the recruiters said that an objective was very important, while the other half paid little attention to it. If you were to ask ten different people what they thought of your resume, you would receive something a little bit different from each of them. People naturally have biases toward certain styles and formats that affect their feedback. When you want some feedback, remember that career counselors are trained to be objective and to assist their clients to do what's best for them. While receiving feedback is fine, you must ultimately do what's best for you. After reading this chapter and Chapter 5, you'll be able to produce the resume that's best for you.

Some Basic Pointers to Get You Started

As you begin identifying what you want to include on your resume, keep the following pointers in mind. First, your resume must look good at first glance. Your resume will make your first impression. What the recruiter sees is what she'll get. If your resume is on cheap paper, you are cheap in the recruiter's mind. If your resume looks sloppy, you are sloppy. If your resume is overloaded with text, you're long-winded and unorganized. Print your resume on good, cotton-bond paper. Balance your resume by having enough white space and not too much text. Use a good, quality laser printer to print your final draft.

Next, the most important experiences and skills must be easily detected by recruiters. Use highlighting, indentation, spacing, and bulleted statements to make it easy for the recruiters to pick out the information that's important. If recruiters have to look too long and too hard for information, they'll stop looking! Emphasize your important points and present them in a way that make them stand out.

Finally, be a fanatic when it comes to accuracy and attention to detail. Spellcheck doesn't check everything. One wrong letter can take you out of the race. "*Running* a large marketing division" is very different from "*Ruining* a large marketing division." If you misspell or misuse a word, you can kiss your chances goodbye! Recruiters make it clear that one minor spelling error sends the resume to the recycling bin. Spelling errors indicate that you don't pay attention to detail and you're not reliable.

WHAT'S IMPORTANT ENOUGH TO PUT ON A RESUME—THE COMPONENTS

Remember, there are no exact rights and wrongs when it comes to a resume. Many items are *optional,* and their inclusion depends on your overall situation and the career fields you're pursuing. However, there are many components of a resume that are *highly recommended.* Therefore, in describing the various parts of a resume I'll tell you what I highly recommend putting on your resume and what I consider optional. When needed, I'll also describe differences that exist between the entry-level resume and the experienced resume. And, since different resumes require different elements, I'll show you where to put the different items on *your* resume.

Differences between entry-level and experienced resumes are covered in detail in Chapter 6. However, it's good to have a basic understanding of the differences as you review the resume components. Entry-level resumes contain less work experience and accomplishments than experienced resumes. Therefore, the writers of most entry-level resumes start off with the education section and keep their resumes to one page. Experienced resumes often begin with their work experience and present more results. Going to two pages for experienced resumes is more acceptable. Due to the lack of experience, entry-level resumes present a wider range of other types of experience, including academic projects, volunteer and extracurricular activities, part-time jobs, and internships. Experienced resumes list full-time work experience as the main type of experience.

Heading
Highly Recommended
Starting from the top, your heading consists of your full name (typically first, middle initial, and last), mailing address, phone number(s), and e-mail address. This information is usually centered, as shown in Heading Sample 1. Notice that the name is one size larger than the contact information. If you're working while job searching, you must decide whether it's appropriate to put your work phone number on your resume. If you need to preserve space, you can separate your address from your phone number and e-mail address, as shown in Heading Sample 2. For college students, it's recommended that you enter your campus address and campus phone number as well as your permanent/home address and permanent/home phone number (Heading Sample 3).

Heading Sample 1

Joe C. Jobs
514 Bakery Lane
Williams, VA 22222
203-555-4780
joejobs@whatever.com

Heading Sample 2

Joe C. Jobs
514 Bakery Lane   203-555-4780
Williams, VA 22222   joejobs@whatever.com

Heading Sample 3

Anita Career

Current Address	Permanent Address
8888 Campus Box	514 Bakery Lane
Elon College, NC 27244	Williams, VA 22222
336-555-2538	203-555-4780
careeranita@elon.edu	

Objective

Entry-Level: Highly Recommended; Experienced: Optional

If you're preparing an entry-level resume, you want to show that you have a sense of direction. If you are an experienced job seeker, you may start with a Summary of Qualifications section instead. The summary of qualifications section is described in the next section. If you choose to put an objective on your resume, recruiters overwhelmingly want to see a succinct, focused objective. Don't make the mistake of presenting a lot of fluff, as illustrated in Objective Sample 1. There aren't many people out there who want a non-challenging position with a low-class company, where they are unable to use any of their skills and where there is no chance for advancement. When you write your objective, remember to keep in mind that recruiters are looking for two things and two things only: the type of job you want and where you hope to get it (Objective Sample 2).

Objective Sample 1

The Too-Much-Fluff Objective

To obtain a challenging position in a top-notch company where I am able to use my skills and advance within the company.

Objective Sample 2

The Objective Recruiters Want

To obtain a sales position within the pharmaceutical industry.

Summary of Qualifications

Optional

This section is highly recommended only for those job seekers that have substantial skills and experience relating to their perfect job. If used, the Summary of Qualifications should be placed near the top, right after the heading. The summary should contain bulleted statements of facts only. Opinions carry little weight. Summary samples 1 and 2 show the distinction between an opinion-oriented summary and a fact-oriented one.

Summary Sample 1
Opinion-Oriented Summary of Qualifications
- Excellent communication and organizational skills
- Ability to get along with a wide range of people
- Ability to solve problems and conflicts
- Strong work ethic and very responsible

Summary Sample 2
Fact-Oriented Summary of Qualifications
- Public-speaking skills: Participated in two weeklong public-speaking seminars
- Ten years of event-planning experience
- Strong computer skills: Developed 14 PowerPoint presentations and 7 Access databases
- National certification in conflict resolution

Education/Training
Highly Recommended
If you're an entry-level candidate, especially a recent graduate, place your Education section immediately after the Objective section. If you're an experienced candidate, you'll probably want to place this section at the end of your resume, since your work experience is more recent and, typically, more pertinent. While the overall section of Education is highly recommended, some of its parts are optional. Following is a breakdown of those parts that are highly recommended and those that are optional.

Highly Recommended Items in Education Section
The following items are highly recommended within the Education section:

- Schools/Colleges: Name, location (city/town and state only)
- Degrees, Licenses, and Certifications
- Majors, Minors, and Specializations

The following items provide samples for the high school, college, and graduate school levels as well as other random examples of training.

Highly Recommended Items
High School Level
Shippensburg Area Senior High School, Shippensburg, PA

Completed College Prep and Business Curriculum, June 1999
Associate-Degree Level
A.S. in Business, May 1999

Brady Community College, Stonebrook, WA

Bachelor's-Degree Level
B.A., May 1999

Elon College, Elon College, NC

Major: Communications (Corporate emphasis)

Minor: Business Administration

Graduate-Degree Level
D.Ed. in Counselor Education, May 1995

Pennsylvania State University, University Park, PA

Dissertation Topic: *Career Uncertainty and Involvement Among College Students*

M.A. in Student Affairs in Higher Education, May 1989

Indiana University of Pennsylvania (IUP), Indiana, PA

B.A. in Mathematics, May 1988

Shippensburg University, Shippensburg, PA

In addition to formal education and degrees, you can list any relevant training courses you may have taken or certification programs you've completed. See the various samples:

Associated Builders and Contractors, Inc. Graduated May 1999

Certification: Computer Accounting Assistant, May 1998

The Charles P. Young School of Accounting

Notary Public: State of New York

Licensed Insurance Agent: Pennsylvania

Dale Carnegie Institute: 1997

Optional Items in Education Section

Many items in the Education section are optional. Putting them on your resume depends on your situation and what you're pursuing. The bottom-line question you must answer is, "How does putting this on my resume benefit me?" Following are two of the most common items job seekers wrestle over regarding whether or not to include them on their resume.

Grade Point Average (GPA)

Probably the biggest resume debate is whether or not to include your grade point average (GPA). If you are an experienced candidate, you'll probably want to leave your GPA off your resume, since your experience and skills overshadow your academic record. If you are an entry-level candidate, the long-standing rule of thumb has been as follows: if you have a 3.0 or above, put your GPA on your resume. There are exceptions to this rule, however. If you were heavily involved in substantive activities (e.g., vice president of the senior class), or you were obligated to work a high number of hours per week, then a 2.75 GPA combined with your active involvement is a respectable overall picture. Another exception to the 3.0 rule relates to the field you're pursuing. For example, for those individuals pursuing an advanced degree in physical therapy, a 3.0 is not an impressive GPA. You must know the type of GPA that is respected for the field you're pursuing.

Relevant Course Work

Relevant course work is only beneficial if you're an entry-level candidate and have taken courses relevant to your perfect job that are outside of your major or minor. For example, if you are a history major pursuing a career in banking, it would be a good idea to list any business or finance courses you've taken. If your perfect job calls for public speaking, you should include any completed public speaking or communication courses. The sample below shows an education section that includes both GPA and relevant course work.

BACHELOR OF ARTS, May 1999

Elon College, Elon College, NC
Major: *History*
Minor: *Psychology*
GPA: *3.1 on 4.0 scale*

Relevant Course Work:
Finance, Accounting, Economics, Business Logistics

Experience

Highly Recommended

The experience section is highly recommended and as close to "required" as you can get. Recruiters are very interested in seeing what you've done in the past and how it may relate to the job at hand. If you are an entry-level candidate, place your Experience section after the Education section; if you are experienced, do the opposite.

Each experience includes up to six parts: organization name, organization location (city and state), position title, start and end date, position responsibilities, and accomplishments. The first four parts—organization name, location, position title, and dates—are highly recommended for all experience levels. Including the latter two depends on the level, substance, relevance, and self-explanatory nature of the experience. It also depends on how many other experiences you want on your resume. Review the following sample:

Waiter—*The Restaurant Inn,* Oakland, CA, Summer 1999
- Effectively communicated a wide range of food and beverage options to customers
- Handled customer complaints with grace and diplomacy
- Balanced my time effectively; juggled multiple duties simultaneously

The general responsibilities of a waiter or waitress are well known. To take up five extra lines with a fuzzy, long-winded description of the obvious is a waste of precious resume space. In this case, unless the person was pursuing a career in hotel/restaurant management, the experience was self-explanatory, not relevant, and not from a high-level position. Therefore, including the responsibilities and accomplishments was not necessary. Chapter 5 covers the issue of *emphasizing the right experiences* in much more detail.

While results and accomplishments are important to express on a resume, they are much more effective for experienced job seekers. They have had much more time to build a list of accomplishments and achievements than entry-level job seekers. Take a look at the experience highlighted on the following salesperson's resume:

Account Executive—ABC Corporation, Madison, PA,
March 1995–Present

Consistently exceeded company and local market revenue goals and quotas while managing a territory that consisted of more than 3,000 businesses.

Accomplishments

- Won 1997 company-wide sales incentive trip to Maui, Hawaii. (Recognized as one of the top six account executives from approximately 500 representatives—167 percent quota.)
- President's Club Award Winner, 1996–1997.
- Won 1996 company-wide sales incentive trip to Cancun, Mexico. (Recognized as one of the top six account executives from approximately 500 representatives—140 percent quota.)
- Club 60 Award Winner, 1997.
- Club 50 Award Winner, 1996.
- Won 1995 company-wide sales incentive trip to Paradise Island, Bahamas (180 percent quota).
- Top Account Executive for the Madison Market, 1995, 1996, 1997.
- Won 1996 regional sales contest trip to Miami Beach, FL.
- Won 1995 regional sales contest trip to New York City, NY.

Notice the results-oriented approach of this experienced salesperson. When you have the results and accomplishments, don't be shy. The more you can show a potential employer, the better. Realize, however, that you may not be able to use accomplishments to the extent that our sample shows. Certain career fields are prone to generate concrete, quantitative results more naturally than others are. An experienced psychologist, for example, has a much more difficult time quantifying results than a salesperson. For a psychologist, presenting a statement such as, "Assisted client in feeling approximately 75 percent less anxiety when talking to people," is not a good way to list accomplishments. So if you're in a field that doesn't produce quantitative results, don't force something in that's not there. The recruiters will begin to question your honesty.

Various Types of Experience

Realize that there are many types of experience you can include on your resume. Many job seekers think of experience solely as work experience, but that's just not true. Just because you were paid for doing a job does not necessarily mean the experience is substantial enough to impress a recruiter. For many people, volunteer work, unpaid internships, and community service have had a greater impact on their career than their paid experiences. Following are five subcategories of experience and a sample of each. Where these categories should be placed on a resume, what their headings should be, and how much description is necessary is covered in Chapter 5.

Work Experience

Work experiences are simply those experiences for which you get paid. If you're an entry-level job seeker, part-time and summer jobs are perfectly acceptable as work experience, while experienced job seekers ultimately will include more full-time jobs.

Program Analyst—May 1992 to December 1993

Office of Research and Special Studies—XYZ Company

- Coordinated all facets of the department's research program, including developing requests for proposals, evaluating researchers, and monitoring financial reports.
- Coordinated the procurement and maintenance of all computer hardware and software.

Volunteer/Community Service

Recruiters like to see that you get involved in your community. It indicates that you're active and not solely driven by money. If you haven't been involved much up to this point, it's never too late. There are thousands of volunteer organizations that need help. Notice how community service is often presented as a list of events.

Community Service

- Sara County Speakers Bureau: Speak on benefits of exercise—1996 to Present
- Team Leader, American Heart Walk, Sara County, Easton, MD—1998

Extracurricular Activities

Extracurricular activities are much more prevalent and important to present for entry-level candidates. Experienced professionals should focus more on full-time positions and community service on their resume. Recruiters differentiate club membership from active involvement in an activity. Top value is placed with those who obtained a leadership position, were heavily involved in coordinating an event, or deeply engaged in a project.

President—*Gamma Sigma Sigma,* Moravian College, Spring and Fall 1999

- Served as president of a national service sorority, consisting of approximately thirty local members
- Presided at weekly meetings and enforced policies and rules
- Supervised approximately eight committees

Internships

Internships, cooperative education, student teaching, clinical experience, or practicum experience are all forms of hands-on training. These experiences usually are very relevant, due to the professional training element involved. Internships are extremely important for high school and college students. They serve as the best way for students to obtain relevant experience and skills.

Recruiters perceive internships as "the new springboard to employment." They want to see that you performed duties and responsibilities that a full-time professional would perform. Some internships are more "meaty" than others. Make sure you're specific in describing the types of projects you completed and any results that were generated. Also reveal with whom you worked closely. They want to see that you've experienced working within a team.

Intern—*City Life Magazine,* Chapel Hill, NC

- Researched and interviewed for feature stories
- Wrote, proofed, and edited stories
- Targeted articles to audience of more than 5,000
- Worked closely with the Senior Editor on a four-part story

Academic Experience

Academic experience is, by far, the most under-utilized type of experience. Examples of academic experience are projects, case studies, international study (study abroad), laboratory experiments, field studies, and research. Some of the most substantive, enlightening experiences are academic by nature. However, most job seekers either completely overlook them or minimally present them. Job seekers have been conditioned to believe that *work experience* is the only real experience that belongs on a resume. This is just not true.

Climatic Water Budget Analysis—University of ABC, 1999

- Examined the effect of land-use change on ground water recharge
- Computed daily and monthly water budgets of Key West, FL, and Bonners Ferry, ID
- Applied water budget factors, including leaching through landfills, irrigation scheduling, plant/crop yield, and forest fire prediction

Skills

Highly Recommended

There are three types of skills that are widely included on a resume: computer skills, language skills, and relevant skills/training. Skills can be found in many different places on a resume. They can be incorporated into the Summary of Qualifications section, or they can be presented in their own section, called Summary of Skills, Relevant Skills, or Professional Training. They can even be split into more than one section, such as Computer Skills and Language Skills. The strength, number, and relevancy of your skills will dictate where they are placed and how much they are emphasized. Below are some examples of how skills are presented on a resume.

Information Technology/Computer Skills

Internet/World Wide Web—Solely produced XYZ Career Center home page

Database Development—Designed, developed, and implemented a relational database used to maintain employer relations, track students' career involvement, and access job leads and internships

Multimedia Presentation/Design—Designed, produced, and implemented numerous automated slide presentations using Astound (animated graphics) and PowerPoint software

IBM—Microsoft Word, Microsoft Access, Microsoft PowerPoint, Astound (slide presentation design)

Macintosh—MacWrite, MacPro, Managing Your Money (budget design and management)

Computer Skills

Experience using Microsoft Office (Excel, Word, Access, Power Point) and the Internet

Professional Training

First Aid (adults and children), CPR, Consumer Safety, Fire Safety, Multicultural Education Training, OASHA Regulation Training, DSM IV, CASSP Training

Language Skills

Proficient in writing and speaking Spanish

Lived in Spain for one year, 1998

Honors and Awards

Highly Recommended

Don't underestimate the importance of honors and awards. We all have the tendency to think that the awards and honor societies we receive aren't that big of a deal. Recruiters don't think that way. Any honor or award you've been given must go on your resume. You never know which one or two things on your resume may make the difference. Remember, recruiters are very different, and they value different things. Putting an award on your resume gives you a chance of it being valued. Not putting it on gives you no chance!

Honors and Awards

- Who's Who of Students in American Colleges and Universities
- Dean's List (5 Semesters)
- Honors Program
- Omicron Delta Kappa—National Leadership Honor Society
- Psi Chi—National Psychology Honor Society
- Sigma Tau Delta—National English Honor Society
- Alumni Fellowship Scholarship Award

Interests and Hobbies

Optional

Interests and hobbies are optional, yet they can be a smart addition. They tell the recruiter more about you as a person and may help make you more of a person in their eyes and less of a "number." If you have the space, you may want to consider adding this section. However, be careful what you include. Certain political activities, for example, may rub someone the wrong way. On the flip side, your interest in skiing may be the recruiter's favorite pastime, thus increasing the chance for building positive rapport.

Personal Interests
Tennis, Foreign Travel, Antique Furniture Restoration, Military History

Member of Naval Academy Athletic Association

Professional/Trade Associations
Highly Recommended
If you belong to any professional or trade associations, it's highly recommended that you put them on your resume. This section applies mostly to experienced job seekers. Be sure to highlight any involvement you've had in your organizations. Following are examples of local involvement and national involvement, respectively.

Professional Memberships and Certification
- Aerobic and Fitness Association of America—1997 to Present
- Advanced Cardiac Life Support: American Heart Association—1995 to Present
- Basic Cardiac Life Support: American Heart Association—1987 to Present

Professional Organizations
- National Association of Colleges and Employers (NACE)—Conducted book reviews for NACE and its Journal of Career Planning and Employment
- American Association For Higher Education (AAHE)
- North Carolina Association of Colleges and Employers (NCACE)
- Mid-Atlantic Association of Colleges and Employers (MAACE)—Selected to serve on MAACE Professional On-Site Consulting Committee
- American College Personnel Association (ACPA)

Publications and Presentations
Highly Recommended
This section again applies more if you're an experienced job seeker, especially if you're in education. Many professors and higher-education professionals write articles and books and present at conferences. Following are examples of both publications and presentations.

Publications
"Learning to learn: Finding your course in college." *Ted's Place, http://www.regiononline.com*. Bethlehem, PA: Regional Network Communications, Inc. (October, 1996)

"A comparative study of declared and undeclared college students on career uncertainty and involvement in career development activities." *Journal of Counseling and Development*, 74(6), 632–640. Edwin L. Herr, co-author. (August, 1996)

"Career uncertainty and career development involvement among college freshmen and sophomores: A quantitative and qualitative analysis." Doctoral dissertation. The Pennsylvania State University, University Park, PA. (May, 1995)

Presentations

Transition Tactics, National Association of Colleges and Employers Conference, Dallas, 1998

Institutional Commitment to Career Development, Student Affairs in Higher Education Conference, Appalachian State University, 1998

Transition Tactics, Southeastern Association of Colleges and Employers Conference, New Orleans, 1998

Getting The Most Out Of College, high school students and parents, North Carolina and Pennsylvania, 1998–1999

The Strategic Job Search, National Association of Colleges and Employers Conference, San Francisco, 1992

References

The odds are that if you're creating an entry-level resume, you've left room for references. Don't bother. An actual list of references is important to have—but not on your resume. Space is too precious. You should have a separate page of references. Chapter 7 covers the topic of references. The statement, "References available upon request" is often seen as the last sentence on resumes. If you have a line to kill, it won't hurt, but it will have little meaning to recruiters since they'll contact references with or without that statement.

THE FUNDAMENTAL DO'S AND DON'TS

We've covered a lot of ground talking about resumes, but if you're ever in doubt, remember that there are no absolutes when it comes to resumes. There are, however, some definite do's and don'ts that you should always keep in mind.

The Dos
Make It Easy to Review
- Catch the recruiter's eye. Most recruiters spend less than 30 seconds on the initial review of your resume.
- Choose the resume style that works best for you.
- Use appropriate highlighting (bold, italic, uppercase), indentation, and spacing.

- Begin with strong action verbs when describing your experiences.
- See Appendix E, "Action Verbs and Skills for Resumes."

Make Sure It's Accurate

- Check spelling, punctuation, grammar, and style.
- Get an objective eye. Have other people proofread your resume.

Present Strong Content

- Think strategically about the experiences and skills you want to emphasize and the overall format (headings) of your resume.
- Write a concise objective, including position level and type of industry you are seeking.
- Be descriptive and results-oriented, when possible, yet not too wordy.

Make It Eye Appealing

- Generate a well-balanced resume—not too busy, not too bare.
- Print on high quality paper: 25 percent to 100 percent cotton-bond paper.

The Don'ts

- Use "I."
- Write "Resume" at the top.
- Include an objective that is unfocused and flowery.
- Present personal information, such as health, gender, and marital status.
- List references on the resume. Have a separate reference sheet.
- Send a photo along with the resume.
- Begin your descriptions with "Responsible for" or "Duties include."
- Throw your information into someone else's format.
- Constrict yourself to the "Resume Rules of Thumb," such as "keep resume to one page." It depends on how much substantive information you have and the field you are pursuing.

Resume Bloopers

The following bloopers are real, taken from actual resumes, cover letters, and applications. They're generated from Robert Half International. Enjoy!

Personal Information

1. Qualifications: I am a man filled with passion and integrity, and I can act on short notice. I'm a class act and do not come cheap.
2. I procrastinate—especially when the task is unpleasant.

3. Personal: I am married with 9 children. I don't require prescription drugs.

4. Here are my qualifications for you to overlook.

Reasons for Leaving Last Job

1. Responsibility makes me nervous.

2. They insisted that all employees get to work by 8:45 every morning. Couldn't work under those conditions.

3. The company made me a scapegoat—just like my three previous employers.

4. Was met with a string of broken promises and lies, as well as cockroaches.

Special Requests and Job Objectives

1. Please call me after 5:30pm because I am self-employed and my employer does not know I am looking for another job.

2. My goal is to be a meteorologist. But since I have no training in that area, I suppose I should try stock brokerage.

3. Note: Please do not misconstrue "job-hopping." I have never quit a job.

Small Typos that Greatly Change Meaning

1. Work experience: Dealing with customers' complaints that arouse.

2. Develop and recommend an annual operating expense fudget.

3. I'm a rabid typist.

4. Instrumental in ruining the entire operation for a Midwest chain of department stores.

THE WHOLE IN ONE

- The main goal of a resume is to present your selling points to prospective employers.

- The nature of the resume is very subjective, and there are no absolute rights and wrongs.

- The components that come highly recommended are education, experience, and skills.

- An objective is recommended as well, as long as it's focused and concise.

- Honors, interests, publications, presentations, and professional associations are additional components that should be included if you have more than one of each.

- Overall, you want your resume to be easy to review, accurate, descriptive, and appealing to the eye.

Chapter 5

Crafting the Perfect Resume

GET THE SCOOP ON . . .

- Inside strategy for crafting the perfect resume
- Your selling points and message to recruiters
- Top resume styles and when to use them
- Choosing the style that's perfect for you

THE INSIDE STRATEGY FOR CRAFTING THE PERFECT RESUME

How many times have you heard the saying, "It's not *what* you say, it's *how* you say it"? Well, when it comes to resumes, it's more than a saying, it's a strategy that will make your resume *perfect*. Now that you know what goes on a resume—the components—it's time for you to learn how to present these components in a way that will impress prospective employers.

Writing a resume is a lot like working in advertising. Ad agencies must constantly restructure their strategies and selling points depending on their target audience. They know that ads appealing to teens usually don't appeal to the elderly and may even turn the elderly away from their product. Creating the perfect resume is no different. It's crucial for you to structure your resume in a manner that presents you in the best possible light, but you should never forget to keep your audience in mind: the recruiter.

The inside strategy for crafting the perfect resume consists of a two-step process. The first step is to identify your *selling points*—those experiences, skills, accomplishments, and training that are most important to your prospective employers. The second step is to find the resume style that accentuates your selling points.

IDENTIFY YOUR SELLING POINTS AND YOUR MESSAGE TO RECRUITERS

Before you jump right in and start writing that resume, you need to take some time to identify your selling points and the message you want to send to a recruiter. Your selling points are experiences, accomplishments, education, and skills that will help you stand out to recruiters, and the selling points that you choose to emphasize will definitely send a message to recruiters regarding who you are and what you have to offer. Since your resume is most often the first point of contact, the recruiters form an image or first impression of you based on the message you send them. Because recruiters spend less than 30 seconds on the initial review of your resume, that image they form usually determines whether your resume gets a second look! The good news is that you've already done most of the work required to identify your selling points.

Your selling points are directly related to the job you want. So, by identifying your perfect job, you've also identified your selling points. Your perfect job includes the type of position you want as well as the industry in which you want to work. Based on this information, you can identify the relevant experiences, accomplishments, education, and skills. For example, if your perfect job is selling medical equipment, your selling points would consist of skills, experiences, accomplishments, and education relevant to both the sales occupation and to the field of medicine.

Conducting information interviews is one of the best ways to identify or confirm your selling points. Meet with professionals or recruiters in your chosen field and/or occupation. Discuss your skills, training, and experience and ask their advice on which aspects are most impressive or relevant. You could also meet with a career counselor to receive similar advice. In addition, many of the recommended resources in Appendix A and under "Exploring Careers" in Appendix C include a section that describes the types of skills and qualifications desired for each occupation and industry.

THE TOP RESUME STYLES AND WHEN TO USE THEM

Now that you know your selling points, you're ready for the second step to crafting the perfect resume: choosing the resume style that emphasizes your selling points and sends the message you want to send to recruiters. It's very important to find the style that allows your selling points to stand out. To accomplish this, you first must learn about the top resume styles and the advantages and disadvantages of using each style.

Most resume experts agree on three common styles: *Chronological*, *Functional*, and *Combination*. A fourth resume style, the *Combination-Internal* resume, is one that not many resume guides will tell you about, but that I find particularly useful. Each style has a different purpose, and which one you use depends on your particular situation as well as the job for which you're applying. You'll see each style in action using actual resumes from a real job seeker, disguised as "Anita Job." Most resume books present completely different resumes for each style. I think you'll find it very beneficial to see how the same resume, with the same basic information, can look very different based on the style used. Each style emphasizes different aspects of your qualifications and sends different messages to recruiters.

Chronological Style

FYI

When inexperienced job seekers are asked, "Do you have any experience?", they usually respond "No" due to their lack of full-time work experience. Full-time work experience is not the only type of experience that counts. Recruiters view internships, extracurricular activities, volunteer work, academic projects, and part-time jobs as "experience."

The Chronological Resume focuses on your work experience, listing the jobs you've had in reverse-chronological order (from most recent to least recent). If you're an inexperienced job seeker, you should use internships, part-time jobs, extracurricular activities, hands-on projects, and community service in place of full-time work experience. The Chronological style is most common among job seekers and easiest to review for recruiters. The typical heading is generic, such as "Experience" or "Work Experience." Refer to Anita Job's Chronological Resume. Notice how her experiences are presented in reverse-chronological order, with the most recent experience being the Program Coordinator/Research Analyst position.

The Chronological Style Is Recommended When

- Your titles and company names alone are relevant or impressive.
- The most recent experience is relevant or impressive (since you list this experience first and it's most visible).
- You have consistently advanced or progressed from your least recent position to your most recent position.
- Your length of time at each organization is respectable.

The Chronological Style Is NOT Recommended When

- You have gaps in your work history (sporadic, spotty).
- You have changed employers too often.
- Your position titles and employers are not relevant.
- Your most impressive, relevant experience was one of your least recent.

Functional Style

The Functional Resume style highlights and emphasizes functional skill sets rather than titles, organizations, and dates. Basically, the duties and responsibilities are separated from their titles and organization names and are presented within their own Skills section. The titles, organization names, dates, and locations are presented in an entirely separate section of the resume. The Functional style lets you highlight your transferable skills that are relevant to your perfect job. It also lets you combine similar responsibilities from more than one job, placing the more important skill sets first and making them more visible.

Chronological Resume

Anita Job

337 Maple Lane	717-555-1111 (W)
Long, PA 17777	E-mail: tah1@ttt.com

EDUCATION

Bachelor of Arts in Government, Spring 1994—*Shippensburg University, PA*

EXPERIENCE

Program Coordinator/Research Analyst—December 1993 to Present
XYZ Transportation Institute—The XYZ State University
- Coordinate outreach activities of the Local Technical Assistance Program (LTAP).
- Serve as Editor of the LTAP quarterly newsletter, which is distributed to all Pennsylvania local governments, all fifty state DOTs, and legislative institutions.
- Coordinate LTAP government relations activities.
- Conduct training for local governments on basic computer applications.
- Coordinate the strategic planning process for the LTAP center.
- Manage a multistate government relations project to facilitate the implementation and evaluation of research products developed by the Federal Highway Administration.
- Administer all facets of contracted research program, including writing proposals, collecting and disseminating data, managing financial resources, reporting to sponsor, and generating reports.
- Supervise support staff and graduate students.

Program Analyst—May 1992 to December 1993
Office of Research and Special Studies—ABC Department of Transportation
- Coordinated all facets of the department's research program, including developing requests for proposals, evaluating researchers, monitoring financial reports, submitting progress reports to management, and ensuring completion of final reports.
- Coordinated the procurement and maintenance of all computer hardware and software.

Research Analyst—December 1991 to May 1992
Legislative Office for Research Liaison (LORL)—The XYZ General Assembly
- Conducted policy research for members of the state legislature.

Legislative Aide/Intern—May 1989 to September 1989 *The Office of State Representative Kyle Heckman*

COMPUTER SKILLS

MS Windows, MS-DOS, MS Word, MS Excel, MS PowerPoint, MS Access, Lotus 1,2,3 WordPerfect 6.1, SPSS 6.0, SAS, Harvard Graphics, Internet (Eudora, Netscape, FTP).

When you look at Anita Job's Functional Resume on page 72, notice that she presents four skill sets under the Transferable Skills section: "Training and Management," "Project/Event Coordination," "Research and Writing," and "Computer." One of the greatest advantages to using the Functional style is that you can easily move skill sets and order them in a way that brings the highest visibility to the skill set that is most relevant. Notice, too, that the titles, organization names, dates, and locations are presented in a different section called "Experience." This makes it difficult for recruiters to determine which skills and responsibilities belong to what job. So, this feature is something like a double-edged sword. By taking your skills and responsibilities out of context, you force the recruiter to try to figure out what you did at what job, something that can sometimes be annoying to the recruiter.

The Functional Style Is Recommended When

- The skills you developed are more relevant or impressive than your titles and organization names.
- You have gaps in your resume (periods of time when you didn't work).
- You are changing career fields or industries.

The Functional Style Is NOT Recommended When

- Your skill areas are not relevant to your perfect job target.
- You want to demonstrate advancement within one field.
- Your titles and organization names are impressive or relevant.
- Other styles will work as well or better (no need to put the recruiters through the difficulty of reviewing this style if other styles that are easier to review work just as well).

Combination Style

The Combination style essentially *combines* the Chronological and Functional styles. Specifically, the Combination style presents experiences in reverse-chronological order within their appropriate Functional skill headings. The Functional headings are placed outside or external to the experiences. This style lets you have the best of both worlds—highlighting skill sets (Functional) *and* keeping the whole experiences together (titles, organization names, and dates are not separated from the description of responsibilities). From the recruiter's standpoint, the Combination style enables them to quickly and easily identify candidates' skill sets and review their experiences. For this reason, the Combination style is very popular among recruiters.

The Combination style usually works best for the experienced job seeker who has held many different positions. If you're an entry-level job seeker, your greatest challenge may be coming up with the number and types of experiences needed to make this style work. For example, if your perfect job dictates that your skill headings should include "Management," "Mar-

Functional Resume

Anita Job

337 Maple Lane   717-555-1111 (W)
Long, PA 17777   E-mail: tah1@ttt.com

EDUCATION

Bachelor of Arts in Government, Spring 1994—*Shippensburg University, PA*

TRANSFERABLE SKILLS

TRAINING AND MANAGEMENT

- Conduct training for local governments on basic computer applications.
- Coordinate the strategic planning process for the Local Technical Assistance Program (LTAP) center.
- Supervise support staff and graduate students.
- Managed all facets of the department's research program, including developing requests for proposals, evaluating researchers, monitoring financial reports, submitting progress reports to management, and ensuring completion of final reports.

PROJECT/EVENT COORDINATION

- Coordinate LTAP government relations activities.
- Coordinate outreach activities of the LTAP.
- Manage a multistate government relations project to facilitate the implementation and evaluation of research products developed by the Federal Highway Administration.

RESEARCH AND WRITING

- Conducted policy research for members of the XYZ legislature.
- Serve as Editor of the LTAP quarterly newsletter, which is distributed to all XYZ local governments, all fifty state DOTs, and legislative institutions.
- Administer all facets of contracted research program, including writing proposals, collecting and disseminating data, managing financial resources, and generating reports.

COMPUTER

- Coordinated the procurement and maintenance of all computer hardware and software.
- MS Windows, MS-DOS, MS Word, MS Excel, MS PowerPoint, MS Access, Lotus 1,2,3 WordPerfect 6.1, SPSS 6.0, SAS, Harvard Graphics, Internet (Eudora, FTP).

EXPERIENCE

Program Coordinator/Research Analyst—December 1993 to Present
XYZ Transportation Institute—The XYZ State University

Program Analyst—May 1992 to December 1993
Office of Research and Special Studies—ABC Department of Transportation

Research Analyst—December 1991 to May 1992
Legislative Office for Research Liaison (LORL)—The XYZ General Assembly

Legislative Aide/Intern—May 1989 to September 1989
The Office of State Representative Kyle Heckman

keting," and "Writing," you must have enough experience in each of these three areas to make the Combination style work.

Look at Anita Job's combination resume on page 74 and notice the two external functional headings, "Training and Project Management" and "Research." See how the experiences within each of these headings are presented in reverse-chronological order. Like the Functional style, the Combination style makes it very easy for you to change the order of experiences, moving the skill set that is most relevant to the top. Unlike the Functional style, the Combination style presents each experience—including titles, organization names, dates, location, and description of responsibilities—all as one unit.

Notice how much space Anita devotes to the Program Coordinator/Research Analyst position compared to the others. It is very common for job seekers to have one or two experiences that are much more meaty or substantive than other experiences (due to the length of time on the job or the position level). The longer you've had the job, the more likely it is that you've developed multiple skills and worked in a wide variety of settings. Within the Program Coordinator/Research Analyst position, Anita has developed skills in the following Functional areas: research, project management, supervision, training, and strategic planning. However, using the Combination style, Anita is forced to choose only one Functional heading.

The downside of the Combination style is that it doesn't let you highlight the multiple skills developed in your more meaty individual experiences. Since the functional headings are placed outside the experience, you are forced to choose one functional heading that best summarizes all the experiences inside that heading.

The Combination Style Is Recommended When

- The skill headings matching your experiences are skills that are consistent with your perfect job.
- You've held an adequate number and diversity of positions needed to fit under your various Functional skill headings.
- You want to present skills not represented in recent experiences (moving these experiences towards the top).
- Both your skills, as well as your position titles and organization names, are impressive and relevant.

The Combination Style Is NOT Recommended When

- The skill headings are not relevant or impressive in relation to your perfect job.
- You don't have enough experiences to fill the Functional skills headings.
- You have impressive, relevant multiple skills within one or each experience.

Combination Resume

Anita Job

337 Maple Lane, Long, PA 17777   717-555-1111 (W)   E-mail: tah1@ttt.com

EDUCATION

Bachelor of Arts in Government, Spring 1994—*Shippensburg University, PA*

EXPERIENCE

TRAINING AND PROJECT MANAGEMENT

Program Coordinator/Research Analyst—December 1993 to Present
XYZ Transportation Institute—The XYZ State University
- Coordinate outreach activities of the Local Technical Assistance Program (LTAP).
- Conduct training for local governments on basic computer applications.
- Coordinate the strategic planning process for the LTAP center.
- Supervise support staff and graduate students.
- Manage a multistate government relations project to facilitate the implementation and evaluation of research products developed by the Federal Highway Administration.
- Manage all facets of contracted research program, including writing proposals, collecting and disseminating data, managing financial resources, reporting to sponsor, and generating reports.
- Coordinate LTAP government relations activities.
- Serve as Editor of the LTAP quarterly newsletter, which is distributed to all state local governments, all fifty state DOTs, and legislative institutions.

Program Analyst—May 1992 to December 1993
Office of Research and Special Studies—ABC Department of Transportation
- Coordinated all facets of the department's research program, including developing requests for proposals, evaluating researchers, monitoring financial reports, submitting progress reports to management, and ensuring completion of final reports.
- Coordinated the procurement and maintenance of all computer hardware and software.

RESEARCH

Research Analyst—December 1991 to May 1992
Legislative Office for Research Liaison (LORL)—The XYZ General Assembly
- Conducted policy research for members of the state legislature.

Legislative Aide—May 1989 to September 1989
The Office of State Representative Kyle Heckman

COMPUTER SKILLS

MS Windows, MS-DOS, MS Word, MS Excel, MS PowerPoint, MS Access, Lotus 1,2,3
WordPerfect 6.1, SPSS 6.0, SAS, Harvard Graphics, Internet (Eudora, Netscape, FTP).

Guidance

*I would encourage
inexperienced job
seekers to be
sensitive to the
reader but to err
on the side of
using too many
examples of
experiences. New
graduates are
especially likely
to overlook how
an office in a
school club or
volunteer experi-
ence might relate
to the position for
which they are
applying.*

—Glaxo
Wellcome

Combination-Internal Style (A New Alternative)

From my extensive experience as a career specialist, the Combination-Internal style has been used very rarely. Similar to the Combination style, the Combination-Internal style combines the Functional and Chronological styles. The difference, however, is that the Combination-Internal style highlights multiple functional skill areas *within* selected *individual* experiences. Many people have had jobs or experiences where they have developed multiple skills and have worked in multiple functional areas. The Combination-Internal style empowers you to highlight these areas and visibly get credit for obtaining multiple skills.

When you look at Anita Job's Combination-Internal Resume on page 76, notice the three functional skill sets highlighted under her position as "Program Coordinator/Research Analyst": "Project and Event Coordination," "Training and Supervision," and "Research and Writing." See how these functional headings are indented to clearly show where they belong. Also notice that the other experiences were not substantive enough to incorporate subheadings. The titles of these other experiences are self-explanatory, yet another reason to avoid a functional breakdown of subheadings. The only real downside to this style is that it's not always conducive to giving Functional headings to all experiences.

If you have individual experiences in which you've developed skills relevant to your perfect job, the Combination-Internal style is highly recommended. Anytime you can hit the recruiter between the eyes with relevant skill headings, you should do it. What recruiter wouldn't want to see Functional headings relating to their job opening? Over and over again, recruiters stress the importance of highlighting skills relevant to the job. The Combination-Internal style offers you a more realistic way to do this.

The Combination-Internal Style Is Recommended When

- You have individual experiences that used multiple skill sets.
- The skill sets within your experiences are relevant and significant to your perfect job target.

The Combination-Internal Style Is NOT Recommended When

- You have many shorter, less substantial experiences.
- The Functional skill headings are not relevant to your perfect job target.

CHOOSING THE STYLE THAT IS PERFECT FOR YOU

Remember, to craft the perfect resume, you must identify your selling points and then choose the resume style that promotes them the most, sending the right message to recruiters. It's crucial to accept the fact

Combination-Internal Resume

Anita Job

337 Maple Lane, Long, PA 17777   717-555-1111 (W)   E-mail: tah1@ttt.com

EDUCATION

Bachelor of Arts in Government, Spring 1994—*Shippensburg University, PA*

EXPERIENCE

Program Coordinator/Research Analyst—December 1993 to Present
XYZ Transportation Institute—The XYZ State University

PROJECT AND EVENT COORDINATION
- Coordinate outreach activities of the Local Technical Assistance Program (LTAP).
- Manage a multistate government relations project to facilitate the implementation and evaluation of research products developed by the Federal Highway Administration.
- Coordinate LTAP government relations activities.

TRAINING AND SUPERVISION
- Coordinate the strategic planning process for the LTAP center.
- Conduct training for local governments on basic computer applications.
- Supervise support staff and graduate students.

RESEARCH AND WRITING
- Manage all facets of contracted research program, including writing proposals, collecting and disseminating data, managing financial resources, reporting to sponsor, and generating reports.
- Serve as Editor of the LTAP quarterly newsletter, which is distributed to all state local governments, all fifty state DOTs, and legislative institutions.

Program Analyst—May 1992 to December 1993
Office of Research and Special Studies—ABC Department of Transportation
- Coordinated all facets of the department's research program, including developing requests for proposals, evaluating researchers, monitoring financial reports, submitting progress reports to management, and ensuring completion of final reports.
- Coordinated the procurement and maintenance of all computer hardware and software.

Research Analyst—December 1991 to May 1992
Legislative Office for Research Liaison (LORL)—The XYZ General Assembly
- Conducted policy research for members of the state legislature.

Legislative Aide/Intern—May 1989 to September 1989
The Office of State Representative Kyle Heckman

COMPUTER SKILLS

MS Windows, MS-DOS, MS Word, MS Excel, MS PowerPoint, MS Access, Lotus 1,2,3 WordPerfect 6.1, SPSS 6.0, SAS, Harvard Graphics, Internet (Eudora, Netscape, FTP).

that there isn't one perfect resume style for everybody. Some job seekers have had much success using the Chronological style, while others benefited more from using the Functional or Combination styles. The worst thing that you can do is to take your information and throw it into someone else's format. You must take the time to determine which style is perfect for you! To illustrate how you can do this, we'll continue to work with Anita Job and her experience. Once we walk through the process for Anita Job, you'll be able to apply this process to your own situation.

Case Study: Crafting the Perfect Resume for Anita Job

The first step is for Anita to identify her selling points. Remember, you must know what you want to pursue (your perfect job) in order to identify your selling points. Anita Job's perfect job target is a process consulting position for a large consulting firm. Areas associated with process consulting include change management, organizational development, strategic planning, training, and project and operational management. Based on her perfect job and information interviews with contacts in consulting, Anita identified five key selling points:

- Project/event coordination skills
- Training experience
- Strategic planning experience
- Computer skills
- Supervisory experience

The second step for Anita is to choose the resume style that places the most emphasis on these selling points. Within this best style, there is additional tweaking that she can do to make her selling points even stronger. Changing the order of the description of duties, paying close attention to word choice, and condensing or removing extraneous or irrelevant experiences are all methods of tweaking. You'll see some of this tweaking as we move along with Anita's case study.

The best way to learn how to choose the perfect resume style is to get in the mind of the recruiter. Therefore, to help Anita pick the best style, you'll be asked to play the part of a recruiter, reviewing the various resume styles within the standard 30-second scan. Pay close attention to how the different styles accentuate selling points, thus changing the message Anita is sending and the corresponding image that is formed. You'll determine which style(s) is most advantageous according to Anita's perfect job target and selling points.

Analyzing the Chronological Style

Imagine you are the recruiter; review Anita's Chronological Resume for 30 seconds. What stands out? What message is being sent or image formed? The image formed in this brief period of time is probably something like this:

- Background in government
- Research and program coordination skills
- Experience working in politics and public administration
- Solid computer skills

Is this style most advantageous for Anita? Does the Chronological style cover her selling points?

Effectiveness of Chronological Style

Essentially, two out of the five selling points were highlighted: project coordination skills and computer skills. Training, strategic planning, and supervision were three selling points that were not effectively highlighted using this style. The image formed is probably a little too research- and politics-oriented to be considered for consulting positions. A different style is most likely needed.

Analyzing the Functional Style

Imagine you are the recruiter; review Anita's Functional Resume for 30 seconds. What stands out? What message is being sent or image formed? The image formed in this brief period of time is probably something like this:

- Background in government
- Training and management skills
- Project/event coordination skills
- Research and writing skills
- Solid computer skills

Is this style most advantageous for Anita? Does the Functional style accentuate her selling points?

Effectiveness of Functional Style

Essentially, three out of the five selling points were highlighted, while a fourth was briefly mentioned. The heading "Training and Management" may imply supervision experience; strategic planning was not empha-sized, but it's related to training. This style is successful in shifting the focus away from research and politics and closer toward Anita's selling points. The concern, however, is the difficulty in determining the extent of experience and strength of each skill due to the nature of this style. With the descriptions and skills separated from their titles, organization names, and dates, it's difficult to determine how much time was spent developing the various skill sets and the context in which they were used. So, the number of selling points highlighted was high, but the quality of these selling points is in question.

Analyzing the Combination Style

Imagine you are the recruiter; review Anita's Combination Resume for 30 seconds. What stands out? What message is being sent or image formed? The image formed in this brief period of time is probably something like this:

- Background in government
- Training and project management experience
- Research experience
- Solid computer skills

Is this style most advantageous for Anita? Does the Combination style accentuate her selling points?

Effectiveness of Combination Style

Three out of the five selling points were highlighted: training, project coordination, and computer skills. Strategic planning and supervision were not emphasized but may be slightly implied. The "Training and Project Management" section is much larger than the "Research Experience" section, thus emphasizing these two selling points well. It's difficult to pick out the training and project management skills within Anita's first experience listed, due to the large number of responsibilities described. Overall, this was a fairly effective style for Anita.

Analyzing the Combination-Internal Style

Imagine you are the recruiter; review Anita's Combination-Internal resume for 30 seconds. What stands out? What message is being sent or image formed? The image formed in this brief period of time is probably something like this:

- Background in government
- Project and event coordination experience
- Training and supervision experience
- Research and writing experience
- Solid computer skills

Is this style most advantageous for Anita? Does the Combination-Internal style accentuate her selling points?

Effectiveness of Combination-Internal Style

Four out of the five selling points were highlighted: training, supervision, project coordination, and computer skills. Strategic planning was moved to the first responsibility described under the "Training and Supervision" heading. Therefore, it has a better chance of being noticed. The subheadings within Anita's largest experience made it easier to pick out relevant responsibilities. Due to the size and scope of Anita's most recent work experience, the Combination-Internal is the style that's most effective for her to use.

Revised Combination-Internal Resume

Anita Job

337 Maple Lane, Long, PA 17777 ♦ 717–555-1111 (W) ♦ E-mail: tah1@ttt.com

EDUCATION

Bachelor of Arts in Government, Spring 1994—*Shippensburg University, PA*

EXPERIENCE

Program Coordinator/Research Analyst—December 1993 to Present
XYZ Transportation Institute—The XYZ State University

PROJECT AND PROGRAM MANAGEMENT

- Coordinate outreach activities of the Local Technical Assistance Program (LTAP).
- Manage a multistate government relations project to facilitate the implementation and evaluation of research products developed by the Federal Highway Administration.
- Coordinate LTAP government relations activities.
- Manage all facets of contracted research program, including writing proposals, collecting and disseminating data, managing financial resources, reporting to sponsor, and generating reports.

TRAINING AND SUPERVISION

- Coordinate the strategic planning process for the LTAP center.
- Conduct training for local governments on basic computer applications.
- Supervise support staff and graduate students.

Program Analyst—May 1992 to December 1993
Office of Research and Special Studies—ABC Department of Transportation

- Coordinated all facets of the department's research program, including developing requests for proposals, evaluating researchers, monitoring financial reports, submitting progress reports to management, and ensuring completion of final reports.
- Coordinated the procurement and maintenance of all computer hardware and software.

Research Analyst—December 1991 to May 1992
Legislative Office for Research Liaison (LORL)—The XYZ General Assembly

- Conducted policy research for members of the state legislature.

Legislative Aide/Intern—May 1989 to September 1989
The Office of State Representative Kyle Heckman

COMPUTER SKILLS

MS Windows, MS-DOS, MS Word, MS Excel, MS PowerPoint, MS Access, Lotus 1,2,3
WordPerfect 6.1, SPSS 6.0, SAS, Harvard Graphics, Internet (Eudora, Netscape, FTP).

Tweaking within a Style to Make It Perfect

Once a style has been chosen, there's still some tweaking or shifts in emphasis that you can make to draw more attention to your selling points. Look at Anita's revised Combination-Internal Resume on page 80. Just by moving one of the former "Research and Writing" responsibilities under slightly revised heading "Project and Program Management" and eliminating the other "Research and Writing" responsibility, the emphasis is even more stronger toward Anita's selling points. De-emphasizing less relevant experiences (research) can strengthen your focus on the more relevant experiences.

Tweaking puts the finishing touches on your resume. Pay attention to the terms you're using and the way you're wording things. Constantly ask yourself how these words and terms will be received by the recruiter, and determine if there's a better way. Have a friend, colleague, or career counselor review your resume. Ask them what message they get and what stands out in their minds. If you know someone in your career field, ask them to offer advice on how you could tweak your resume a bit to highlight the most relevant and important information.

THE WHOLE IN ONE

- To craft the perfect resume, you must first identify your selling points. Selling points should be consistent with what you are pursuing—your perfect job.

- The second step is to choose a resume style that best promotes or highlights your selling points. Since recruiters spend less than 30 seconds initially reviewing your resume, it's critical that your selling points are presented in such a way that the image or first impression that is formed is most favorable.

- No one style fits all job seekers.

- To craft your perfect resume, choose one of the four styles— Chronological, Functional, Combination, or Combination-Internal— and do some tweaking within the chosen style to further accentuate your selling points.

ASSIGNMENT

Complete the "Resume" section of Goal 3 of your Personal Job Search Trainer.

Chapter 6

Special Types of Resumes: When the Other Styles Don't Work

GET THE SCOOP ON . . .

- Multiple versions of your resume
- Producing computer-friendly resumes
- Differences between experienced and entry-level resumes
- Selling multiple skills
- Marketing your academic experiences
- How to make a results-oriented resume

THE ADAPTABLE RESUME: MULTIPLE VERSIONS OF YOUR RESUME

Most job seekers have more than one skill they would enjoy using in a career. For example, in your Professional Self-Profile, you identified your top five skills that you would most enjoy using on the job. In today's volatile workforce, it's important that you produce multiple versions of your resume that correspond to your multiple skills of interest. This enables you to market yourself to a wide range of career opportunities and prospective employers. Don't worry, with today's technology, you won't have to write five or six resumes from scratch. By using the current tools of word processing, such as cutting, copying, and pasting, designing multiple versions of your resume is a snap.

The Consulting-Oriented resume that follows uses the Combination-Internal style that was presented in the last chapter. Notice the order of the functional subheadings within the Program Coordinator/Research Analyst position. This version is emphasizing the "Project and Event Coordination" and "Training and Supervision" subheadings because of its intended use for consulting opportunities.

Anita is also considering job opportunities related to research and development (R&D), so she's created a second version of her resume that places a higher emphasis on her research skills. Review the Research-Oriented resume that follows. Notice how the image of a resume can drastically change just by moving things around, and that

Consulting-Oriented Resume

Anita Job

337 Maple Lane, Long, PA 17777   717-555-1111 (W)   E-mail: tah1@ttt.com

EDUCATION

Bachelor of Arts in Government, Spring 1994—*Shippensburg University, PA*

EXPERIENCE

Program Coordinator/Research Analyst—December 1993 to Present
XYZ Transportation Institute—The XYZ State University

PROJECT AND EVENT COORDINATION

- Coordinate outreach activities of the Local Technical Assistance Program (LTAP).
- Manage a multistate government relations project to facilitate the implementation and evaluation of research products developed by the Federal Highway Administration.
- Coordinate LTAP government relations activities.

TRAINING AND SUPERVISION

- Coordinate the strategic planning process for the LTAP center.
- Conduct training for local governments on basic computer applications.
- Supervise support staff and graduate students.

RESEARCH AND WRITING

- Manage all facets of contracted research program, including writing proposals, collecting and disseminating data, managing financial resources, reporting to sponsor, and generating reports.
- Serve as Editor of the LTAP quarterly newsletter, which is distributed to all state local governments, all fifty state DOTs, and legislative institutions.

Program Analyst—May 1992 to December 1993
Office of Research and Special Studies—ABC Department of Transportation

- Coordinated all facets of the department's research program, including developing requests for proposals, evaluating researchers, monitoring financial reports, submitting progress reports to management, and ensuring completion of final reports.
- Coordinated the procurement and maintenance of all computer hardware and software.

Research Analyst—December 1991 to May 1992
Legislative Office for Research Liaison (LORL)—The XYZ General Assembly

- Conducted policy research for members of the state legislature.

Legislative Aide/Intern—May 1989 to September 1989
The Office of State Representative Kyle Heckman

COMPUTER SKILLS

MS Windows, MS-DOS, MS Word, MS Excel, MS PowerPoint, MS Access, Lotus 1,2,3
WordPerfect 6.1, SPSS 6.0, SAS, Harvard Graphics, Internet (Eudora, Netscape, FTP).

re-ordering subheadings and adding an objective can change the overall image that is formed. Also notice that the Program Coordinator/Research Analyst title was changed to Research Analyst/Program Coordinator. This subtle change can make a difference when a recruiter is scanning a resume in less than 30 seconds.

If Anita was pursuing research positions, this version of a Combination-Internal Resume would work well. Isn't it amazing how the same person, with the same experiences, can have two very different-looking resumes. Anita has adapted her resume to fit the two different types of jobs she's pursuing.

The days of making 50 copies of the same resume are over. Just as no one resume is perfect for everybody, no one resume is perfect for every job for which you apply. You must be ready to revise your resume to fit the career opportunity at hand. The most important copy of your resume for you to have is the electronic version you have saved to a disk. If your resume is electronic, it can easily be updated and/or revised as different job opportunities surface. If you don't have easy access to a computer, there are many printing and copying businesses that will print and make copies of your resume for a nominal fee. Keep one original copy of each different version of your resume so you are ready to make copies of them when you need to.

THE ELECTRONIC RESUME: PRODUCING COMPUTER-FRIENDLY RESUMES

Guidance

Resumes remain the primary resource for employers to get a quick assessment of a prospective employee. With today's technology in scanning resumes, content of the resume, not appearance, makes the vital difference in differentiating one prospective employee from the next.

—Johnson & Johnson

Technology hasn't just made it easier on you, the job seeker. It's also simplified things for recruiters; their use of technology to recruit job candidates has dramatically increased. In 1997, 88 percent of employers used electronic sources to find job candidates. (Source: Lee Hecht Harrison) There are two primary methods of technology that recruiters use to review resumes. They can scan a hard copy of your resume into their computer to be electronically reviewed, or they can review a copy of your resume that you posted on the Internet. Therefore, another version of your resume that you must create is a computer-friendly version.

The Scanable Hard-Copy Resume

For those employers that scan your resume into their computer for review, you must produce and send a scanable version of your resume. If you're unable to determine whether they will scan your resume, there's nothing wrong with submitting two versions of your resume: one attractive version (using bolding, italics, etc.) on cotton-bond paper and one plain version on standard white paper. Doing this shows that you cover all your bases and leave nothing to chance. Mention in your cover letter that you have sent two versions.

Research-Oriented Resume

Anita Job

337 Maple Lane, Long, PA 17777   717-555-1111 (W)   E-mail: tah1@ttt.com

OBJECTIVE
To provide writing and research skills to the research and
development division of a corporation.

EDUCATION
Bachelor of Arts in Government, Spring 1994—*Shippensburg University, PA*

EXPERIENCE
Research Analyst/Program Coordinator—December 1993 to Present
XYZ Transportation Institute—The XYZ State University

RESEARCH AND WRITING
- Manage all facets of contracted research program, including writing proposals, collecting and disseminating data, managing financial resources, reporting to sponsor, and generating reports.
- Manage a multistate government relations project to facilitate the implementation and evaluation of research products developed by the Federal Highway Administration.
- Serve as Editor of the LTAP quarterly newsletter, which is distributed to all state local governments, all fifty state DOTs, and legislative institutions.

PROJECT AND EVENT COORDINATION
- Coordinate outreach activities of the Local Technical Assistance Program (LTAP).
- Coordinate LTAP government relations activities.

TRAINING AND SUPERVISION
- Conduct training for local governments on basic computer applications.
- Coordinate the strategic planning process for the LTAP center.
- Supervise support staff and graduate students.

Program Analyst—May 1992 to December 1993
Office of Research and Special Studies—ABC Department of Transportation
- Coordinated all facets of the department's research program, including developing requests for proposals, evaluating researchers, monitoring financial reports, submitting progress reports to management, and ensuring completion of final reports.
- Coordinated the procurement and maintenance of all computer hardware and software.

Research Analyst—December 1991 to May 1992
Legislative Office for Research Liaison (LORL)—The XYZ General Assembly
- Conducted policy research for members of the state legislature.

Legislative Aide/Intern—May 1989 to September 1989
The Office of State Representative Kyle Heckman

COMPUTER SKILLS
MS Windows, MS-DOS, MS Word, MS Excel, MS PowerPoint, MS Access, Lotus 1,2,3
WordPerfect 6.1, SPSS 6.0, SAS, Harvard Graphics, Internet (Eudora, Netscape, FTP).

Keep Your Scanable Resume Plain and Simple

Recruiters scan your resume into their computer system so that the computer rather than people can review your resume. This saves the recruiter time, but it also means that a resume that would normally impress him or her may be overlooked if the computer either doesn't "like" your resume or can't "read" it. You must realize that the computer doesn't review resumes in the same way that a human recruiter does. The computer recruiter doesn't like fancy script, italics, or underlining. In fact, it can't even read fancy print. Therefore, the first rule is to keep it plain and simple. Review the tips below to help you keep your scanable resume plain and simple.

- **Paper:** Use standard-size (8½ × 11), white paper, printed on one side only.
- **Highlighting:** Use all caps or bold; do not use italics, script, or underlined highlights.
- **Font Size:** The font size should be between 10 and 14 points.
- **Font Type:** Stay away from fancy fonts; use a plain font (e.g., Courier, Arial, Times New Roman, Helvetica).
- **Graphics:** Don't use graphics, shading, boxes, or lines; do not compress spaces between letters.
- **Folding/Stapling:** Avoid folding or stapling your resume.

Take a look at the computer-friendly resume sample on page 88 and notice its plain, simple nature. This is the kind of resume you should submit if you think the recruiter may scan it and have a computer look at it. Notice how boldface and all caps are ways to highlight the text. The font is Times New Roman, and the font size ranges from 10 to 14. There are no graphics, fancy bullets, or lines.

Load Up with Keywords

When a company scans your resume for a computer to look at it rather than a human being, the way your resume is reviewed is dramatically affected. Rather than look at your resume as a whole, a computer looks only for specific keywords that it has been programmed to recognize. If the computer finds enough keywords on your resume, it is flagged and set aside for review by a recruiter. If the computer doesn't find enough keywords, your resume is ignored, eliminating any chance of you being called in for an interview. Keywords are field-specific terms and functional skills relevant to a job, industry, or employer. On traditional resumes, you are highly advised to use action verbs, such as develop, create, and produce. This is good advice for traditional resumes, but these action verbs rarely make it on the computer recruiter's list of keywords. Therefore, you must find ways to incorporate relevant field-specific terms and functional skills into your resume.

FYI

Choosing the right words to put on your resume has always been important. When it comes to scanable resumes, choosing the right words to put on your resume means everything! Keywords make or break your chances of getting a second look.

Computer-Friendly Resume

Mary Elon

Local Address
1997 East Haggard Avenue
Elon College, NC 27244
336-555-0000

Permanent Address
One Oak Road
Home, PA 07871
717-555-9999

OBJECTIVE   To obtain a full-time position in hotel and restaurant management.

EDUCATION   ELON COLLEGE, Elon College, NC
Bachelor of Arts in Psychology, May 1998

RELEVANT EXPERIENCE

Intern, THE HOMETOWN COUNTRY CLUB, Home, NC, December 1996 to May 1997

Coordinated events that included the grand opening, golf tournaments, and invitationals, which entailed promoting events, establishing relationships with food and beverage vendors, managing the budget, providing cost estimates, and implementing all other event responsibilities.

Presented membership privileges and registration information to new-member prospects.

Managed the marketing, coordination, and presentation of merchandise.

Assisted in managing the overall budget using Microsoft Excel.

Managed the snack bar, including hiring and training staff, and overall operation.

Wrote press releases and contacted local newspapers for coverage of events.

Sales and Catering Assistant, THE INN, Burlington, NC, Fall 1997

Solicited new clients and developed sales contracts.

Assisted Banquet Manager, Food and Beverage Administrator, and Sales and Marketing Director.

Performed administrative duties that included providing telephone coverage, screening mail, distributing memos and faxes, and mailing service contracts and invoices.

WORK EXPERIENCE

Waitress, LONGBRANCH STEAKHOUSE AND SALOON, Burlington, NC, 1994 to 1996

Trained new wait staff and assisted with coordinating parties.

Banquet Staff, ALAMANCE COUNTRY CLUB, Burlington, NC, 1994 to 1995

Served as waitress and bartender during weddings and other private functions.

VOLUNTEER SERVICE

Assisted in charity race for breast cancer awareness for the Women's Hospital of Greensboro.

COMPUTER SKILLS

Experience using Microsoft Office: Excel, Word, Access, and PowerPoint and the Internet.

Review the following resume statement that is found in the "Experience" section of a resume:

Developed various computer skills.

The term "various" most likely will not be a keyword. So, despite all the computer skills you've developed, your resume could very well be ignored because the computer didn't find what it was looking for. You must describe the *various* computer skills in order for them to be detected by the computer. Review the revised statement.

Developed various computer skills, including Microsoft Access database software and Microsoft Excel spreadsheet software.

Guidance

In resume building, it is essential to list all prior activities and experiences that relate to the job in which you have interest. With computerized key word search capabilities, the content of your resume will get you on the employer's "radar screen."
—Johnson & Johnson

Now there are six new potential keywords that the computer may recognize: Microsoft, Access, database, software, Excel, and spreadsheet. It may seem like splitting hairs to you, but choosing the right words for this kind of resume could make all the difference in the world.

Finally, make sure that your name is the first item on your resume. You want to be the one to get credit for all those keywords!

Take another look at the computer-friendly resume sample, and identify the potential keywords. For this particular resume, Mary Elon is pursuing a job in hotel/restaurant management, so keep this in mind as you look for words you think a computer has most likely been programmed to look for. Remember, too, that keywords can be functional skills or field-specific terms.

Keywords on Mary's resume that the computer has most likely been programmed to detect include the following:

Field-specific terms:

hotel, restaurant, management, intern, country club, events, golf, food, beverage, vendors, membership, registration, catering, inn, press releases, waitress, parties, served, bartender, weddings, functions

Functional skills and areas:

coordinated, promoting, budget, marketing, wrote, sales, bachelor, telephone, mail, faxes, contracts, invoices, trained, volunteer, computer, Microsoft Office, Excel, Word, Access, PowerPoint, Internet

The Internet-Posted Resume

There are many job search sites on the Internet where you can post your resume on line. See "Posting Your Resume" in Appendix A for a listing of Internet posting sites. Also, more and more companies are adding a

Inexperienced Resume

Justin Time

50 Hitthe Road
Jobsville, PA 11111
777-555-7777

EDUCATION   **ABC UNIVERSITY,** Carburg, Pennsylvania
Major: History   Current Status: Second Semester Junior

XYZ COLLEGE, Toadville, Pennsylvania
Major: Elementary Education—1994 to 1995

**WORK
EXPERIENCE**   **Student Assistant—***Football Office*
ABC University—Spring Semester 1997

- Conducted tours for prospective student-athletes and their parents.
- Assisted with the general student-athlete recruitment process, including the coordination of student-athlete files and data entry.

Sales Clerk—Stack Outlet
Hanes, Pennsylvania—Summer 1996

Staff Assistant—Turnersville Recreation
Turnersville, Pennsylvania—Winters 1995 and 1996

- Assisted in coordinating a basketball clinic for children from 2nd grade to 6th grade.
- Coached 6th grade all-star team and officiated basketball games.

Student Assistant—Athletic Department
ABC College—Summer 1995

- Assisted the Sports Information Director.
- Coached 4th graders and assisted in fundamental skills training during Youth Developmental Football Camps.
- Videotaped football games and led quarterbacks through various drills during ABC College Football Camp.

Stock Clerk—*Harrison Store*
Turnersville, Pennsylvania—Summer 1994

ACTIVITIES   Volunteer for Special Olympics
Varsity Football—ABC College
Volunteer: Cleaning Up, The College Project, ABC College
Intramural Sports—Basketball, Softball, XYZ University

Experienced Resume

Gene P. Lakes

280 Long River Road
Beachtown, CA 17777
555-555-5555
E-Mail: yyyy@co.org

SUMMARY OF QUALIFICATIONS

- More than twenty years of sales experience
- More than ten years of high-level sales as Senior Account Executive
- Received numerous sales awards and achievements
- Strong leadership skills through participating in seminars and military training
- Experience and skills in developing computer databases and Web pages

EXPERIENCE

XYZ Engineering Systems, Harrisburg, PA
Senior Account Executive—1987 to Present
Copier Sales Representative—1978 to 1987

- Responsible for the sale and lease of XYZ engineering products in central Pennsylvania with an annual budget of more than $1 million.
- Acquired computer skills and working knowledge of electronic document distribution systems and network connectivity in response to a recent shift of the XES product mix to a digital environment.
- Sold CAD workstations, plotters, scanners, and associated software, which are now digital parts of global solutions costing well over $1 million when third-party vendors are included.

PROFESSIONAL ACCOMPLISHMENTS

- Recipient of 18 President's Club Awards (One of only two XES employees who have attained 18 President's Club Awards, which is the highest XYZ sales award given).
- Sales Representative of the Year—two years (Highest percent of sales budget).
- General Manager's Award for Sales Excellence—three-time recipient.
- Received special invitation as one of only nine U.S. Sales Representatives who attended a two-week program in Japan and Hong Kong, May 1988.

Gene P. Lakes—Page 2

MILITARY SERVICE
- Active duty attached to the District Intelligence Office in New York City—1968 to 1971.
- Earned several commendations, including one from the Captain of USS *Nautilus*.
- Active in Naval Reserve from 1971 until retirement as LCDR in 1988.

COMPUTER SKILLS

Internet/World Wide Web—Produced home page for local business group.

Database Development—Designed, developed, and implemented a relational database used to maintain records of sales, report statistics, and produce the annual report.

Multimedia Presentation/Design—Designed, produced, and implemented numerous automated slide presentations using Astound (animated graphics) and PowerPoint software.

IBM—Microsoft Word, Microsoft Access, Microsoft PowerPoint, Astound (Slide presentation design).

Macintosh—MacWrite, MacPro, Managing Your Money (Budget design and management).

PERSONAL INTERESTS
- Tennis, foreign travel, antique furniture restoration, and military history study.
- Member of Naval Academy Athletic Association.

EDUCATION

St. Joseph's University, Philadelphia, PA: Bachelor of Science in Political Science, 1966

Temple Law School, Philadelphia, PA: One-year scholarship awarded, 1976–1977

TRAINING

XYZ International Center For Management Training, Leesburg VA

Formal training sessions included:

Leadership Through Quality, Effective Sales Presentations and Proposals, and PC Skills

Defense Language School, Monterey, CA:
Special Russian Language Course, 1978

Naval Officer Candidate School, Newport, RI:
Commissioned, July 1970

section to their home page where you can submit your resume on line. There are some concerns to posting your resume on the Internet. First, you must realize that once you post your resume on line, it's out there for the world to see. Some people are uncomfortable with their personal address and phone number being accessible to the world. Therefore, you must determine what information you want to include on your Internet-posted resume. In addition, you should explore the legitimacy of the Internet site or company to which you are electronically submitting your resume. Ask who will be able to view your resume.

DIFFERENCES BETWEEN EXPERIENCED AND INEXPERIENCED RESUMES

Whether you have thirty years of experience or you're fresh out of high school or college with no experience, the resume's purpose remains the same: to promote your selling points to prospective employers. However, there are some differences between the experienced and inexperienced job seeker that are important to note, and these differences have a direct impact on the way a resume should be written and structured. Note that "inexperienced job seeker" refers to a person who has little *work* experience, rather than a person with little *job-seeking* experience. As you read about these differences, refer to the *Inexperienced Resume* sample and the *Experienced Resume* sample presented on the following pages.

Resume Length

If you're an inexperienced job seeker, you should stick with the general rule of thumb and keep your resume to one page. Exceptions to this rule are those of you in education (student teaching and practicums take up space), health/psychological care (clinical, practicums, and internships take up space), and others of you who have been extensively involved in internships and leadership activities. If you're a more experienced job seeker, you typically have more flexibility and can go to two pages due to your extensive experience.

Description Length

If you're an inexperienced job seeker, you'll have fewer experiences to present, so the descriptions of your responsibilities can be a little longer, especially those responsibilities relevant to what you're pursuing. If you're an experienced professional, you'll list the more important, big-picture responsibilities. As a general rule of thumb, the more relevant the experience, the longer the descriptions should be. Recruiters will spend more time reading those areas that are important to them.

Multiple Skills Resume

Hirem N. Hurry

ABC College, Box 000, 200 Jake Street, Cassidy, IN 18018 555-555-5555

EDUCATION

Bachelor of Arts in Political Science, May 1997   **ABC College,** Cassidy IN
Minor: Philosophy   GPA: 3.27   Major GPA: 3.48

RELEVANT COURSES

Independent Study: American Women in Politics   Public Administration and
                                    Politics of Labor   Public Policy
                                                                            Labor Economics

LEADERSHIP EXPERIENCE

Resident Director—*Residence Hall Staff,* ABC College—Fall 1995 to
                    Spring 1996

Programming: Initiated and coordinated dorm-wide educational and social work-
                        shops.

Management: Supervised a five-person staff; facilitated weekly staff meetings.

Discipline: Enforced college and dorm regulations.

Liaison: Acted as direct link to Office of Student Services and Dean of Students.

Advising: Served as confidant for both residents and staff members; acted in
                        times of various emergencies.

Teamwork: Facilitated community development and intergroup norms and goals.

President—*United Student Government,* ABC College—Fall 1996 to
                    Present

Financial: Managed a $95,000 budget that is allocated to eighty-five student
                        organizations.

Management: Supervised twenty student senators and sixteen class officers and
                        presided over meetings.

Liaison: Served as student link to the college faculty and administrators.

Vice President—*United Student Government,* ABC College—Fall 1995
                    to Spring 1996

Financial: Developed a $95,000 budget; designed financial allocation policies for
                        all student organizations.

Programming: Initiated various forums/discussions with administrators.

Recruiting: Coordinated and oversaw campus-wide election process.

President—*Zeta Tau Alpha Sorority,* ABC College—Fall 1995 to Present

Development: Active in coordinating the transition from a local chapter to a national
                        sorority.

Supervision: Presided over weekly membership and executive board meetings.

Management: Coordinated all official sorority business with the national office and
                        the college greek adviser.

Plain-Jane Resume

Jane Academic

PERMANENT
1000 Bottleneck Street
Jesse, CA 11111
302-555-7777

CAMPUS
10 Oak Street
Carle, CA 11111
302-555-0000

CAREER OBJECTIVE

To secure a full-time, entry-level position in environmental consulting

EDUCATION

Bachelor of Science in Environmental Science, May 1996
University of ABC, Carle, CA

Major GPA: 3.0/4.0   Concentration: Atmospheric
Financed 100 percent of college education

COMPUTER EXPERIENCE

Operating Systems: UNIX, DOS, Windows   **Programming:** FORTRAN
Statistics/Graphics Packages: SAS, DI3000, GIS

ACTIVITIES AND INTERESTS

University of ABC varsity crew team member—received Gold Medal at 1993 Regatta
Intramural sports: girls lacrosse, field hockey
Member of University Outing Club

WORK EXPERIENCE

Beach Lifeguard for North Shores Beach Club—Summers 1993 to 1994
- Responsible for the overall safety of the North Shores Beach Club members.
- Trained in first aid and CPR.

Pool Lifeguard for the North Shores Beach Club—Summer 1992
- Responsible for the overall safety of the North Shores Beach Club members.
- Trained in first aid and CPR.
- Organized private tennis lessons.

XYZ Company—Part time 1992 to 1993
- Scored perfect on the product exam and assisted in managing incoming shipments.

VOLUNTEER WORK

Wilmington Rowing Club—Assisted in building a new dock for the rowing club, March 1994.

YMCA of Rehoboth—Provided daycare for local residence, April 1990.

Academic-Jane Resume

Jane Academic

PERMANENT
1000 Bottleneck Street
Jesse, CA 11111
302-555-7777

CAMPUS
10 Oak Street
Carle, CA 11111
302-555-0000

CAREER OBJECTIVE
To secure a full-time, entry-level position in environmental consulting

EDUCATION
Bachelor of Science in **Environmental Science,** May 1996, **University of ABC,** Carle, CA
Major GPA: 3.0/4.0 Concentration: **Atmospheric** Financed 100 percent of college education

COMPUTER EXPERIENCE
Operating Systems: UNIX, DOS, Windows   **Programming:** FORTRAN
Statistics/Graphics Packages: SAS, DI3000, GIS

ENVIRONMENTAL SCIENCE EXPERIENCE
Microclimate Analysis—University of ABC, 1996
- Measured and analyzed flux of heat energy and radiation of a small area.
- Instruments utilized: pyranometer, net radiometer, and infrared temperature guns.

Coastal Environmental Research—University of ABC, 1995
- Researched the transgression of the Carle and northern California barrier island systems.
- Examined the beach environments and erosion caused by longshore drift.
- Studied coastal change, dune migration, and spit advance at Cape Mickencarla.

Modeling and Evaluation of Climatic Processes—University of ABC, 1995
- Used FORTRAN programming to build and evaluate mathematical and statistical models of climatic processes that describe the receipt, transformation, storage, and disposal of radiation.

Climatic Water Budget Analysis—University of ABC, 1994
- Examined the effect of land use change on ground water recharge.
- Computed daily water budgets of Wilmington, DE; Key West, FL; and Bonners Ferry, ID.
- Application of water budget factors, including leaching through landfills, irrigation scheduling, plant/crop yield, and forest fire prediction.

ACTIVITIES AND INTERESTS
University of ABC varsity crew team member—received Gold Medal at 1993 Regatta
Intramural sports: girls lacrosse, field hockey; Member of University of ABC Outing Club

WORK EXPERIENCE
Beach Lifeguard for North Shores Beach Club—First aid and CPR—Summers 1993 to 1994.
Pool Lifeguard for the North Shores Beach Club—Organized private tennis schedules, Summer 1992.

XYZ Company—Part time 1992 to 1993
- Scored perfect on the product exam and assisted in managing incoming shipments.

VOLUNTEER WORK
Wilmington Rowing Club—Assisted in building a new dock for the rowing club, March 1994.
YMCA of Rehoboth—Provided daycare for local residents, April 1990.

Qualifications Summary

Experienced job seekers have many more meaty experiences and skills worth summarizing. Therefore, a "Summary of Qualifications" section or "Summary of Skills" section is much more likely to be seen on an experienced resume. Remember that recruiters just want the facts, so this section should be included only if you have from four to seven factual selling points worth reporting.

Experience vs. Education

If you're an inexperienced job seeker, you have gained most of your experience and skills in the classroom. Therefore, it's appropriate to start off your resume with the "Education" section. Conversely, experienced job seekers have acquired professional skills and experiences that are very important to prospective employers. Since these experiences are more important and much more impressive, it's more common to begin your resume with "Experience" rather than "Education."

SELLING MULTIPLE SKILLS: THE NEW COMBINATION-INTERNAL RESUME

Many job seekers have had experiences in which they've developed multiple skills. However, in a typical 30-second scan of your resume, most recruiters overlook the majority of these skills. The Combination-Internal resume introduced in the previous chapter allows you to highlight your multiple skills. A slightly different version of a Combination-Internal resume is presented on page 94. Notice that the "functional skill" subheadings in this sample are presented on the same line as each individual responsibility rather than on top of a few responsibilities, as presented earlier. This version allows for a greater number of highlighted skills. The version that you choose depends on the number of skills that you want to highlight and how well the responsibilities fit under each skill.

WHEN IT'S ALL ACADEMIC: MARKETING YOUR EDUCATION

I've worked with hundreds of young job seekers who have stated that they don't have any relevant experience to put on their resume. They've been engrossed in their studies and have not had a chance to gain experience out in the real world. After probing with a few questions, most of these young job seekers revealed academic experiences that were indeed relevant. What these job seekers didn't realize was that recruiters care more about the substance and relevance of the experience than whether it was paid or volunteer. Review your

Results Resume

Phil W. Facts

1000 Accomplishments Lane
Resultsville, NH 11111
555-222-5000 (H)
222-333-6000 (W)

OBJECTIVE

Full-time position in pharmaceutical sales.

SALES EXPERIENCE

Account Executive—XYZ Corporation, Resultsville, NH *March 1995–Present*

Consistently exceed company and local market revenue goals and quotas while managing a territory consisting of more than 3,000 businesses.

ACCOMPLISHMENTS

- Won 1997 company-wide sales incentive trip to Maui, Hawaii (Recognized as one of the top six Account Executives from approximately 500 representatives—167 percent quota).
- President's Club Award Winner, 1996–97.
- Won 1996 company-wide sales incentive trip to Cancun, Mexico (Recognized as one of the top six Account Executives from approximately 500 representatives—140 percent quota).
- Club 60 Award Winner, 1997.
- Club 50 Award Winner, 1996.
- Won 1995 company-wide incentive trip to Paradise Island, Bahamas (180 percent quota).
- Top Account Executive for the Resultsville Market, 1995, 1996, 1997.
- Won 1996 regional sales contest trip to Miami Beach, FL.
- Won 1995 regional sales contest trip to New York City, NY.

Sales Manager—XYZ Corporation, Othertown, NH, *March 1994–March 1995*

Consistently exceeded company and local market revenue goals and quotas while managing the Long County territory consisting of more than 3,000 businesses.

ACCOMPLISHMENTS

- President's Club Award Winner, 1994–95.
- Top Account Executive in the New Hampshire region and company wide (1994).
- Won 1995 Jeep Grand Cherokee—the 1994 company-wide sales incentive prize—presented to the top Account Executive (220 percent quota).
- XYZ's top performing Account Executive for September 1994.

Phil W. Facts—Page 2

Sales Representative—XYZ Company, Benny, NH, *July 1993–March 1994*

Consistently exceeded company and local market revenue goals and quotas.

ACCOMPLISHMENTS

- Recognized on XYZ's Elite list for September, October, November, December, January, and February for high sales productivity.
- Won 1993 regional sales contest to Orlando, Florida (240 percent quota).
- XYZ's top performing inside sales representative for October 1993.

Sales Representative—ABC Store, Resultsville, NH *October 1991–July 1993*

- Recognized as highest fine jewelry salesperson, store wide and company wide.
- Maintained this job while a full-time student at ABC University.

EDUCATION

Bachelor of Science in Education, May 1993
ABC University, Resultsville, NH
Elementary Education Major with an Early Childhood Certification
Major GPA: 3.4

ASSOCIATIONS

Resultsville Trading Group
Resultsville County Chamber of Commerce, Membership Committee
Resultsville Jaycees

PROFESSIONAL TRAINING

Consistently participates in company-wide sales training seminars and workshops.

experiences that are related to your high school or college course work. There may be a project, term paper, experiment, case study, research study, practicum, internship, or some other field work that you're overlooking.

This point is clearly illustrated through the *plain-jane resume* and the *academic-jane resume*. Both resumes are actual resumes from a real client, disguised as "Jane Academic." Jane was pursuing a career in environmental consulting. The plain-jane resume was the actual resume Jane started with. She had very little luck obtaining interviews. The academic-jane resume was the version of her resume after agreeing to incorporate her classroom field-work into a section called "Environmental Science Experience." Notice how Jane condensed her less relevant "Work Experience" section to leave more room for the more relevant "Environmental Science Experience" section. Jane had much success generating interviews with this version and ultimately obtained a job with an environmental consulting firm in Pennsylvania.

HOW TO MAKE A RESULTS-ORIENTED RESUME

Guidance

Don't just list what your responsibilities were; indicate how you contributed or made a difference.

—Enterprise Rent-A-Car

Results and accomplishments are powerful parts of a resume. However, as mentioned in Chapter 4, listing results on a resume doesn't work for everybody. If you have measurable results, make sure to highlight them on your resume. The most effective way to present your accomplishments is by describing your individual experiences across two categories: responsibilities and accomplishments. Review the following Results-Oriented resume. Notice how Phil Facts' accomplishments subsections, see pages 98 and 99, consist of measurable outcomes. There are no opinions presented, just facts.

THE WHOLE IN ONE

- There are many different types of resumes. One size definitely does not fit all. Your resume must be adaptable to different types of jobs.

- You should develop and produce a computer-friendly version of your resume, one that can be scanned by a computer and contains detectable keywords.

- While the purpose of any resume is to accentuate your selling points, there are some differences between experienced and inexperienced resumes. Experienced resumes tend to be longer, are led by experience, and are results oriented.

- The new Combination-Internal Resume that was introduced offers an effective way of selling your multiple skills that were developed from one experience.

- The most overlooked experiences for younger job seekers are academic projects, experiments, and field work. These experiences can be extremely relevant to recruiters.

- If you have measurable results from various experiences, make sure to highlight them. Incorporating an "Accomplishments" section within an individual experience is the best way to sell your results.

ASSIGNMENT

If you haven't already, complete the "Resume" section of Goal 3 of your Personal Job Search Trainer.

Chapter 7

Cover Letters and Portfolios: Completing Your Self-Marketing Package

---

GET THE SCOOP ON . . .

- Cover letters
- Open cover letters
- Hidden cover letters
- Crafting the perfect cover letter
- Portfolios
- Web-based portfolios

THE PURPOSE AND NATURE OF COVER LETTERS

The cover letter is an important part of your self-marketing package. It's often the very first point of contact you have with the recruiter. Cover letters allow you to introduce yourself to prospective employers in a more personal way than the resume does.

The cover letter has four main purposes. First, it serves as an introduction to your resume. You should never send your resume without an accompanying cover letter. If a resume shows up on the recruiter's desk without a cover letter, the recruiter may not know why you're submitting your resume. Usually, your resume gets tossed if it doesn't have a cover letter with it. Second, the cover letter offers you your only written opportunity to express why you're interested in the job, company, or career field you're pursuing. The objective on your resume simply states *what* you're interested in pursuing, not *why* you're interested in pursuing it. Third, the cover letter allows you to highlight those two or three most relevant selling points from your all-inclusive resume. It directs the recruiter to areas of your resume that you want them to notice, and it lets you mention them at greater length. Finally, the cover letter communicates the next steps, as you see them. You can let the recruiter know that you intend to call them on a certain date to check the status of the search or to set up an information interview.

The nature of the cover letter is different from that of a resume. While the resume is a comprehensive presentation of experience, skills, and educational background, the cover letter is a specific, targeted presentation of a few of your most relevant skills, experiences, and interests; while the resume is formatted in fact-oriented phrases beginning with action verbs, the cover letter is written in complete sentences in business-letter form.

THE PARTS AND FORMAT OF COVER LETTERS

FYI

Cover letters give you your first chance of "talking" to the recruiter. If your writing style is unorganized and choppy, the recruiter will naturally think that you have trouble expressing yourself in a clear and effective way.

Essentially, there are four parts of a cover letter. In the introduction, explain why you're writing and who referred you. Second, you should reveal your interest in the job, company, and career field. Third, highlight key selling points that are most relevant to the job opportunity. Finally, in the closing, state what you see as the next steps. On the following page is a general explanation of the parts of a cover letter, presented in its typical format.

Following, you'll see the similarities and differences between the two major types of cover letters: open-market cover letters and hidden-market cover letters.

OPEN-MARKET COVER LETTERS: PERSONALIZED LETTERS FOR ANSWERING ADS

Guidance

A cover letter should reinforce themes present on the resume, rather than introduce new information. Employers focus more on candidates' resumes and may overlook important information mentioned in the cover letter.
—Bell Atlantic

Open-market cover letters are written for jobs in the open job market. The open job market consists of jobs announced as open or vacant through newspaper ads, job listings at career centers, company vacancy listings, and Internet job boards or Web sites. With open-market cover letters, you are responding to a specific job opening listed by a particular organization. In other words, you are being reactive, following the organization's lead. Take a look at the open-market cover letter sample on the following page.

The first part of the open-market cover letter (introduction: why you are writing) is usually straightforward. Anthony was simply writing in response to their recent advertisement and wished to apply for the job. Notice how he effectively expressed why he is interested in this opportunity (part two). He identified three aspects that were appealing and presented them in the second paragraph. When expressing your interest, it's important not to just say that you are interested. You must present concrete reasons that describe *why* the opportunity is appealing.

The Parts and Format of Cover Letters

Your Present Address
City, State Zip Code
Date

(quadruple space)

Ms./Mr. Employer Name
Title
Company
Mailing address
City, State Zip Code

Dear Ms./Mr. _____:

Opening Paragraph—Tell why you're writing and how you learned about the opening or organization. Mention a contact name on the first line, if you have one.

Middle Paragraph(s)—Present your most relevant selling points, tailoring your remarks to the employer's point of view. Support your claims with statements showing evidence of your skills. Tell why you're interested in the position, company/organization, location, or industry.

Closing Paragraph—Refer the reader to your enclosed resume.

If this is a letter of inquiry, request an information interview over the phone or in person.

If this is a letter of application, state that you look forward to the possibility of further discussing your interests and qualifications during an interview.

Sincerely,

(quadruple space)

(Your handwritten signature—black or blue ink)
Type your name

Open-Market Cover Letter Number 1

102 Zullinger Lane
Ockersville, MD 27777
December 17, 2000

Mr. Patrick Long
Human Resource Manager
Benhart Pharmaceuticals, Inc.
266 Beaver Court
Franklin, MD 22222

Dear Mr. Long:

I am applying for the pharmaceutical sales position that appeared in the *News Sun* on December 14. After reviewing the position description, I found every aspect of this professional opportunity appealing.

During my professional internship, I enjoyed working with the same types of clients that you serve. Also, your management philosophy and teamwork approach are consistent with my values. Finally, the region for which this position is responsible is in an area that interests me greatly.

Through my relevant, professional experience and master's-level work in exercise physiology, I have gained knowledge, experience, skills, and self-confidence to help rehabilitation programs reach higher levels of productivity and efficiency that last. I feel that my ability to adapt in new situations, as well as my motivational and communication skills, are major reasons for the success I have experienced. Currently, I am excited to take these skills and experiences and use them within the pharmaceutical industry. With the combination of my education and professional experiences, I believe I could contribute to the success of Benhart Pharmaceuticals, Inc.

I have enclosed a copy of my resume for you to review. I would enjoy the opportunity to discuss my interests and qualifications with you in greater detail. Thank you in advance for your consideration.

Sincerely,

Anthony Heckman

Open-Market Cover Letter Number 2

8888 Campus Box
Elon College, NC 27244
March 5, 2000

Mr. Rocky Brent
Vice President of Marketing
Kelly Enterprises
2345 Bo Avenue
Jeffrey, MN 56789

Dear Mr. Brent:

While searching the Internet yesterday, I discovered the Kelly
Enterprises home page and was very impressed with the company
information. I found the position description of Public Relations
Assistant on your Employment Opportunities page. Upon reading the
job description, I feel my skills and experience would make me a
strong candidate, and I would like to be considered for the position.

Along with my class work at Elon College, I have been able to gain
valuable, practical experience through my internships. A generous
portion of my internship at Woodstone College involved assisting
with the creation of a marketing plan. This assignment required a
great deal of research and collaboration, and from this experience, I
gained a better understanding of communication tools and how to
use media to reach various publics. The job description also stated
that you need a self-starter. While at Elon College, I recognized a
need to assist new students with the adjustment to college and
worked with Elon's Student Government Association to initiate the
Student to Student Program and to recruit volunteers.

Enclosed you will find my resume and list of references. If you need
to see samples of my work, I can arrange to forward them to you. I
will call within the week to check the status of my application and
inquire about the hiring timeline. Thank you very much for your time
and consideration.

Sincerely,

Mary Bair

Part three of writing open-market cover letters is to highlight a few selling points. Anthony identified his adaptable, quality communication skills and self-confidence as a few of the selling points related to sales. Again, it's important to reveal where and how you developed your skills, not just to mention that you have them. Finally, notice Anthony's closing paragraph. He refers the recruiter to his resume and thanks him for his time and consideration. Anthony is basically saying that the company has the next move.

In the closing paragraph of open-market cover letters, you have the option of either conveying to the recruiter that you'll be calling to inquire about the position or letting the company make the next move. There are pros and cons to each option, which are discussed in detail in Chapter 9, "The Best Job-Search Strategies in the Open Job Market."

FYI

Recruiters frequently complain that job seekers are too vague when explaining their selling points. Using generic strengths such as "responsible" and "people-person" won't help you stand out from the crowd. Specify your selling points by describing where you acquired them.

Two main differences exist between these two open-market cover letter samples. First, notice how part two of a good cover letter—expressing interest—was not included in the second letter. Mary focuses most of her attention on part three, highlighting selling points. Overall, her cover letter is strong, but she could potentially strengthen it further by expressing why she's interested in this opportunity. The second difference is found in the closing. Notice how Mary, unlike Anthony, states that she'll take the initiative and call to find out about the status of her application and hiring timeline. By taking the initiative and calling, Mary may have an opportunity to express her interest in the position. On the flip side, there's a slight risk involved in taking the initiative. You may be perceived as somewhat pesty or desperate by calling. The pros and cons to taking the initiative when responding to a job opening are covered in detail in Chapter 9.

HIDDEN-MARKET COVER LETTERS: NETWORKING LETTERS THAT GET YOUR FOOT IN THE DOOR

Hidden-market cover letters are those cover letters written for jobs in the *hidden job market*. The hidden job market consists of jobs that are *not* announced as open or vacant. Every organization experiences turnover (employees leaving the company) and job growth (creating new positions), resulting in job opportunities. However, many companies don't advertise their openings. Rather than sift through hundreds of resumes sent in response to an ad, they'll hire from their network of contacts, people who are on file with their personnel division, or employees from different departments. Strategies for tapping into the hidden job market are thoroughly presented in Chapters 10 and 11.

The one factor that influences hidden-market cover letters the most is not knowing what, if any, positions are available. This means that you'll

Hidden-Market Cover Letter Number 1

333 Charles Lane
Littlestown, PA 11111
May 13, 2000

Ms. Anne Mummert
Recruiting Manager
Koontz Consulting
1601 Timothy Lane
Philadelphia, PA 19103

Dear Ms. Mummert:

I am writing to express my interest in pursuing consulting opportunities at Koontz Consulting. After reviewing your home page and reading your 1999 annual report, I am very excited about the possibility of working as a consultant for Koontz Consulting. The emphasis on developing a world-class team, creating a lasting positive change, and providing excellent client services is particularly attractive. Furthermore, I am committed to using my consulting skills in the dynamic and ever-changing private sector. I believe that my abilities and interests match these values, as demonstrated in my resume.

Through my relevant professional experience and my master's- and doctoral-level work in strategic planning, change management, and organization development, I have gained the knowledge, experience, skills, and self-confidence to help empower companies to reach higher levels of productivity and efficiency that last. I am confident that my prior experience in facilitating strategic planning sessions, training organizations on computer applications and budgeting, and leading research projects on topics that include transport logistics and customer service has provided me with the skills needed to become a successful consultant at Koontz Consulting.

I have enclosed a copy of my resume for you to review. I would greatly appreciate the opportunity to learn more about Koontz Consulting and its various professional opportunities. I will call you next week to see if there may be a convenient time to meet with you. Thank you for your time and consideration.

Sincerely,

Julie Brent

have to be somewhat conservative when you write your cover letter and try to cover as many bases as possible. Review the sample hidden-market cover letter from Julie Brent (see page 109), and notice the differences and similarities between it and an open-market cover letter. In part one, notice how Julie is *expressing an interest in opportunities* rather than *applying for a specific job*. When writing hidden-market cover letters, there's no job opening of which you're aware. Parts two and three (expressing why you're interested and highlighting selling points, respectively) of the hidden-market cover letter are very similar to those parts of the open-market cover letter. The only slight difference is that you're expressing your interest and highlighting selling points that relate to *types of jobs* rather than *one particular job*. In part four, the closing, I highly recommended that you take the initiative and attempt to generate a networking contact. See how Julie takes initiative by informing the recruiting manager that she will be in contact with her.

A second version of hidden-market cover letters is called the networking letter. When a contact of yours refers you to someone who is in a company or industry that you want to pursue, your cover letter turns into a networking letter. With your contact's permission, you should state in the very first sentence that you have been referred to that particular recruiter by your contact. The referral sentence often carries more weight than anything else you express on the cover letter. In the letter on the following page, see how Julie's first paragraph changes with the addition of a referral source.

As you are job searching, you'll more than likely run into someone who wants you to send them a resume. Even social events can lead to job opportunities. During a party, a friend of a friend might tell you to submit your resume on Monday. In this case, you have actually spoken to the contact directly. In the cover letter on page 112, notice that Erik doesn't just jump right into his job search situation. He spends two paragraphs explaining how he enjoyed their previous time together and offering compliments about Ms. Logan's daughter and her commitment to education. It's important to express common points of interest with your contacts to further strengthen your relationship. The more your contacts like you and are comfortable communicating with you, the more likely they are to want to help you.

Guidance

Cover letters are a good way to accentuate an individual's accomplishments and lend specificity to the desire for a particular job or function. In many cases, however, they aren't thoroughly read by employers. The substance of a prospective employee's skills and objectives are still seen on the resume.
—Johnson & Johnson

THE 5-STEP PLAN FOR CRAFTING THE PERFECT COVER LETTER

Most job seekers take what I call the *cover letter shortcut*. They write one generic cover letter for every job opening they apply for, no matter what the position is or who they'll be sending it to. For each new job opening,

Networking Letter Number 1

Dear Ms. Mummert:

Scot Hess, Senior Consultant for Mosebach Consulting, recommended that I contact you. I am very interested in pursuing consulting opportunities at Koontz Consulting. Scot informed me of your company's quality and consulting services. After reviewing your home page and talking to Scot, I am very excited about the possibility of working as a consultant for Koontz Consulting. The emphasis on developing a world-class team, creating a lasting positive change, and providing excellent client services are particularly attractive. Furthermore, I am committed to using my consulting skills in the dynamic and ever-changing private sector. I believe that my abilities and interests match these values, as demonstrated by my resume.

they simply change what is minimally necessary, such as the recruiter's name and title, company name, and the name of the open position. Some job seekers don't even address their cover letters to an individual. They'll start with a statement like, "To whom it may concern," or "Dear Personnel Representative."

When it comes to crafting the perfect cover letter, there are no shortcuts. You must take the time to write a well-thought-out, detailed, and personalized cover letter. Following are the recommended steps to crafting the perfect cover letter.

Step 1: Research the Company, Industry, and Job

In order to identify key selling points and specific areas of interest, it's necessary to know about the company, the industry, and the job. Most

Networking Letter Number 2

44 David Bair Court
Chrisroberts, PA 11111
May 1, 2000

Ms. Jessica Logan
Principal
Peter-Alexander Elementary School
600 Gregory Road
Coatsville, PA 18960

Dear Ms. Logan:

I wanted to express to you how much I enjoyed our conversation at the leadership banquet last Thursday. Also, I wish to congratulate you and your husband on your daughter's achievements. I am sure that you are very proud of her and what she was able to accomplish during her college career.

It was refreshing to hear your commitment and enthusiasm for the field of education. The Somersville School District sounds like a special place where students are enriched and challenged in a positive environment. I am extremely interested in the possibility of becoming a part of the Somersville experience.

I am confident that my academic background and full-time teaching experience with elementary school students, combined with my current experience in working with young students with special needs, will enable me to become a positive addition to your teaching staff. At the Adkins School, in particular, I was pushed to new heights through living out the beliefs of treating each student as an important individual and that "education is a journey, not a destination."

Thank you again for the positive encouragement that you shared with me and for the excitement and optimism you expressed toward the education field. I would love the opportunity to further discuss my background and skills and how they could benefit students within your school district. As you suggested, I will call you this summer to arrange a time to meet. Take care and good luck with the rest of this school year!

Sincerely,

Erik Bair

companies have a Web page with current, comprehensive information. (For specific resources on researching companies, see "Researching Organizations/ Employer Profiles" in Appendix A and "Researching Organizations" in Appendix C). Determine the company's products or services, management philosophy, mission, competitors, organizational structure, work atmosphere, and where the job opening or occupation of interest fits into the larger picture. Closely examine the job responsibilities on the ad or posting. If the advertisement is vague, don't shy away from calling the company and asking them to send you a more detailed job description. The worst thing that can happen is they say no.

For hidden-market cover letters, you'll want to learn about the types of positions for which you would be best suited. If you have a contact in the company or industry you're pursuing, learn about the company through them. Ask the contact if you can use their name as a reference in your cover letters.

Step 2: Personalize Your Cover Letter

Once you know more about the company, industry, and job, you can identify your selling points and areas of interest. The strength of a cover letter depends on your ability to tie together your selling points and interests with the company's values and needs. Don't just state the obvious. Telling a certain Fortune 500 textile company that it's appealing to you because it is a "large, well-established, respectable textile company" is not going to help you stand out. You must dig for more unique, concrete information. From your research, you must first identify specific aspects of the company and the positions that are genuinely appealing to you. Next, you must identify those selling points (skills, qualities, and experiences) that are most important to highlight. These areas of interest and selling points should be validated through past experiences, further personalizing the letter. For hidden-market cover letters, you will have to relate your selling points and areas of interest to types of positions in which you're interested.

Step 3: Target the Cover Letter to an Individual

Addressing your letter, "To Whom it May Concern" isn't going to get you very far. Find the name of the person who will be reviewing your materials, and address the letter specifically to them. If the advertisement provides the name of the contact person, you're all set. If it doesn't, your best bet is to get on the phone and find out who will be reviewing your resume. Before you call, think of some other questions about the position or company that you genuinely would like to ask. The receptionist may forward you to someone in the division with the open position to answer your questions, giving you the chance to build rapport with a key employee.

For hidden-market cover letters, it's usually best to send your cover letter and resume to someone outside Human Resources (HR). Try to find the name of the person in the appropriate division who has hiring authority, and submit your materials to this person (if you're successful in finding them). If not, at least get the name of the HR person who reviews or maintains the resumes.

Step 4: Write a Well-Written, One-Page Letter

With the information you gathered from Steps 1–3, you're ready to write your letter. Write, rewrite, and edit your cover letter carefully. Have a career counselor or someone you respect review your letter. It's good to have an objective eye review your letters. Proofread your document for appropriate spelling and grammar. Remember, you're demonstrating your communication and writing abilities, both of which are highly sought-after skills, through your cover letter. Most likely, this is the first correspondence that you've had with the recruiter. Finally, keep the cover letter to one page or less. Recruiters don't have time to read long cover letters, and they're anxious to get to your resume.

Step 5: Produce a Professional Document

Make sure your cover letter is as professional looking as possible. If at all possible, print your cover letter with a laser printer. If you don't have access to one, it's worth taking your letter on disk to a printing and copying place. Match the cover letter paper with the resume paper. Both should be printed on 25 percent to 100 percent cotton-bond paper.

THE PORTFOLIO: REFERENCES AND OTHER SUPPORTING DOCUMENTS

The resume and cover letter are your two primary job-search documents. There are some additional, supporting documents that are important in completing your self-marketing package. The most common and widely used supporting documents are reference sheets and letters of recommendations. Other supporting documents include writing samples, field-specific work samples, research papers, and projects. Developing a portfolio can give you an edge. A portfolio is simply a professional binder used to organize, maintain, and present all your job-search documents, both primary and supporting. During interviews, the portfolio enables you to show your past work and accomplishments rather than just talk about them.

References

As another means of evaluating you, recruiters often contact your references. For references, choose people you have worked with or known in similar settings. Keep in mind that your references may be asked questions about you or may be asked to write a letter of recommendation. As a job seeker, you'll need to prepare for both. There are three steps you must take regarding references.

Step 1: Identify Your References

Your references can make or break your chances of landing that perfect job, so it's important for you to pick the best ones possible. The three main criteria for selecting good references are how relevant they are, how impressive they are, and how strong a relationship you have/had with them. Recruiters want to contact references who are in the same career field as the job you're pursuing. Also, if your reference has an impressive title or is known in the field, their recommendations will carry more weight. Finally, recruiters would rather talk with references who have worked closely with you, since they would be able to talk more specifically about your skills and qualities.

Typical references include prior or current supervisors, professors or teachers who had you in class, associates from volunteer or extracurricular activities, or coaches and other mentors. The ideal number of references you should get is between three and five, but the final number of references that you decide to use depends on how well they meet the stated criteria.

Step 2: Produce a Reference Sheet

Once you've identified prospective references, you must contact them and get their permission. Make sure they're willing to be contacted by prospective employers and write letters of recommendation upon request. Determine where and how each reference wants to be contacted during the day. Get the correct spelling and accurate information on all of the following (assuming they want to be contacted at work):

- First and last name
- Position title
- Organization name
- Organization address
- Organization phone number
- E-mail address

Develop and produce your reference sheet on the same cotton-bond paper that your resume and cover letters are on. Typically, the references are presented as a centered list on one page. See the following sample.

Step 3: Generate Letters of Recommendation

It's good common practice to ask people to write general letters of recommendation soon after your association with them is complete.

References for Anita Job

Ms. Melissa Byerly
Director of Marketing
Clark Corporation
1222 Oak Drive
Hamburg, PA 17777
777-555-5555
cjones55555@lb.com

Dr. Alicia Adkins
Associate Professor of Marketing
Jackson College
12 Old Main Drive
Westen, IA 50000
555-222-5555
011111@yycollege.edu

Mr. Rudy Webber
Vice President
Werner Consulting
244 Chamber Road
Parksville, CA 11111
555-555-2222
11111@OCC.com

Ms. Pat Long
Associate Vice President
Mellor Corporation
4 Maple Drive
Washington, DC 11111
555-111-5555
2222@000.com

That way, they can write the letter while you're still fresh in their minds. Also, they'll have a letter stored in their computer from which they can revise and customize upon request.

Letters of recommendation are much stronger when they're targeted to an individual company and job. Therefore, upon prospective employers' requests of written letters of recommendation, contact your references and ask them to write a personalized, targeted letter. To facilitate this process, I highly recommend that you mail, fax, or e-mail the following documents to your references:

1. A letter from you asking them to write and submit a letter of recommendation. Make sure you include the recruiter's name, title, organization, and address.

2. A copy of the job description. This will help your references write about your skills and experiences that matter most to the prospective employer.

3. A copy of your resume. Don't expect the references to remember everything about you. Refresh their memories and help them pick out some concrete experiences to support their claims about you.

If you send them the listed information, your references will have all the information they need to write a solid letter of recommendation for you. Another issue to take care of is to determine whether the prospective employer wants the letters submitted from you or sent directly from the references. If your references send the letters directly to your prospective employers, you should ask your references to send you a copy of the letter. It's good to see what they're writing about you and it helps to keep track of when they've submitted the letter (some may forget).

Other Supporting Documents: Building Your Portfolio

Inside your portfolio, you should always have professional copies of your resume and list of references. Any other documents you add to your portfolio are optional. Your portfolio should have a professional-looking cover. The supporting documents inside usually are laminated to protect them and give them a more formal, official appearance. Following are supporting documents that you can consider adding to your portfolio.

Letters of Recommendation or Endorsement

Exceptional letters of recommendation can be added to your portfolio. Also, thank-you letters from clients, customers, co-workers, and colleagues may be considered. Even if they aren't relevant to the job you're trying to get, it shows employers that you've impressed one or more of the people you've worked with in the past.

Writing Samples

Writing skills are becoming increasingly important among employers. Articles, term papers, or other writing samples may be beneficial to add to your portfolio, especially if you're pursuing career opportunities in industries or companies that place a high value on writing skills.

Reports

Reports you have developed and produced are excellent forms of supporting documents. With accountability being so prevalent, organizations look highly on candidates who have had experience producing reports.

Advertisements and Handouts

If you've created advertisements or handouts for an organization or certain event, add them to your portfolio. These supporting documents can be some of the more exciting ones included in your portfolio.

Systems, Logistics, and Procedures

If you've been instrumental in creating, developing, or refining certain systems or office procedures, you may want to incorporate them into your portfolio.

Programs and Events

Profiles and summaries of programs or events you have coordinated tend to be strong supporting documents to have. Showing the results, accomplishments, or outcomes of these events would add teeth to your portfolio.

Experiments, Projects, and Case Studies

Academic experiments, projects, or case studies can be powerful supporting documents, especially when the subject matter is relevant to your perfect job. For example, professionals in science may have experiments or projects that they developed in a prior work or academic environment.

WEB-BASED PORTFOLIOS

A new, progressive type of portfolio is the Web-based portfolio. Basically, all the supporting and primary job-search documents introduced can be presented in electronic form within a Web-based portfolio. There are many benefits to producing a Web-based portfolio:

- **Easy to Update**

  If you revise a document or add a new one, the Web makes it easy. You can change something one minute and instantaneously show it off.

- **Wide Distribution and 24-hour-a-day Access**

  If you want a prospective employer to see a supporting document, all you need to do is give them the Internet address. Recruiters can review your Web-based portfolio before, during, and after the interview. This also lets them review it at their leisure.

- **User-Friendly**

  You have the ability to structure your portfolio in a way that allows recruiters to very easily and quickly access the documents of interest. Instead of leafing through a binder, they can simply click on the options in which they're most interested.

- **Creative Display**

  The possibilities of spicing up and creatively presenting your Web portfolio are endless. You can download graphics, link to relevant Web sites, and scan in personalized pictures.

- **Demonstration of Computer Skills**

  By showing your supporting documents through a Web-based portfolio, you're directly demonstrating strong computer skills. These computer skills will make you that much more marketable.

FYI

Web-based portfolios can really knock the socks off of your recruiters, especially during an interview. A very small percentage of job seekers use these portfolios. So if you're looking for a way to stand out, Web-based portfolios will do the trick!

For job seekers who are pursuing a career in the arts or graphic design, the Web-based portfolio is a great way to demonstrate your work. I've worked with technical graphics college students who have produced Web-based portfolios consisting of the graphics they have created in class. Most of these students presented their graphics to recruiters during interviews. While interviewing at the recruiter's place of work, the students directed the recruiter to the Internet site that housed their Web-based portfolio and described their graphics from there.

A Success Story

One student, Joan, was able to show her graphics on a big screen to eight members of the selection committee. During her group interview, Joan mentioned her Web portfolio to one of the committee members, and that member suggested that they move to the conference room to view her graphics on the big screen. They had a projector hooked up to a computer that had access to the Internet. Joan was able to present her work to all eight members at the same time.

To see samples of Web-based portfolios, go to Kalamazoo College's Web page: http://www.kzoo.edu/admiss/portfolio.html.

Kalamazoo College requires all students to produce a Web-based portfolio.

Producing Your Own Web-Based Portfolio

Creating a Web-based portfolio is easier and less time-consuming than you think. If it's something you're interested in doing, see the following steps to get going in the right direction.

Step 1: Develop and Gather Your Portfolio Materials

Identify all the items that you want in your portfolio and make sure they're ready to be placed on the Web for the world to see. For example, if you want to include your resume, two letters of recommendation, an advertisement you created, a writing sample, and a case-study report, you need to make sure each of these five items are complete, free of mistakes, and saved on your computer or a disk. Have other people you respect proof your documents.

Step 2: Identify a Place on the Internet to Put Your Portfolio

Contact your Internet Service Provider (ISP) to see if they offer free Web hosting for personal use. If your ISP doesn't offer free Web hosting, there are some Internet sites that offer free Web space. Visit http://www.geocities.com or http://www.angelfire.com to get some free Web space on their servers.

Step 3: Download Software That Converts Your Portfolio to the Web

Once you have a place to put your portfolio, you'll need a way to transfer it to the Web. There are two software packages that are easy to use and are most likely already on your computer. The first is Netscape Page Composer, which comes with Netscape Communicator (4.74 at time of publishing). The second is FrontPage Express, which comes with Microsoft Internet Explorer (5.5 at time of publishing). To download Netscape Communicator with Page Composer, visit http://www.netscape.com. To download Internet Explorer with FrontPage Express, visit http://www.microsoft.com/ie.

Step 4: Convert Your Portfolio Materials to the Web

Most software packages allow you to paste formatted text directly to the Web page, and both of the previously mentioned packages allow you to do so. Open your portfolio from your word processor, then highlight and copy the whole thing. Now open your Web-publishing software that you downloaded and paste your portfolio on a new page. You may want to go back through the portfolio to make sure that the formatting is still correct. The publishing software is basically a word processor for the Web. Therefore, you can create new documents or edit existing ones within your publishing software.

Step 5: Publish Your Portfolio on the Web

When you're ready to publish the portfolio to the Web, you'll need to save the file (portfolio) to your computer. If you're using FrontPage

Express you'll be able to publish using the Save As command under the File menu. If you're using Page Composer, you need to use the Publish Command under the File menu. You'll be prompted to list the name of your file (portfolio name) and your file's location. Fill in the location with the File Transfer Protocol (FTP) location that your ISP or Web-hosting company gives you. The FTP location is the publishing location. To actually view your Web portfolio, you will also need the http or Web location. This http location is the Web address that you will give to prospective employers to view your portfolio on the Internet. Make sure your service provider gives you both addresses: FTP and http. (Source: Eric Cone, Web Master, Elon College).

Once your portfolio is published on the Web, you should see how it looks. Get on the Internet and enter the Web address (http) that houses your portfolio. Make sure everything looks okay. If changes need to be made, simply go back to the saved file, edit it, and proceed through Step Five again (FTP it to the Web). Then view it again using the http address.

Now that your new Web-based portfolio is up and running, it's time to start selling it! One of the best ways to use your Web portfolio is to mention it in your cover letters. Inform your prospective employers that you produced a Web-based portfolio, and encourage them to take a look at it. Make sure you provide them with the Web address so they can view it. Another time to use your Web-based portfolio is during interviews. When appropriate, inform the recruiter that you published a Web portfolio. Depending on how much time you have and how comfortable you feel, you can access it from one of their computers and show them some work samples. If you don't have the time, you can at least describe the portfolio to them and ask them to take a look at it later, at their convenience.

THE WHOLE IN ONE

- Your resume should never be sent without an accompanying cover letter.

- Cover letters are more narrowly focused and presented in business letter format.

- The purposes of a cover letter are to introduce your resume, express your interest in the career opportunity, highlight top selling points, and demonstrate your writing skills.

- There are two major types of cover letters. Open-market cover letters are used when pursuing job openings, while hidden-market cover letters are used to network and tap into the hidden job market.

- The five steps to crafting the perfect cover letter are researching the company and job at hand, personalizing your selling points and areas of interest, targeting your letter to the appropriate recruiter, writing a well-articulated and grammatically correct letter, and producing a professional-looking document.

- Your primary job-search documents are your resume and cover letters. Supporting documents, such as references and work samples, can be maintained and presented in a portfolio.

- Web-based portfolios are the exciting new wave of portfolios, experiencing much early success.

ASSIGNMENT

Complete the "Cover Letter," "References," and "Portfolio" sections of Goal 3 of your Personal Job Search Trainer.

Part III

Finding the Perfect Job

Chapter 8

The 3 P's to Finding the Perfect Job

GET THE SCOOP ON . . .

- The importance of persevering
- Incorporating a plan into your job search
- Personalizing your job search
- Where most of the jobs are found

AS YOU BEGIN SEARCHING, ALWAYS REMEMBER THE 3 P's

You're all packed up and ready to go! Your perfect job is in sight, and you've crafted a resume that is perfect for you. You have your references all lined up, and you're ready to write powerful cover letters as opportunities arise. You also know how to produce a printed or Web-based portfolio that can give you an edge. Now it's time to take your show on the road and search for that perfect job. You know what you're looking for—you just need to know where and how to find it. Chapters 9 and 10 reveal the best job-search strategies to use in helping you find the perfect job. Chapter 11 then lays out a 7-step networking plan that will empower you to find key job leads.

Before you get out there, though, you need to know the keys to success. As a job search adviser, I'm constantly asked, "What do I have to do to get the right job for me?" My response is always the same: *persevere*, *plan*, and *personalize!*

The 3 P's to finding the perfect job are as follows.

Persevere!

The job-search process goes something like this: "no, no, no, no, no, no, no, no, no, no-way, no, no, no, no, not really, no, no, no, no, no, no, forget it, no, no, no, no, YES!" That one "yes" is all you need. The key is being able to get through the no's! Think about softball or baseball hitters. When they get one hit out of three times at bat, it's been a good day. When they've failed two out of three times—the majority of the time—how can they go home and feel good about themselves? The answer: They've accepted the nature of the game. Getting a hit one out of three times is a .333 batting average. A .333 batting average is universally accepted in the baseball and softball world as a great average.

As a job searcher, you must accept the fact that the failure rate is intensified many more times than it is for the softball or baseball hitter. Receiving feedback from one out of fifty companies that you've sent your resume to is a good day! You cannot take rejections personally! Everyone experiences rejections in a job search. Lots and lots of rejections. That's just the nature of the beast. If you stop job searching because of the frustrations of rejections, guess what? You'll never get a job, at least not the one you want. You must take your rejections in stride and get right back on that job-searching horse! A sense of humor is sometimes the best way to persevere through the rejections. Look on the following page at the creative and funny way this job seeker dealt with his rejections—*a letter like this relieves stress, but don't send it!*

Plan!

The next thing you need to think about is making a plan. Nobody makes you spend time on your job search. It's not a test that you have to study for or a report due to your boss next Wednesday. You could go on for months without ever spending a second on a job search. Also, there are so many things that need to get done in a job search that it can feel overwhelming. This makes it so easy to put the job search on the back burner and deal with it later. The fact of the matter is that *you* are in control of your own career. *You* have to provide the structure needed to get things done within your search.

There are two major areas where structure is needed. First, it's critical that you develop and implement a task-oriented, deadline-oriented, personalized job search plan that will guide your actions. You have the framework already outlined for you in the Personal Job Search Trainer in this book. Hopefully, you've begun building your plan. Keep this plan handy at all times, and refer to it regularly. Take a look at how detailed and task-oriented the Personal Job Search Trainer is. Notice the job search strategies and tasks that are outlined. It's important that you break the strategies down into small, realistic tasks. Performing one task at a time makes the job search feel less overwhelming.

You must also be very organized in how you track your job search activities and progress. With all your meetings and phone calls with recruiters and networking contacts, it'll be important to stay organized and keep track of who you've contacted and when. You don't want to miss out on a job opportunity simply because you forgot to write down when your next call was supposed to take place. Following are two examples of tracking and progress forms that you can use in your job search. The first form tracks the activity and progress of an individual contact. The second form tracks the interaction with multiple contacts.

222 Maple Drive
Gardner, NC 13456
November 4, 2000

Mr. Charles Jones
Vice President of Marketing
XYZ Corporation
159 East Third Street
Greensville, CA 15559

Dear Mr. Jones:

I am writing in response to your recent letter notifying me that I did not get the job of Assistant Manager with your firm. After long discussions with my mentors, colleagues, and significant others, I have decided to decline your rejection.

Although your rejection letter was carefully worded and professionally written, I felt that it lacked the level of empathy that I am looking for in a company. Specifically, I found your statement "Good luck in your search" to be vague and impersonal. In order for me to accept your rejection, I must be convinced that your interest in my future is sincere.

Please send a more heartfelt rejection letter at your earliest convenience. Until then, I will initiate employment with your company starting on Monday. I look forward to seeing you then.

Sincerely,

Ima Jobless-Still

PROSPECTIVE EMPLOYER CONTACT SUMMARY

Use this worksheet to keep a record of your contacts with employers.

Name of Employer	Address/ Phone/Contact	Letter of Inquiry Sent	Resume Sent	Applications Completed	Letters of Recommen- dation Requested	Interview Scheduled	Notes

Tracking Form

Contact _____ Title _____

Organization _____

Address _____

_____

Phone Number _____ E-mail _____

Referred by _____ of _____

Contact Record

Date	Type of Contact (phone call, interview, etc.)	Notes on Discussion
_____	_____	_____
_____	_____	_____
_____	_____	_____
_____	_____	_____
_____	_____	_____
_____	_____	_____
_____	_____	_____
_____	_____	_____
_____	_____	_____
_____	_____	_____
_____	_____	_____
_____	_____	_____
_____	_____	_____

Personalize!

The third P to success is personalizing. Take a look at a typical job search scenario: You've recently sent your resume to an organization that advertised an opening. You're excited about this opportunity because it seems perfect for you. You have relevant skills and experience and have spent days presenting these on your resume and cover letter. You know you could be successful in this position, so you wait anxiously for a response with great optimism. Meanwhile, the recruiter is sitting in her office with more than 100 pieces of cotton-bond paper on her desk, each having only subtle differences in color, style, and typed content. With so many resumes to deal with, she executes a quick, 30-second scan of each resume to dwindle down the stack. The months and years that you spent acquiring relevant knowledge and practical experience through courses, full- and part-time jobs, extracurricular activities and internships, not to mention the hours you spent on your resume, comes down to a 30-second scan of your piece of cotton-bond paper. Was this a thorough examination of your potential? Did the recruiter get a chance to explore your skills and experience and learn about your ambition and excitement for this job? Did they really get to know the person behind that piece of paper? There's a big difference between who you are as a person and what you can offer and how a recruiter sees you based on that 30-second scan.

This is not to say that the recruiter is an evil or inconsiderate person. The job-search process is impersonal by nature. Think about it. The recruiter's first impression of you is usually based on the words on a fancy piece of paper. Your resume and cover letter are being analyzed—not your enthusiasm, communication skills, positive attitude, self-confidence, interpersonal skills, or sense of humor.

Imagine you were responsible for hiring someone to take care of your grandmother or your newborn baby. Would you feel comfortable hiring people solely on the basis of what was on their resumes and cover letters? Would a 30-second scan of that person's resume be enough of an assessment to make the decision to hire them? No! You need more of a look than that to feel comfortable with your decision. When employers assess you solely on the basis of your resume, they're only seeing a small part of the big picture. It is necessary to use your personal and professional contacts to create ways for you to personalize the job search. These contacts can recommend you, the whole person, to colleagues and potential employers, pointing out your personal qualities and characteristics not expressed on your resume. They can also help you set up information interviews and meetings with their contacts.

When you personalize a job search, you become more than a resume. You become a person with a positive attitude and a sense of humor, a person who is enthusiastic and committed to the field, and a person who can look the recruiter in the eyes with confidence and poise. Networking and information interviews are the best strategies to help you personalize the job search. Chapter 10 thoroughly covers these topics.

WHERE THE MAJORITY OF JOBS ARE FOUND

Now that you know the three Ps to finding the perfect job, you're ready to begin searching. However, it's helpful for you to know where most of the jobs are found before you start. All jobs can be broken down into two job markets: the open job market and the hidden job market, as introduced in the prior chapter. The open job market consists of jobs that are announced as open or vacant, such as want ads and Internet job listings. Today, there are hundreds of Internet sites that list job vacancies all over the world. Looking for jobs is one of the top three uses of the Internet. Therefore, with the emergence of the Internet, most jobs must be found through job advertisements, right? Wrong. Only 15 percent of all available jobs are advertised. More specifically, less than 3 percent of all jobs are advertised in the newspaper want ads.

The hidden job market consists of jobs that are *not* advertised. Most companies hire through their various networks and personal referrals. Networking is, by far, the most effective job search strategy in the hidden job market. In fact, close to 80 percent of all jobs are obtained through some form of networking.

Where Job Seekers Spend Their Job-Hunting Time

Since networking is the king of the job-search methods, you would think that most job seekers actively network. The fact of the matter is, they don't. Many job seekers spend more time answering job ads than they do networking. In the 1998 Current Population Survey (CPS) conducted by the U.S. Department of Labor, more than six million (6,210,000) unemployed job seekers were surveyed, asking them to reveal the job-search methods they've used. Of the 6,210,000 job seekers, 15.9 percent placed or answered ads, while only 14.8 percent networked with friends or family.

Why do more job seekers respond to ads than network? First, answering ads is a very structured, step-by-step process that's easy to follow. The advertisement usually lays out very clear directions. See the following example, based on an actual job advertisement.

To apply, please send a letter of application, your resume, and a list of references to Mr. Joe Recruiter, Director of Human Resources,

Guidance

Use all resources that are available to you in your job search.

—Glaxo
Wellcome

FYI

Don't let the percentages discourage you from answering ads. You never know where your big break could be. Just because it's statistically less successful doesn't mean it won't work for you. Just be prepared to spend more time networking than answering want ads. Exhaust all your job-search strategies.

XYZ Corporation, 23 Maple Drive, Jobtown, NY 12345. The application deadline is November 1, 2000.

In addition, answering ads is often seen as a more direct and immediate way to get a job. Submit your cover letter and resume, acquire an interview, and get offered the job. Simple! Networking, on the other hand, is often perceived as overwhelming, scary, shady, and time-consuming. It's hard to see the light at the end of the tunnel. Finally, for many people who aren't naturally gregarious or outgoing, networking can be uncomfortable or awkward. It's not something that comes naturally to most people.

So, if you want to get an edge on most job seekers, there are three things you should do: network, network, and network!

THE WHOLE IN ONE

- You'll experience many rejections throughout your job search. It's just part of the process. Keep your sense of humor handy, and remember that the rejections don't reflect poorly on you. It's just part of the process.

- Nothing will get accomplished in your search without a plan. The job search can feel overwhelming. Laying out a specific plan that contains small, incremental tasks makes it feel more manageable.

- Make sure to track your progress and record the interactions you have with contacts and recruiters.

- The job search is very impersonal by nature. Your goal is to create opportunities for you, the whole person, to sell yourself. Don't let your resume do all the talking. Show your face and personalize the job search.

- As you venture out into job-searching land, realize that most of the jobs (85 percent, actually) are not advertised. Don't put all your eggs in the want-ad basket. Remember that networking is still the job-search king!

Chapter 9

The Best Job-Search Strategies in the Open Job Market

GET THE SCOOP ON . . .

- Responding to job ads
- Posting your resume on line
- Connecting with an employment service
- Getting the most out of job fairs
- Using your college or alma mater career center
- Pros and cons on being assertive in the open job market

STRATEGIES FOR THE OPEN JOB MARKET

Even though most jobs are found in the hidden job market, there are still plenty of employed people out there who credit the open job market to their success. While roughly 15 to 20 percent of jobs are obtained in the open job market, this percentage varies from field to field and person to person. For example, if you're in the computer science field, where employers are begging for live bodies to fill their numerous vacancies, you'll be very successful answering ads, posting your resume on the Internet, and participating in other open job market strategies. Your success in the open job market also depends on your qualifications. If you've acquired relevant skills and experience and have a stellar academic record, your resume may stand strong by itself in the open job market. Whatever your case may be, looking for jobs in the open job market is worth your time. You just don't want to spend the majority of your time here.

Following are the top job-search strategies in the open job market. Each job-search strategy is broken down into three parts: pros and cons, where to find the resources, and the key steps needed to succeed. Note that within the "Where to Find . . ." section, you'll be referred to the appropriate appendix that provides a thorough list of hard-copy and Internet resources that relate to that particular strategy.

STRATEGY 1: RESPONDING TO JOB ADVERTISEMENTS

If you're like most people, the first thing you think about when you start looking for employment is getting your hands on a newspaper and answering job ads. The problem is that thousands of other job seekers across the nation are thinking the same thing. You can help your chances if you don't solely look for job ads in newspapers. Job ads can be found in trade magazines, professional associations, college career centers, employment centers, and on the Internet.

Pros

- **Easily Accessible**
  Most newspapers have a classified ads section. If you have access to the Internet, you'll have access to thousands of current job listings.

- **Straightforward Process**
  The ads usually lay out the necessary steps to apply.

- **Direct Path to an Interview**
  You don't have to network with five different people before getting an interview. You either get an interview or you don't.

Cons

- **Small Percentage of Jobs**
  Only 15 percent of all jobs are advertised.

- **Numbers are Not in Your Favor**
  People swarm to advertised openings. Professional job openings can attract close to 100 applicants per job.

- **Entry-Level and Part-Time Positions**
  For experienced job seekers, responding to ads can be frustrating. A large number of job ads are for entry-level or part-time positions.

Where to Find Job Advertisements

It's tough to find a job when you can't even find the job listings. Looking for jobs in the want ads is just one of many ways to find job vacancies. With the emergence of the Internet, job listings can be accessed all over the world, 24 hours a day. To get your hands on these job listings, you have to know where to look. In this section, you'll learn about the many different sources of job listings. Following are the main categories of job advertisements.

Classified Ads

A large percentage of job advertisements are presented in the classified section of major metropolitan newspapers, such as the *New York Times*, the *Chicago Tribune*, and the *Los Angeles Times*. Even if you don't live in one of these cities, you might want to read these major newspapers' want ads because they sometimes include national and international listings in addition to their own metropolitan areas. Your local newspaper will also list job vacancies, most of which will be available in your area. If working for a smaller company is right for you, be sure to look at the want ads in small-town newspapers. Smaller, local companies tend to advertise in small-town newspapers because the ad rates are lower.

General Career-Related Publications
Certain international, national, and regional career-related newspapers and bulletins contain job listings. The *National Business Employment Weekly* is an example of a larger career-related publication. Many regional and local business offices produce career newspapers or bulletins that list job opportunities.

Field-/Industry-Specific Publications
Many trade and professional associations publish a monthly or biweekly bulletin or newsletter that includes positions related to their respective field. For example, *Spotlight*, a biweekly newsletter produced by the National Association of Colleges and Employers, lists nationwide job vacancies in the career services and human resources–staffing industries.

General Internet Job Listings
The emergence of the Internet has created a whole new world of job advertisements. The number of job-listing sites is overwhelming. Most of the career-related Internet sites allow you to search for job vacancies by geographical area and career field. Some others allow you to search by salary level and experience.

Company Web Pages
More and more companies are adding a section to their Web page that centers on career opportunities. If you have specific companies or organizations in mind, you can head right to their home page and see if they have employment information.

Broadcast/Media Announcements
Television, radio, and telephone job hotlines can serve as additional means to finding job listings. Contact your local stations to see if they announce vacancies. Some local (city or county) employment services provide a telephone job hotline. Look in the local government section of your telephone book under "jobs" or "employment" to see if your area has a hotline.

Regional Business Offices
Contact the Chamber of Commerce, Better Business Bureau, or local governmental employment office in your area to see if they provide job

notices. They can also inform you of relevant trade or professional associations that may produce employment publications. Actually, the yellow pages are as good as any directory to find these phone numbers. If you're looking for jobs in a wide number of places, you can use the Internet to find any chamber of commerce in the world.

College/Alma Mater Career Centers

College career centers typically maintain job listings, including hard-copy listings, database listings, Internet links, or a combination of the three. Many of these career centers are now moving to a Web-based system of maintaining job openings. Listings that are unique to their college are password protected, allowing only their students and alumni to access the system, so see if you need to do anything special to access your school's database. Check with your local college or alma mater to determine the types of job listings that are maintained.

State and Federal Employment Offices

Many government openings are advertised through the Civil Service (State) or Office of Personnel Management (Federal). The state employment agency in your area should provide job listings. If you have access to the Internet, visit www.usajobs.opm.gov, which is directly maintained by the Office of Personnel Management. You can also visit www.fedworld.gov/jobs/jobsearch.html for federal and state listings.

See "Job Openings" in Appendix A, "Job Surfing on the Internet;" and see Appendix C, "Recommended Printed Resources," for recommended Internet and printed resources that list job openings.

The Key Steps for Responding to Ads

Step 1: Identify the Best Job-Listing Resources

Based on the career field you're pursuing and the geographical area of interest, determine the best resources for advertised openings (use the numerous options previously outlined. If you live in Indiana, for example, and are interested in publishing, you should look in the *Indianapolis Star* and *Publisher's Weekly*. Ask career counselors, chamber of commerce representatives, and contacts in the field to direct you to relevant job-ad publications. Use a few of the job-search Web sites listed in Appendix A to search for listings. Contact trade and professional associations in your area to get their advice on available publications.

Step 2: Select the Best Job Openings to Pursue—Less is More

At first, you may logically think that the best way to increase your chances is by applying for as many jobs as you can. It's a numbers game, right? Actually, you'll have a better chance of succeeding if you focus on

---

Guidance

Develop a network of mentors before you get out of college. Use the resources that are available at your college—alumni, professors, professional associations, and, most of all, career planning and placement offices.

—Andersen Consulting

fewer, more closely matched openings. You'll have more time to research and tailor your cover letters if you don't have 20 ads per week to respond to.

Step 3: Carefully Review the Job Notices and Research the Organizations

Closely read each job announcement to determine what you like about it and how your skills, experience, and educational background would be assets. Learn about the company by researching it on the Internet or talking to a contact who is familiar with it. Closely read the application procedures to make sure you submit exactly what they ask you to send. If they want three letters of recommendation, don't send them four. Also, determine whether they want you to send a traditional resume or an electronic one.

Step 4: Craft a Targeted, Tailored Cover Letter

Using the advice and techniques of Chapter 7, address your cover letter to the appropriate person and tailor your letter to the company's needs. Express specific areas of interest and your top selling points. If you know anyone who works at the company, contact them to ask for their advice. They may offer to speak on your behalf. Ask your contact if you can use their name in the cover letter.

Step 5: Promptly Submit All Materials

Take the time to research and personalize your cover letter, but make sure you meet the application deadlines. Don't get in the habit of sending your resume in at the last minute. Even if you get your materials to the recruiter on the deadline day, it will still be perceived as "last minute."

Step 6: Organize Your Search and Track Your Progress

You may have 10 or more ads that you've responded to over the last few weeks. It's critical to keep track of who you applied to, when you applied, and the materials you submitted. Keep this log with you at all times so that you're prepared when the companies call you back. Call the company to check on the status of the search if they've not gotten back to you within two to three weeks. Refer to the section presented at the end of this chapter, "Dealing with the Open Cover Letter Dilemma: To Be, or Not to Be, Assertive," to determine whether or not to initiate a call earlier.

FYI

Subscribing to every newspaper and trade magazine on the east coast to get access to hundreds of job vacancies a day won't get you a job. There's no way you can put together a tailored, targeted cover letter for 40 different job vacancies per week. Focus on a few of the best publications, select the best ads, and put in the time it takes to produce a solid cover letter.

STRATEGY 2: POSTING YOUR RESUME WITH AN ONLINE CAREER CENTER

Don't confuse this strategy with submitting an electronic version of your resume when responding to an ad. A job ad or company on the Internet may ask you to submit an electronic resume to them. This is simply another variation of responding to job ads. Posting your resume with an online career center is most similar to placing your resume with an employment agency. Just as companies pay employment agencies a fee to search for candidates, companies pay online career centers a fee to be able to review candidates' electronic resumes.

Pros

■ **High Visibility**

Placing your resume on line gives hundreds, if not thousands, of companies access to it.

■ **Low Time Involvement**

You don't have to tailor your resume and cover letter 20 different times for 20 different job ads. Numerous companies will view that one resume you post.

Cons

■ **Impersonal**

Many different companies with different needs will review the same version of your resume. You don't even have the opportunity to write a personalized cover letter.

■ **Bland Resume**

The first impression employers get of you is generated from a very dry resume.

■ **Reformatting Your Resume**

Each online career center seems to have their own procedures for posting resumes. Many times, you have to reformat your resume to fit into their online systems. Recently, though, some online career centers have developed format-transfer systems that allow you to copy and paste your resume on line without additional formatting. For example, JOBTRAK has moved to a system where you simply copy your original resume (e.g., Word or WordPerfect) and just paste it in. No formatting is necessary.

Where to Find Online Resume Posting Sites

General Internet Search Engines
Find one of the better search engines, like Yahoo.com or Webcrawler.com, and conduct a keyword search for posting resumes or job searching. A list of links to job-search and resume-posting sites will be presented from this keyword search.

Printed Reference Guides
There is an increasing number of books and other publications on using the Internet in your job search. These publications identify various job-search Internet sites and present a description of their components.

You can find these in bookstores within their career section or through a career-resources catalog (See "Career-Related Catalogs" in Appendix C).

College Career Center Web Pages

Most college career centers have a home page designed to make things easy for their job-hunting students and alumni. However, since Web pages are out there for the world to see, you can visit these sites and benefit, too. Career center Web pages typically include numerous links to the best career-related Internet sites in the world. The career centers make it easy for the user by categorizing and describing the linked sites.

Referrals from a Contact or Career Counselor

Seek advice from a career counselor or a contact in your chosen career field regarding the best online career centers to use.

Field-/Industry-Specific Publications

Many trade and professional associations publish a monthly or biweekly bulletin, journal, or newsletter that includes information on Internet sites relevant to their industry.

See "Posting Your Resume" in Appendix A, "Job Surfing on the Internet," for recommended Internet sites that allow you to post your resume on line.

The Key Steps for Posting Your Resume with an Online Career Center

Step 1 (Optional): Create a Plain-Text Version of Your Resume

For online career centers that have still not worked out the formatting glitches, you may want to create a plain-text version of your resume that lets you easily convert your resume to any online formatting system. (NOTE: If you would rather just identify those sites that can take your resume as it is, you can skip to Step 2). To make a text resume, simply make a copy of your computer-friendly resume (that you learned about from Chapter 6) and save it as a text file. The extension must be .txt. For example, if your resume file was saved as res.doc, you must copy it and save it to plain text under the name, followed by res.txt. Saving it as a text file affects the formatting of your resume, so you'll need to clean up the text version. Don't use tabs, highlighting, or any other special formatting because you need an unformatted resume that can be pasted into any resume-posting Internet site. Once you've posted it on a Web site, you can play around with all the tabs, boldface, and highlighting you want.

Step 2: Determine the Information You're Comfortable Including on Your Posted Resume

As we saw in Chapter 6, one of the drawbacks to online resumes is that they're available to anyone with Internet access. Some job seekers are uncomfortable putting personal information on a resume that can be accessed by anyone, anywhere, at any time. If you choose to post your resume on line, you must decide whether or not you're going to include your home address or telephone number. Some job seekers who post resumes on line give their e-mail address as the sole means of contacting them. Just realize, however, that most recruiters prefer to call candidates to schedule interviews.

Step 3: Research and Choose Appropriate Resume-Posting Sites

Whichever Web site(s) you choose to post your resume with, be sure to ask them for a list of recruiting companies that use their system. Some sites may primarily attract companies in a certain occupation or career field that has no interest to you. Also, be sure to ask about the confidentiality of your resume. Can anyone access your resume, or do recruiters and companies need a password to access your resume? These are important questions to ask.

Step 4: Find Out the Notification Procedures

Find out how or even if the Web site will notify you when your resume is selected and reviewed. Will they let you know when companies review your resume, or will the first contact you receive be from the company itself? You need to know what to expect.

Step 5: Determine How Long Your Resume Stays On Line

Find out if they keep your resume in their system until you ask them to remove it or if you must periodically update your resume in order for them to keep posting it. Some companies charge a fee if you choose to revise your resume a certain number of times. If you wanted to post an updated resume, determine whether or not you can exchange the old one with the new one at anytime.

Step 6: Organize and Track Your Progress

Keep track of where you post your resume on line. Create a list of sites where your resume is posted, and be sure to include a contact name and phone number for each and every site you post your resume on, even if it's a technical support number. Call your contacts every few weeks if you don't get many responses. You may want to shop around for other sites if you're not getting many hits.

FYI

Most job seekers post their resumes on any Internet site that offers free resume posting. While this is a nice feature, it shouldn't be the only factor influencing whether or not you use a particular site. Research and find out how many and what types of companies are registered with each Internet site you're considering. Shop around to find the best resume-posting sites for you!

STRATEGY 3: USING THIRD-PARTY EMPLOYMENT SERVICES

In the traditional job search, there are two parties involved: you and the company. The company places an ad and you directly respond to it. If you choose to use employment services, a third party is thrown into the mix. Employment services act as a liaison or messenger between you and the company. The company places their job ad with the employment service, and the employment service finds appropriate candidates to interview for and (hopefully) fill the position.

Three major types of third-party employment services exist: public employment agencies, private employment agencies, and temporary employment agencies. It's important for you to understand how they're different and which ones are best for you.

Registering with Public Employment Agencies

Approximately 1,700 local public employment agencies exist in the United States. They're funded by the state labor department and operated through the states in conjunction with the U.S. Employment Service. They're referred to as *State Employment Services* or *Job Services* and can be found in the state government section of your telephone book. If you're uncertain about what types of jobs to pursue, employment counselors who work for the agencies can give you career instruments and help you decide. You can look through job listings posted by local companies or identify a specific industry or field in which you'd like to work. Employment counselors will describe to you any job you're interested in and can arrange an interview for you if you'd like to apply for the job.

Pros

- **Free**
  There's no cost involved. The services are funded through the state labor department.

- **Salaried Staff**
  Employment counselors don't work on commission, so they won't be shoving jobs down your throat trying to make a sale.

- **Increased Visibility**
  It's nice to have someone else trying to find a job for you. The employment agency will identify employers that match your criteria in addition to those you've identified on your own.

Cons

- **Few White-Collar Jobs**
  Traditionally, most of the jobs advertised through public employ-

FYI

Members of private employment agencies are salespeople. They care first about making the sale (match), second about keeping their clients happy (employers), and somewhere down on the list, they care about you (the lowly job seeker). Don't let your counselor persuade you into taking interviews you don't want. You're the boss, even though it won't feel that way.

ment services tend to be blue-collar jobs, so if you're looking for a white-collar job, you're not likely to have much luck finding one here.

- **Bureaucratic Process**
  We *are* talking about the Government here. The bureaucratic process can slow things down at times and be frustrating.

Registering with Private Employment Agencies

Private employment agencies, often referred to as *headhunters, executive search firms*, or *recruiters*, are most appropriate for experienced job seekers. These search firms will find work for you in your particular area and will do most of the work for you. They will send companies your resume, call companies that may be interested in you, set up interviews for you, and may even help negotiate your salary. There are two types of search firms: contingency and retainer. Both types of firms are hired by the company looking to fill a position. Contingency search firms only get paid when a company hires someone that the firm presented to them; their pay is contingent on the hire. Retainer firms are paid when they find and present an appropriate candidate to the company. They get paid whether or not the company ends up hiring them.

Regardless of who hires the headhunter, there are three ways that the search firms or headhunters can be paid: by the company, by you, or by both. Most search firms get paid solely by the hiring company. Some firms, however, charge you a percentage of your first-year's salary (typically 5 or 10 percent) in your new job. This is not something that I would recommend you do. There are plenty of search firms out there where the company pays the fee, so save your money and look for one that doesn't charge the job seeker.

Pros

- **Increased Visibility**
  A third party with hundreds of company contacts is searching for professional positions for you.

- **Free Service**
  Most search firms get paid by the company doing the hiring, not by you.

Cons

- **High-Level Positions**
  If you have limited or moderate experience, search firms are not very helpful.

- **You're Not the Client**
  The company doing the hiring is the client of the search firms.

Employment agencies are an option, but be aware that most agencies are paid $2,500 to $10,000 by the employer to find employees, so the agency may not be working in your best interest.
—Enterprise
Rent-A-Car

They care most about making the best decision for the company. Search firms have been known to persuade people into taking jobs they don't want. Making the sale is most important to many search firms.

- **Favor the Employed Job Seeker**
  Most firms look for qualified professionals who are already employed to fill vacancies because they're perceived as a lower risk and more marketable.

- **Small Percentage of Jobs**
  Approximately 7 percent of all managerial, executive, and professional positions are listed with agencies.

Registering with Temporary Employment Agencies

Temporary employment agencies are paid by companies to hire temporary workers, known as *temps*, for positions that last anywhere from a few days to a few months. Temps typically fill the position of a permanent professional who is ill, on maternity leave, or on vacation. Temps are also hired during peak business periods or to complete a special project. Some temporary agencies have what they call *temp-to-perm* jobs. The job starts as temporary but, if things go well, has the potential of moving to a permanent status. Temporary positions are beneficial for unemployed job seekers who need money or want to develop various skills. Temporary work is also a way to directly market yourself to prospective long-term employers. The majority of these jobs tend to be related to technical, financial, and marketing fields.

Pros

- **Availability**
  Today, temporary work is very popular. Plenty of temporary jobs and agencies are accessible.

- **Skill Building**
  Temporary work can provide an opportunity to develop and hone certain skills, including computer skills, communication skills, and organizational skills.

- **Networking Opportunity**
  Temporary positions also enable you to network with a variety of businesses and professionals. As you move from company to company, you gain more and more contacts. You also are given an opportunity to demonstrate your skills first hand.

- **Get Your Blood Flowing Again**
  For those who have been out of work for a significant amount of

time, temporary work can serve as an energizer. Typically, as you're getting a taste of working again, it motivates you to look for that perfect job.

Cons

- **Lacks Variety of Career Fields**

  If you're looking for jobs in human services, science, education, or other nontechnical fields, temporary work is hard to find. The majority of positions available reflect the job market demand. Computer data entry, telemarketing, and low-level accounting positions are examples of common temporary positions.

- **Time-Consuming**

  Working as a temp eats away at your job-seeking time. You'll have to find ways to continue your job search while you're working.

- **Position Level**

  Most agencies primarily fill lower-level positions. However, there are some special temporary agencies that fill upper-level temp jobs.

Where to Find Third-Party Employment Services

Yellow Pages

Look under "Employment" in the yellow pages, and you'll find headings such as "Employment Agencies" and "Employment Contractors-Temporary Help."

General Internet Search Engines

Find one of the better search engines, like Yahoo.com or Webcrawler.com, and conduct a keyword search on "employment agencies," "search firms," "headhunters," "temporary employment," or "placement agencies." A list of links to relevant sites will be presented from this keyword search.

National Directories

You can purchase or see if your library has one of the national directories on employment agencies. (See Appendix C under "Employment Services")

City/Metropolitan Job Banks

There are more than 30 different city job banks within the JobBank series. In addition to listing companies in each metropolitan area, the JobBank series lists both permanent and temporary employment agencies in the area. Contact Adams Publishing at 800-USA-JOBS (toll-free).

College Career Center Web Pages

College career center Web pages typically include numerous links to some of the best career-related Internet sites in the world. Some of these online career centers link to employment agencies.

Referrals from a Contact or Career Counselor

Seek advice from a career counselor or a contact in your chosen career field regarding the best employment agencies for you.

For more Internet listings and printed directories of employment agencies, refer to "Employment Services" in Appendix A and Appendix C.

The Key Steps to Successfully Using Employment Agencies

Step 1: Choose the Best Type of Employment Agency

Be clear about your objectives. Do you want to develop skills, gain networking contacts, or identify additional job leads? Be realistic regarding your level of experience. If you don't have much experience, you'll have more luck using a public or temporary agency.

Step 2: Identify the Agencies That Meet Your Needs

Use one of the previous recommended resources and generate a list of agencies that are free and consistent with your career-field and geographical interests. Many agencies have certain career fields that dominate the positions. Make sure the positions that are most commonly filled are ones that interest you. Also, check to see how long each agency has been in business. The longer they've been around, the better.

Step 3: Use Your Contacts to Help You Choose

Talk to your networking contacts or career counselor to help you identify appropriate agencies. Call professional associations in your area to ask for their advice.

Step 4: Contact the Agencies on Your List

To initiate contact, either call the agencies directly or mail a cover letter along with your resume. Find out the procedures for getting registered. Also, register with more than one agency. Agencies are sometimes territorial, but it's important not to rely on one source. When more people look for you, your chances for finding a job increase. At the same time, however, don't bite off more than you can chew. Keep in mind that you'll have to keep up with all the interviewing activity generated from these agencies.

Step 5: Prepare and Submit Appropriate Materials

Ask your agents what materials you'll need to have on file. Determine whether cover letters, references, or other supporting documents are needed. Keep in mind that your agent may be looking for jobs in many different fields and that your resume should be appropriate for all of them. If your agent will be looking in three different fields, you should ideally submit three different versions of your resume.

Step 6: Be in Control of Your Career Search

Don't simply submit your resume to three agencies and wait to see what happens. Stay on top of things. Periodically check in with your agents or headhunters. Keep a record of the activity that occurs with each agency. Evaluate your progress and determine which agencies are worth staying with and which ones are not. Be polite and courteous. Your agents are human beings with feelings. If they like you, they'll naturally want to help you.

STRATEGY 4: PARTICIPATING IN JOB FAIRS

Job fairs, sometimes referred to as *career fairs* or *career days*, enable job seekers to interview with numerous recruiters under one roof in one day. An employment agency, college career center, or trade/professional association usually coordinates job fairs. Employment agencies and college career centers typically gather local or regional companies that represent a wide variety of career fields. Trade or professional associations most often coordinate a job fair or interview day as part of a larger conference related exclusively to their industry. This can be done on a national or regional level. If it's part of an all-day conference, there may be a fee involved, but it's usually a very affordable one.

Job fairs are structured in one of two ways: preselect or first-come, first-serve. Preselect job fairs allow participating employers to review job-seekers' resumes before the day of the fair and preselect who they want to interview. These interviews are typically scheduled at the convenience of the recruiter, so don't expect a great deal of control over when your interview takes place. With first-come, first-serve job fairs, recruiters don't review resumes prior to meeting with candidates. The job seekers are given a directory to find the booth or table of the employers of interest. Then they simply walk up to each booth and wait in line for their chance to talk with the recruiters. The length of the interviews varies depending on how long the line is and the match between the candidate and employer.

When you participate in a first-come, first-serve job fair, the best time to come is around the halfway point. If you get there right away, you'll experience longer lines. Plus, the recruiters may not remember you as easily if you're the first of many job seekers they see. If you come near the end, you're taking a chance of missing out on companies who packed up and hit the road a little early. Many recruiters go from job fair to job fair and would rather not stay to the bitter end. You'd be surprised how many companies leave a half hour to an hour early.

Pros

- **High Visibility**
  You can interview with many recruiters in one day.

- **Minimal Time Involvement**
  Usually, it takes a month or two to schedule and conduct 10 interviews. A job fair enables you to conduct up to 10 interviews in one day.

- **Networking Opportunity**
  If you do a good job presenting yourself and asking good questions, you can get referrals from recruiters to other company branches and contacts.

Cons

- **Career/Occupation Variety**
  Job fairs primarily attract employers in career fields and occupations that experience high turnover or that currently have a surplus of jobs to fill. Sales, computer science, insurance, and financial services are industries common to see at job fairs.

- **The Frequency of Job Fairs**
  Job fairs don't take place very often in each region.

- **The Eligibility of Some Job Fairs**
  Many college career centers and professional associations will allow only their students and members to sign up for interviews.

Where to Find Job Fairs

General Internet Search Engines

Find one of the better search engines, like Yahoo.com or Webcrawler.com, and conduct a keyword search for job fairs or career fairs. A list of links to job-fair sites will be presented from this keyword search.

Online Career Sites

Some of the larger online career sites have a list of links to job fairs across the country. The National Association of Colleges and Employers (NACE) Web site, for example, offers a comprehensive list of job fairs (primarily college job fairs) across the nation. Visit this site at www.jobweb.org/search/cfairs.

College Career Center Web Pages

Most career-center home pages will announce and describe special career events, including upcoming job fairs.

Referrals from a Contact or Career Counselor

Seek advice from a career counselor or a contact in your chosen career field regarding the best job fairs to attend.

Field-/Industry-Specific Publications

Many trade and professional associations publish a monthly or biweekly bulletin, journal, or newsletter that includes information on when and where job fairs will be held.

Field-/Industry-Specific Web Sites

Some Web sites are exclusively devoted to promoting job fairs. Career Fairs International, for example, has a site, www.efinancialjobs.com, that provides information on career fairs related to accounting, banking, finance, and insurance.

See "Job and Career Fairs" in Appendix A for Internet sites that list job fairs across the country.

The Key Steps to Succeeding at Job Fairs

Step 1: Prepare Important Self-Marketing Materials and Take Them with You

You must come prepared. Bring appropriate versions of your resume, depending on the organizations attending. If you have business cards and it's appropriate to use them, make sure you bring plenty. If you've developed a portfolio that's not too bulky to lug around, bring it with you. Also bring a pen and a professional binder with a notepad inside to take notes.

Step 2: Research Participating Organizations

The biggest complaint among recruiters at job fairs is the lack of company knowledge that candidates demonstrate. The more you can learn about the organizations attending the job fair through their Web pages or company literature, the better. See if the institution coordinating the fair has literature on the participating companies. Know the companies' services and products, management philosophies, missions and goals, leading competitors, markets, and career opportunities.

Step 3: Develop a List of Questions for Each Organization

It's important to ask recruiters questions not only to learn more about the company, but also to show them you've done your homework. You can impress the recruiter most by asking substantive questions that stem from your research. Read the sample question below. Notice how the candidate ties her question to the research.

> "I was reviewing your Web page and was interested to read about the new services that you are providing for the elderly. How have these services been received, and do you plan on continuing them in the future?"

Also, don't be afraid to refer to your list of questions while talking to the recruiter. This shows that you've done your research, you've come prepared, and you leave nothing to chance. It also indicates interest in their company.

FYI

If you're relocating and conducting a long-distance job search, you should still attend local job fairs. Identify the larger corporations that have branches throughout the U.S. and talk to the recruiters from these companies. Once you've built a good rapport with the recruiters, ask them if they can refer you to a contact in your relocation area. Job fairs can help you build your network of contacts.

Step 4: Come Professionally Dressed

Need I say more? Refer to Chapter 14 to gain specific insight on what constitutes professional dress.

Step 5: Present Your Best Self

Recruiters are looking for candidates with strong interpersonal skills. They'll naturally grade you higher if they feel comfortable talking to you. Smile. Be polite, positive, and enthusiastic. Extend your hand and offer a firm handshake when you introduce yourself. Maintain good eye contact throughout your interview. For more specific tips on interviewing, go to Chapters 12, 13, and 14.

Step 6: Take Notes

After each interview, write down your impressions and any next steps that were discussed. Be sure to receive a business card from each person to whom you speak. You need this information to write thank-you letters. If they don't have a business card, ask the recruiter to spell her name and give her title. Check with the sponsoring organization to see if they have a list of participants you can take home with you.

Step 7: Follow Up

Send a thank-you letter to every recruiter you interviewed with, even if there was more than one recruiter for a given company. See Chapter 15 for advice on writing thank-you letters. Read over your notes when you get home, and determine if you should follow up with any of the recruiters. Organize your notes now that you have more time, and be sure to note when organizations said they would contact you.

STRATEGY 5: USING COLLEGE CAREER CENTERS

For college students and graduates, your alma mater career center can serve as an employment service to a certain degree. Unlike the three types of employment services previously described, college career centers offer a comprehensive array of career-related programs, services, and resources. These centers cover issues and topics that relate to career planning, career exploration, self-assessment, career decision making, resume and cover letter writing, interviewing, job search strategies, and graduate school planning. Most centers do all this with a very limited staff, leaving them very little time to focus solely on matching students and alumni with jobs.

Participate in Resume Referral with Your College Career Center

While they can't devote much time to matching students with jobs, most centers have a resume referral system. Some still do it the old-fashioned way, keeping printed resumes on file and matching them with jobs upon request. Many others, though, are maintaining a computer-operated resume referral system, either in house or on line with a third-party Web company. College students and alumni place their resumes on file or on line with their college career center and hope to get selected by a participating company. Just as employment agencies have a list of company contacts that use their services, the career centers have a list of past and present employers. Also, career centers usually have strong connections with their alumni who give special treatment to the students and their fellow alumni who are seeking employment.

Pros

- **Friendly Employers**

  The participating employers usually like to hire graduates of your institution. If they didn't have success with your graduates, they'd stop recruiting there.

- **Friendly Career Staff**

  The career center staff's job is to serve students and alumni. They want to help you because of your association with the college.

- **Alumni Contacts**

  Many alumni who have hiring authority want to take care of their own. Therefore, alumni often will participate in resume referral with their alma mater.

Cons

- **Entry-Level Positions**

  If you're a current student or recent graduate, this is not a problem. If you're an experienced graduate, the typical positions listed in resume referral may not be what you're looking for.

- **Variety of Industries**

  Positions tend to primarily fall within a handful of industries that are constantly trying to hire people. These currently include insurance, sales, and computer science.

- **Scattered Focus**

  Unlike employment agencies, the resume referral service is not a career center's primary focus. It's one of many services that it's trying to juggle.

Participate in On-Campus Recruiting with Your College Career Center

Most college career centers also coordinate an on-campus recruiting program. Since the majority of the positions are entry-level, most programs allow only their students and graduate students to participate.

However, alumni have been known to interview on campus. Similar to job fairs, on-campus recruiting can take place on a preselection or first-come, first-serve basis. It depends on the competitiveness of the program. If it's preselect, you'll submit a resume for each position/company in which you're interested, and you're notified of your interviewing status. If you're selected for an interview, just show up at the career center during the scheduled time. Most interviews last only a half-hour to accommodate as many students as possible. If the system is first-come, first-serve, you can sign up for an interview slot that fits your schedule.

Pros

- **Convenient**

  How much more convenient can job searching be? How many times do jobs and companies come inside your home? Students can walk across campus and interview with companies. They don't even have to mail their own resumes. The career centers do the work for them.

- **Minimal Time Involvement**

  Again, most of the work is done for the students. Today, most career centers have links from their home page to the Web pages of participating companies. Students can roll over in their beds, turn on the computer, and research any company they want. Also, all the hours it takes to network and initiate contact with a company is done by the career center staff.

- **Multiple Interviews**

  Students can potentially interview with many different organizations. This not only provides prospective job opportunities, but also interview practice.

Cons

- **Eligibility**

  Many colleges allow only their students to participate in on-campus recruiting. Alumni and people in the community usually are not permitted to participate in the program.

- **Variety**

  Similar to resume referral, many career fields are not represented through on-campus recruiting. Many career centers are perceived as business and technical oriented due to their highly visible on-campus recruiting programs.

Where to Find College Career Centers

For local college students and alumni, this is pretty straightforward. If you're an alumni, the easiest thing to do is to pick up the phone and talk with a career center staff member. Check to see if you're eligible to participate in their employment programs. You can also visit the career center's Web page. Many career centers have a section on their Web page directed to alumni, describing the services available to them. Most Web pages include descriptions of all their programs and services. If you're a student, make an appointment with a career counselor to talk about the resume referral and on-campus recruiting programs.

For alumni far from your alma mater: Call your the career center and ask if you could take advantage of a local college's career center through a program called "reciprocity." Most college career centers work well together, sharing resources and programs with students and alumni from other colleges. Typically, the career center director writes a letter of reciprocity to the college career center near you, requesting that you be permitted to use their services. This is reciprocated when students or alumni from their institution need to use services from your college career center. Sometimes, there's a fee involved for alumni.

For those who are not students or alumni: Call the local college career center and see if any career services are available for people in the community. Some centers meet with people in the community during slow seasons, such as the summer and spring break.

Key Steps for Successfully Participating in Resume Referral
Step 1: Register with the Center

Most career centers require that you register with them to be included in their resume referral program. Fill out all the registration materials.

Step 2: Prepare an Appropriate Resume

Find out if there are any format guidelines or policies. Some programs advise you not to include an objective since they may be distributing your resume to multiple employers. Also determine what they do with your resume. Some centers scan it into their system, while others mail it out in its original form. Other centers require that you post your resume on line.

Step 3: Learn about the Overall Procedures

Once you submit your resume, what happens next? Find out if you'll be notified when a company selects your resume. Knowing where your resume has been submitted prepares you for calls from those companies.

Step 4: Track Your Results and Progress

Keep a record of the companies that have reviewed your resume and those wanting to interview with you. Check in with the career center periodically, especially if you haven't received any calls from recruiters.

Step 5: Update Your Resume

As you gain additional skills and experience, make sure you submit an updated resume to the career center to replace the old one.

FYI

Don't just sign up to interview with companies that have a big name or that you're familiar with. Research each company to determine whether you should interview with them. There could be a company you've never heard of that has your perfect job and is trying to fill the position. If you don't research the companies, you may miss out.

Key Steps for Succeeding in On-Campus Recruiting

Step 1: Learn the Program Procedures and Deadlines

Each program has a set of procedures to follow, such as submitting a resume and filling out forms. Some programs require that you participate in a certain workshop to be eligible. Others require that you register by a certain date. Contact a career center staff member to learn the procedures and deadlines.

Step 2: Sign Up for Interviews that Interest You

Review the list of companies that are interviewing on campus and research those that you don't know much about. Sign up to interview for those positions/organizations that interest you.

Step 3: Prepare Your Self-Marketing Materials

Develop and submit appropriate versions of your resume, depending on the organizations that you choose. Ask a career center staff member whether or not to submit a cover letter along with each resume. If you've developed a portfolio, bring it to the interviews. Also bring a pen and a professional binder with a notepad inside to take notes.

Step 4: Research the Organizations You're Interviewing with and Develop a List of Questions

Learn about the organizations through their Web page or company literature. Know the companies' services and products, management philosophies, missions and goals, leading competitors, markets, and career opportunities. As stated earlier, you'll impress the recruiter most by asking intelligent questions generated from your research.

See "Researching Organizations/Employer Profiles" in Appendix A and "Researching Organizations" in Appendix C for recommended resources to help you research companies.

Step 5: Come Professionally Dressed

Refer to Chapter 14 to gain specific insight on what constitutes professional dress.

Step 6: Present Your Best Self

As stated earlier in the job fair section, it's critical to be yourself. Refer to Chapter 14 for more specific tips on how to present yourself.

Step 7: Take Notes

After each interview, write down your impressions and any next steps that were discussed. Be sure to receive a business card from the interviewer for future correspondence. If they don't have a business card, get the recruiter's contact information from the career center.

Step 8: Follow Up

Send a thank-you letter to every recruiter with whom you interviewed. See Chapter 15 for advice on writing good thank-you letters. Determine if you need to follow up with any of the recruiters.

DEALING WITH THE OPEN COVER LETTER DILEMMA: TO BE, OR NOT TO BE, ASSERTIVE

As you apply for positions within the open job market, you have a decision to make regarding your cover letters. As discussed previously, the closing paragraph of your open-market cover letters can end in one of two ways. You can express that you'll contact the company to inquire about the status of the search or simply wait to hear from them. Is it better to let the chips fall where they may or try to make something happen? Job search experts constantly debate over this issue.

On one hand, it's best not to be overly assertive, for it can go against you. Job openings typically attract many applicants. If every applicant called to get an edge, the recruiter would get bombarded with calls. You take a chance of being perceived as a pest or even a little desperate.

On the other hand, how can you stand out from the crowd if you just sit there and do nothing? You could call the recruiter to ask some questions about the position and be perceived as someone who is genuinely interested in the job and the company. When you directly talk to the recruiter, you bring your resume to life. You're not merely assessed on paper; your communication skills and level of interest also are assessed.

The bottom line is that you take a risk either way. By calling, there's a small risk of being perceived as a pest or desperate. By not calling, you take the risk of blending in with all the other candidates.

So how do you decide what to do? You need to assess the situation and your chances of getting an interview. If your resume stands strong by itself, you may be better off leaving it in the hands of the company. For example, if your academic background, past experience, and skills closely match the job description, you'll stand out through your credentials alone. However, if you feel your background and experience aren't very competitive for this particular job, you may want to call and try to build rapport with one of the company representatives to give you an edge.

Another factor to consider is whether or not you know anyone in the organization who has an opening listed. If you have a contact, you should call that contact and ask for their advice. Let them know you're applying for a position in their company, and that you have a few questions to ask them. Making your contact aware that you're applying can prove to be beneficial. Your contact may offer to serve as a reference for you, speaking on your behalf to those who have the hiring power.

If you decide to call, try to identify the person who heads up the division to which you're applying. Generate a list of questions related to the position and the company. Asking the right professionals good questions can indicate a level of knowledge and interest that enables you to stand out from the rest. Chapter 11 thoroughly covers information interviewing and the best questions to ask prospective employers.

THE WHOLE IN ONE

- Many worthwhile job-search strategies exist in the open job market.

- Getting your hands on the best job advertisements can be beneficial. Researching the organizations that are hiring, writing a personalized cover letter, and promptly responding to the ads are critical tips to keep in mind.

- Posting your resume with an online career center can generate more visibility for you. One electronic version of your resume can potentially be reviewed by hundreds of recruiters.

- Connecting with an appropriate third-party employment service can also increase the breadth of prospective employers. Make sure you choose an employment service that frequently fills positions of interest and doesn't charge the job seeker.

- Although there aren't many of them, job fairs can be a very efficient way to look for a job. What other time during your job search do you have the luxury of 50 to 100 prospective employers under one roof?

- Your college or alma mater career center can offer employment services of their own. Resume referral programs and on-campus recruiting are two programs worth looking into. For alumni, you should contact your alma mater and determine your eligibility regarding various employment services.

- Whichever strategies you decide to engage in, you must make a decision regarding how assertive you'll be when pursuing opportunities. It's a risk when you take initiative, and it's a risk if you don't. It depends on how competitive you are for each position and if you know anyone who works for the hiring company.

ASSIGNMENT

Complete the first five strategies of Goal 4 of your Personal Job Search Trainer.

Chapter 10

The Best Job-Search Strategies in the Hidden Job Market

GET THE SCOOP ON . . .

- Mass mailing
- Targeted mailing
- Networking and information interviews
- Creative networking ideas

CONTACTING ORGANIZATIONS THROUGH MASS AND TARGETED MAILINGS

Mass mailing and *targeted mailing* are two common job-search strategies used in the hidden job market. Each strategy has its own strengths and weaknesses, and both can seem a little daunting to some job seekers. Mailing out dozens of resumes at one time isn't the most effective way to go about getting your perfect job, but if you know where to find the right resources and the key steps you need to take to succeed, you can improve your odds.

STRATEGY 6: MASS MAILING

Mass mailing is a job search strategy that has been around for a very long time. Job seekers submit a resume and a generic cover letter to a long list of prospective employers in their chosen career field and geographic location. Remember that in the hidden job market, you don't know of any existing job openings in the companies in which you're interested. Therefore, you're just expressing an interest in the companies and asking them to keep your resume on file until an appropriate job opportunity surfaces. The cover letters are usually not targeted to an individual. They're addressed as "To whom it may concern," "Dear Sir/Madam," or "Dear Personnel Department." The only items that change from one cover letter to the next are the company name and its address.

Pros

- **High Visibility**

  You can get your resume out to a large number of prospective employers.

- **Little Time Commitment**

  Since you're not tailoring the cover letters, you don't have to spend time researching and personalizing your cover letters.

Cons

- **Extremely Low Percentage of Success**

  On a good day, you'll receive feedback from 1 out of 50 companies that received your resume. Only one half of these companies that get back to you offer an interview. Now you're down to 1 interview per 100 resumes. On average, organizations hold 10 interviews for every offer made. Thus, the grand total comes out to be 1 offer for every 1,000 resumes.

Where to Find Large Lists of Organizations

Following are sources for finding large lists of organizations.

Local Library

Your local library will have numerous CD-ROMs and printed employer directories to help you generate lists of company names and addresses.

College Career Centers

Call the local college career center and see if you can use their directories to photocopy some lists of organizations. Many centers have directories categorized by industry and geographical regions. Visit their Web pages. Many centers categorize online directories by industry for their students and alumni, but most of the information is accessible to all.

Career-Related Internet Sites

Many of the online career centers enable you to search for lists of companies by career field and region.

Web Sites for Fortune *and* Forbes *Magazines*

Visit www.fortune.com to receive lists of links to the Fortune 500 (the nation's top 500 companies based on revenues) and the world's 500 largest corporations. Visit www.forbes.com to receive the Forbes 500 (the nation's top companies compiled by *Forbes* magazine).

Field-/Industry-Specific Publications

Many trade and professional associations publish membership directories. For example, the Society of Human Resource Management (SHRM) produces membership directories per geographic region.

Regional Business Offices

Contact the Chamber of Commerce, Better Business Bureau, or state employment office in your geographical area of interest to see if they have listings of companies.

See "Researching Organizations/Employer Directories" in Appendix A and "Researching Organizations" in Appendix C for a long list of relevant Internet sites and printed resources. Also check out Appendix B to find resources related to the field you're pursuing.

The Key Steps to Mass Mailing

Step 1: Identify the Best Resources

Based on the career field and location of your perfect job, determine the best resources for generating lists of organizations (use the numerous options outlined above). Ask career counselors, chamber of commerce representatives, and contacts in the field to direct you to relevant directories. Use some of the directories listed in Appendix C and the Internet sites listed in Appendix A that are most applicable to your job search. You can also contact trade and professional associations in your area to see if they produce membership directories.

Step 2: Enter the Company Names and Addresses in a Database

The most efficient way to produce a large number of cover letters and envelopes is to enter the company names and addresses in a database and perform a mail merge. Today's database software makes it easy to perform mail merges. You can buy sheets of labels that feed right into your printer and correspond to your database mail merge. No more duplicate typing necessary. Type the company names and addresses once and use them on the cover letter as well as the envelopes. If you don't have a computer or the right software, many libraries or copy centers will let you use their computers for a minimal fee.

Step 3: Write a Strong Cover Letter

Even though the mass-mailing cover letters are not tailored to each company, they can still be tailored to your occupation and industry of interest. State why you're committed to your chosen occupation and industry and what you have to offer (your selling points). For more information on cover letters, refer to Chapter 7.

Step 4: Keep a Record and Track Results

Keep a record of all the organizations to which you mailed your materials. Record results when you hear something back from the companies. Because you mailed your resume and cover letters to a large number of employers, it's critical that you stay organized. Use the forms provided in Chapter 8.

STRATEGY 7: TARGETED MAILING

Targeted mailing is much more focused and tailored to individual companies than mass mailing. When using targeted mailing, you create a prioritized list of organizations you're interested in and submit a tailored cover letter addressed to the appropriate person. You don't know of any jobs that are available, but you still want to express your genuine interest in working for their company in the near future. Not only are your cover letters targeted to a specific person, but they're also tailored to the company and occupation. Therefore, research is involved when conducting a targeted mailing campaign. Finally, you should follow up with a call to each representative who receives your letter. This gives you much more control and knowledge of your status than you have with mass mailing.

Pros

- **Personalized Correspondence**

  Through your research, you're able to express genuine interests and highlight specific selling points that relate to each company's needs.

- **More Control**

  You're taking the initiative and have a clear understanding of your status with each company thanks to your follow-up calls. You don't just sit around and wait for calls from the companies.

Cons

- **Time-Intensive**

  There's a price to personalizing your direct contact with prospective employers. It takes a significant amount of time to conduct the research and write a different cover letter for each organization.

- **Low Success Rate**

  Even with the more personalized approach, the success rate is still low. You'll frequently hear things like "We're currently not hiring" or "Check back with us in six months." Remember one of the three P's to success: Persevere!

Where to Find Organizations for Targeted Mailing

The best way to research for targeted mailings is to combine the sources identified for mass mailing with the sources identified for responding to ads. Think about it—you must generate the correct names and addresses of your selected organizations (just as you did for mass mailing), but you then need to conduct research on each one (as you did for responding to ads). Therefore, use the recommended sources for mass mailing above and the recommended sources for responding to ads in the previous chapter.

The Key Steps to Targeted Mailing

Step 1: Identify the Best Organizations to Target

Based on the career field and location you're pursuing, determine the best organizations for you. Ask career counselors, chamber of commerce representatives, and contacts in the field to refer you to the companies that are growing and well respected. Contact trade and professional associations to get their advice. Many associations produce lists of the largest and fastest-growing organizations in the field.

Step 2: Enter the Company Names and Addresses in a Database

As described thoroughly in the mass-mailing section, use a database, mail merge, and sheets of labels to efficiently print the contact information of your selected companies on both cover letters and envelopes. Again, if you don't have a computer or the right software, you can rent computer time at your library or copy center for a very minimal fee.

Step 3: Research Each Organization on Your Targeted List

Through the company Web page or employer literature, identify specific aspects of the organizations that are appealing to you. Look for projects or new initiatives that somehow connect to your education, experience, or skills.

Step 4: Craft a Targeted, Tailored Cover Letter

Using the advice and techniques in Chapter 7, address your cover letter to the appropriate person and tailor your letter to the company's needs. Try to find the name of the person who heads up the division you're most interested in, and address your cover letter accordingly. Express specific areas of interest and your top selling points. If you know anyone who works at the companies you're pursuing, contact them for advice. They may offer to speak on your behalf. Ask your contact if you can use their name in the cover letter. Be sure to inform the company contacts that you'll be calling them on a certain date. An important part of targeted mailing is making follow-up calls.

Step 5: Produce and Submit Your Materials

Print each cover letter on the same quality paper as your resume. Submit your resume and tailored cover letter.

Step 6: Generate Substantive Questions for Your Follow-Up Calls

Based on your research, generate substantive questions about the company and career opportunities. The following list of topics will help

Guidance

We like to see candidates do some research on our company because that shows us that they are interested in the career opportunity and that they have their act together.
—Jefferson Pilot

you generate questions, but for a complete list of questions to ask contacts, see Chapter 11 and Appendix D, "Information Interview Questions."

- Products and services

- Mission and philosophy

- Competitors

- Foreign and domestic markets

- Work atmosphere

- Division and larger company structure

- Number of workers in division of interest and company

- Career opportunities for people with your background

- Advice on how to pursue opportunities with their company

- Referrals to other companies and contacts

- Contact's likes and dislikes of the company

- Contact's impression of the current status of the industry

Step 7: Make the Follow-Up Calls

Make every effort to talk to the person you targeted in your cover letter. If you get a general receptionist, ask to speak to your targeted contact. If the receptionist asks what your call is in reference to, respond by saying, "It's in reference to a document she received from me." Don't say that you're inquiring about a job. Receptionists are trained to direct job seekers to Human Resources or Personnel. Ask the receptionist for a more direct number for future correspondence. If you have trouble getting through this time, you'll have a better number to call next time.

If you get the targeted contact's voice mail or answering machine, you can leave a message if you're comfortable doing so. Some people feel more comfortable breaking the ice through the one-way correspondence of voice mail. If you do leave a message, inform your contact that you wanted to make sure she received your resume and that you just have a few questions for her. Whatever you do, don't ask your contact to call you back. Asking someone who doesn't know you to add yet another task to her list of things to do is not a good way to start things off.

When you finally get a hold of the contact, introduce yourself and ask her if she has time to answer a few questions or if there would be a more convenient time for you to call back. Ask the questions on your prepared list and take notes. At the end, express your deepest gratitude for her time and ask for her general advice on how you should pursue opportunities with her company and within the field in general. If you feel good about your rapport, ask your contact if you could visit the company to get a better feel for the work atmosphere and to ask further questions. You're basically requesting an information interview, which is described at length in the next chapter. Also ask for referrals to other organizations or contacts in the field. Use good judgement regarding your requests. You don't want to overstay your welcome and damage the positive rapport that was established with your contact.

Step 8: Keep a Record and Track Results
Keep a record of your impressions of the follow-up calls and any next steps that were established. Make sure to follow up with any requests or recommendations made by your contacts.

STRATEGY 8: NETWORKING AND INFORMATION INTERVIEWS: THE KING OF THE JOB-SEARCH JUNGLE

The best job-search strategy—hands-down—is networking. Some studies have shown that up to 80 percent of all jobs are obtained through some form of networking. Networking can be defined as generating information, job leads, and referrals to prospective employers through personal and professional contacts. Why is networking so powerful? First, it's human nature to want to hire someone you know over a stranger. When you have to call a plumber, set your friend up with a date, or find a babysitter, wouldn't you rather choose someone you know or someone a friend or relative speaks highly of? Also, hiring and turnover costs companies a lot of money. Recruiters are responsible for hiring strong candidates who won't leave within six months of taking the job. The process of hiring the best person for the job is not an exact science. You try to get as much information about the candidates as you can, but you never have as much information as you'd like to make a sound, educated decision. The additional information generated from networking helps recruiters feel more certain of their hiring decisions. Finally, with teamwork and interpersonal skills so highly valued, it's important to find people who will get along well with their co-workers. Networking contacts can inform recruiters of a candidate's personal characteristics and assets that, in turn, helps them choose candidates who will fit in well with the organization.

Where Networking Takes Place
Networking can take place just about anywhere. Wherever and whenever you tell people that you're looking for a new job, you're networking. Networking can occur on a professional level, during your temporary, full-time, or part-time jobs. For high school and college

students, internships and cooperative education serve as a great way to network. Professional conferences or trade shows are great for networking. Networking can also occur on a more personal level. You can network with people in your hometown community, church community, or with friends and relatives. So as a job seeker, it's your job to let everyone know that you're on a job search. You never know where that key referral may come from.

The Best Method of Networking: Information Interviews

One of the best ways to network is to conduct information interviews. Information interviewing is a structured method of networking in which you interview personal contacts or referrals for information, advice, and referrals. The goals of information interviews are different depending on the job-search stage you're in. If you're trying to decide on a career, the goal is to simply learn about various career fields. If you already know what you want to do, the main goal is networking toward a job. The focus in this section is using information interviewing as a job-search strategy.

Information interviews can be conducted either face-to-face, over the telephone, or even through e-mail. It's your responsibility to take the initiative in arranging the information interviews and leading the conversation through your questions. When using some of your close personal contacts, the information interviews will be less formal and structured. The next chapter lays out a thorough plan for mastering your information interviews.

Networking Can Be a Positive Experience for All

Too often, networking gets a bad rap. It's been perceived as a slick way of using people to get a job. This is the case only if you make it so. Through information interviewing, the networking experience can be positive for contacts as well as the job seeker. As long as you don't bulldoze your way into asking for a job, the information interview can be flattering to your contacts. Think about it—you're asking your contacts for advice and information about their chosen line of work. In other words, you're showing genuine interest in what they do and the field they've chosen. How many other opportunities at work do people have to talk about themselves and reminisce over how they got to where they are now? The information interview can be the most pleasant part of your contact's day, maybe even their week! You're giving them the rare opportunity to travel down memory lane. So, the first thing that you need to do is to view the networking experience as a positive experience for everyone involved.

A Couple of Creative Networking Ideas

Be creative in thinking of innovative ways to network. The ideas are limitless! Following are a couple of creative ideas that have been very successful when implemented.

Develop and Implement a Career Exploration Project

For high school, college, and graduate students, initiate a career exploration project (with information interviewing at its core) through one of your courses or as an independent study project (most colleges allow you to work with a professor on an independent-study basis). The project could look something similar to this:

- Identify 15 different organizations within your chosen career field.

- Research each organization and generate questions using the P-O-W-E-R model (see Chapter 11).

- Arrange an information interview with each organization. Explain to the contacts that you're doing this as part of a class project.

- Conduct the information interviews with the questions you generated.

- Write a report on each company, including topics such as products and services, mission and goals, competitors, work atmosphere, and size.

- Write a separate report on your impressions, interests, values, and how this experience impacted your career direction.

- Share the first report with the career center or guidance office. This will be helpful information for them.

One benefit of this type of project is that you have a good excuse for calling your favorite companies. It's a class project! It's a great way to get your foot in the door with some very competitive companies. A second benefit is that the course will make you structure this experience and bring information interviewing to life. You'll engage in it because your grade depends on it.

Observe or Work Shadow Professionals

As described in Chapter 3, work shadowing (observing professionals at work) is a great technique for exploring careers of interest and determining how much you may enjoy certain occupations. In some cases, work shadowing can also be used for networking purposes among job seekers. Teaching is a good example of this. One of the best ways for aspiring teachers to network is to observe various classrooms. Experienced teachers are usually very receptive to aspiring teachers' requests to observe them. During your day of observation, you'll have opportunities to talk with (information interview) the teacher during breaks, introduce yourself to the principal, and network with other teachers in the staff lunchroom. Sure, you'll learn a lot just by observing, but the networking opportunities that go along with it are invaluable. Consider whether or not your field lends itself to work shadowing.

In the next chapter (Chapter 11), a 7-step plan for mastering information interviews is presented. You'll learn who to contact, how to arrange and conduct the information interviews, and the best questions to ask. You'll be introduced to the P-O-W-E-R Model, teaching you the inside strategy for mastering information interviews and networking.

THE WHOLE IN ONE

- You should plan on spending the majority of your job-seeking time tapping into the hidden job market since 85 percent of jobs are found there.

- Mass mailing is a way to get your name and resume out there to numerous prospective employers. However, the cover letters and overall correspondence is not targeted or tailored, resulting in a very low return rate.

- Targeted mailing takes on a much more tailored and personalized approach. You target your cover letters to the appropriate contact, research each company, write a personalized cover letter, and make follow-up calls to your contacts. While it's more time-consuming, targeted mailing increases your chances for success and gives you more control over the job search.

- Networking is, by far, the king of the job-search jungle. Close to 80 percent of all jobs are obtained through some form of networking. It's all about building relationships.

- Networking can be a very positive experience for everyone involved, if you approach it the right way.

- Information interviewing is the most effective method of networking for job seekers. Information interviewing is a structured, proactive way to interact with networking contacts and prospective employers.

- Consider some creative ways to network. Designing a career exploration project and work shadowing are two creative ways to bring networking to life.

ASSIGNMENT

Complete the "Mass Mailing" and "Networking" sections of Goal 4 of your Personal Job Search Trainer.

Chapter 11

Mastering Information Interviews

GET THE SCOOP ON . . .

- How to generate the best networking contacts
- THE P-O-W-E-R Model
- Sample questions
- Arranging information interviews
- Effectively conducting information interviews

THE 7-STEP PLAN FOR MASTERING INFORMATION INTERVIEWS

When you respond to job ads, you follow procedures outlined by the organization doing the hiring. When it comes to networking and information interviewing, there are no procedures for you to follow or react to. You're in charge! You must be proactive in designing a concrete, thorough plan that will bring information interviewing to life. Here's a thorough 7-Step Plan for conducting exceptional information interviews:

1. Identify relevant contacts and helper contacts.
2. Get additional referrals from your helper contacts.
3. Accept the critical success factor of networking.
4. Generate a list of questions to ask your relevant contacts using the P-O-W-E-R Model.
5. Arrange information interviews with your relevant contacts.
6. Conduct the information interviews using the P-O-W-E-R Model.
7. Follow up and track your results.

Step 1: Identify Your Relevant and Helper Contacts

The first step to conducting information interviews is determining the best people to interview. These people will be referred to as your *relevant contacts*. Relevant contacts are people who work in relevant career fields or organizations that you're interested in pursuing. Relevant contacts aren't always easy to get in touch with, so you'll often have to go through *helper contacts*. Helper contacts are contacts that don't directly work in your chosen career field or prospective organizations but may be able to *help* you by referring you to a relevant contact.

There's a reason for distinguishing helper contacts from relevant contacts. The correspondence you'll have with helper contacts will be different from your correspondence with relevant contacts because your goals are different. When you speak with a helper contact, your goal is to receive referrals to relevant contacts. The goal of initially getting in touch with relevant contacts is to arrange an information interview.

To create your list of helper and relevant contacts, it's best to consider everyone you know and everyone you're associated with. This can be an overwhelming task. An effective way to do this is to think of your contacts in three categories: personal, professional, and community.

Identifying Helper and Relevant Contacts through Your Personal Contacts

It's wise to start looking closest to home. Your personal contacts typically are the most willing to help you. Personal contacts include the following:

FYI

It's important to realize that relevant contacts can be either personal contacts (people you know directly) or referrals (people you don't know but have been referred to you). Therefore, you'll most likely conduct information interviews with people that range from close personal contacts to referred strangers.

- Friends
- Neighbors
- Parents
- Children
- Uncles
- Aunts
- Cousins
- Nieces
- Nephews
- Grandparents
- In-laws

Once you've written down the names of all your personal contacts, determine which ones are relevant contacts and which ones would make good helper contacts. To determine relevant contacts, you simply need to pick out those personal contacts that work in relevant career fields or organizations of interest. For example, if you were pursuing banking and your cousin Joan works as an investment banker, Joan would be a relevant contact.

In determining helper contacts, identify those personal contacts that don't work in your chosen field but are likely to know someone who does. Think about the unlimited possibilities. Take your uncles and aunts, for instance—do you know the majority of your uncles' and aunts' friends or associates? Do you know *any* of their friends or associates? Think about your own friends. Do you have any idea what your friends' parents, uncles, aunts, or cousins do for a living? The possibilities are great only if you open your mouth and start asking questions. Wouldn't it be a shame if your friend's uncle works for one of the top three companies in your field and you never knew it? You never know where that perfect contact is hiding!

Theoretically, everyone potentially could be a helper contact. It's not a bad idea to let all your personal contacts know you're looking for a job. However, you want to identify those personal contacts that you think can help the most and contact them individually. For example, if your Uncle Bob is a full-time engineer, active in his community, and someone you respect, he would be a likely choice for a helper contact. It's very possible he knows someone who works in a field in which you're interested. Conversely, your 13-year-old nephew Rocky, whose biggest concern is hitting a home run, would not make the best helper contact.

Identifying Helper and Relevant Contacts through Your Professional Contacts

People you've worked with in one capacity or another can serve as good professional contacts. Professional contacts include the following:

- Past and present full-time employers
  Co-workers
  Supervisors/Bosses

- Past and present part-time employers
  Co-workers
  Supervisors/Bosses

- Past and present internship or co-op employers
  Co-workers
  Supervisors/Bosses

- Colleagues/associates from other organizations

- Members of trade or professional associations

- Chamber of Commerce

- Members of Rotary

- State Employment Office

If your perfect job is in the same field as any past or present employers, you automatically have many relevant contacts. Realize, however, that just because someone is in the same field doesn't necessarily mean they'd make a *good* relevant contact. Select those past and present co-workers or supervisors whom you respect. If your perfect job isn't in the same field as any past or present employers, you can still use some of these co-workers and supervisors as helper contacts.

Members of trade and professional associations that you've met at conferences or trade shows can make excellent relevant contacts. Even if you've never met any trade or association members, you can still contact them to see if they'd be receptive to an information interview. Many members of associations have a high level of commitment to the field and want to help others trying to get their foot in the door. Likewise, members of Rotary (top business members in the community), Chamber of Commerce, and state employment offices often have numerous contacts and are willing to network.

Identifying Helper and Relevant Contacts through Your Community Contacts

People in various communities to which you belong can be great relevant or helper contacts. Community contacts include the following:

- School or college community (educational)
  Teachers
  Coaches
  Professors
  Advisers
  Guidance counselors
  College career counselors
  Mentors

- Church and service community (religious/service)
  Members of your church
  Committee members
  Members of volunteer organizations to which you belong

- Local and hometown community (geographical)
  Professionals in your career field
  Your doctor(s)
  Your dentist(s)
  Your neighbors
  Your real estate agent
  Your accountant
  Your plumber or carpenter
  Your hair stylist or barber (they know everybody in town)
  (The list could go on forever!)

- Social and recreational community (social)
  League members: softball, volleyball, bowling, etc.
  Club members: bridge, theater, music, art, gourmet cooking, etc.
  Parents of youth sports and activities: Little League, youth camps, dance, swimming lessons, etc.

You can tell by this long list of contacts that getting involved in your community can be very beneficial to your job search. Just as you did for your personal and professional contacts, identify community contacts that are relevant contacts and those that would make good helper contacts.

Compile All Your Relevant and Helper Contacts

Now that you've identified helper contacts and relevant contacts through your personal, professional, and community contacts, it's a good idea to organize them and present them together on one form. List your relevant contacts and helper contacts under the last section of your Personal Job Search Trainer.

Step 2: Get Referrals from Your Helper Contacts

Remember that helper contacts are not relevant contacts who work in your career field of interest. Therefore, you're not trying to arrange a structured information interview with them. You simply want to ask them for recommended referrals to organizations or contacts that *are* in your career field. Be polite, but don't take up much of their time.

Choose a Type(s) of Correspondence

You can correspond with your helper contacts in a variety of ways. You can meet with them, call them, write to them, or e-mail them. It depends on the type of relationship you have with your contacts, how close they live, your preferred way of communicating, and your time. There really isn't one best way to correspond with your helper contacts. Some people are more comfortable introducing their request through a letter and following up with a call. Others feel more comfortable just picking up the phone and asking away. Still others would rather get in the car and visit their contacts in person. Typically, people perform better when they are comfortable, so choose the type of correspondence that's most comfortable for you.

Keep in mind that the type of correspondence may differ from one helper contact to the next. For example, you may feel very comfortable picking up the phone and calling your cousin but not as comfortable calling your old boss out of the blue. Determine what type of correspondence is most appropriate for each helper contact on your list.

When and Where Should You Contact Them?

You first need to identify where and what part of the day would be best to contact each helper contact. For example, it would be appropriate to call your aunt at her home number during the evening. However, it may not be appropriate to call your former supervisor at home on a weekend. If you're writing or e-mailing a letter, you should decide which address would be more appropriate to use for each contact: business or home. This, again, depends on the type of relationship you have with each helper contact.

Gather Contact Information (Phone Number, E-mail Address, Etc.)

Once you know the type of correspondence and where you'll be contacting them, gather the corresponding contact information for each helper contact (phone numbers, mailing addresses, e-mail addresses, etc.).

Prepare for Your Calls and Write Your Letters

Before you get on the phone, think about how you're going to introduce yourself and request referrals. For those contacts that you know well, you won't have to prepare very long. If you feel a little nervous or awkward, you may want to jot down some key points to discuss once you're on the phone. Below is a sample script for calling helper contacts. Notice how Anita doesn't jump right into her job search. She starts by asking a series of questions that relate to her contact. Also notice Anita's careful wording. If she bluntly says she's looking for a job, it may scare her helper contact off from wanting to refer Anita to her friends and associates.

> Hi, Jane. This is Anita Job calling. How have you been? How's your family doing? Are you still active in the choir? The reason I'm calling is that I'm considering advertising as a career, and I'm trying to identify some people in the field that I could talk to. I want to learn more about it and see what kind of jobs are available here in the area. I know you're not in advertising, but I was wondering if you happened to know anyone that you would recommend me talking to who *is* in advertising.

If you decide to write a letter, follow the same friendly tone Anita established. Begin the letter asking how your helper contact is doing. Introduce your career situation. Then ask for their referrals. In your letter, inform them that you will be calling on a certain date to see if they have any referrals or advice for you. See the sample cover letters in Chapter 7 to help with the format of your letters.

Make sure you call back on the date you established. After seeing how they're doing, ask your helper contact if they've received your letter. Then reiterate your career situation and ask them about any possible referrals.

If you e-mail your helper contacts, you have the option of asking them to reply via e-mail or informing them that you will call them. Replying by e-mail is less to ask of your contacts than writing a letter, so don't be afraid to ask for this kind of response.

Add Your Referrals to Your List of Relevant Contacts

When your helper contacts refer colleagues and associates to you, make sure to get the correct spelling of their names, organizations, and titles. Also determine where and how the referrals would prefer to be contacted, and get the appropriate contact information. Be sure you get your helper contacts' permission to use their name as a reference in contacting their referrals.

Add your new referrals' names, titles, organizations, and contact information to your list of relevant contacts.

Step 3: Accept the Critical Success Factor of Networking

Let's re-examine the goal of information interviews. The ultimate goal is to receive help from an insider in the field (relevant contact) in finding a job. Among other things, "help" could entail pointing out a job lead, referring you to another company that's hiring, or speaking on your behalf to the hiring authorities. The more that your relevant contact *wants* to help you, the more that he or she *will* help you. Herein lies the most critical success factor of networking that most job seekers overlook. The main goal you should focus on is building rapport with, and gaining respect from, your relevant contacts. If your relevant contacts like you (building rapport) and are impressed with you (gaining respect), they'll want to help you that much more!

Networking is all about relationships. The more positive relationships you have with relevant contacts, the better chance you have of landing a job. Focus first on building rapport and developing relationships, and the job leads and key referrals will follow. Most job seekers do it the other way around. They focus on the immediate concern of finding a job, and the relationship dwindles away. Patience is a big-time virtue when it comes to networking.

Step 4: Use the P-O-W-E-R Model to Generate a List of Questions to Ask Your Relevant Contacts

Now that you've generated a strong list of relevant contacts through your personal, professional, community, and helper contacts, and you understand the critical success factor of networking, you're ready to arrange and conduct information interviews. However, sometimes when you call to arrange an information interview, your relevant contacts will say that they're too busy to meet with you at a later date, but that they have time *right now* to answer some quick questions. To prepare for this scenario, it's wise to generate your list of questions prior to arranging information interviews.

The secret to conducting exceptional information interviews is not in the questions you ask but the progression or order in which you ask them. The majority of job seekers make the common mistake of jumping right into their own issues and concerns during information interviews. They're anxious to receive advice on pursuing various career opportunities in their contact's company or in the field in general. In doing so, they miss out on building rapport and strengthening their networking relationships. Incorporating the P-O-W-E-R Model will enable you to build rapport with your contacts and get the most out of the information interviews.

The P-O-W-E-R Model offers a particular progression of questions that's effective to incorporate during information interviews. POWER is an easy-to-remember acronym. Ask questions relating to

P–Person you are interviewing (relevant contact)

O–Organization of relevant contact

W–Work Field of relevant contact

E–Exploring opportunities with their company or within the field

R–Referrals to other relevant contacts and organizations

In the following section are the types of questions to ask within each phase of the P-O-W-E-R Model and why this order of questions can be so effective.

Questions Relating to the Person (Phase 1)

You learned in the previous chapter that networking can be a positive experience for both parties—you and your contact. The best way to make the experience positive for the contact is to give them the opportunity to talk about themselves and their career path. Ask them about their present position and how they got to where they are today. There are two reasons for starting with questions about the person. First, you can learn a lot about a field and its various career opportunities through the career path and perspective of relevant contacts. Second, there's no better way to build rapport with someone than to ask questions about them and show that you're interested. It's usually a very flattering and pleasant experience for the contacts. It's hard not to like someone who's interested in you and your career.

Sample Questions Relating to the Person
- What are your main responsibilities in your current position?
- Which responsibilities take up most of your time?
- Can you describe your typical day?
- What do you like most about your job?
- What do you like least about your job?

- What is the most challenging part of your job?

- With whom do you work most closely?

- To whom do you report?

- How did you get to where you are today? Where have you previously worked, and what did you do there?

- Why did you choose _____ as your profession?

- What skills and personal qualities have helped you most during your career?

- Where do you see yourself in the future?

Questions Relating to the Organization (Phase 2)

The second phase of questions is related to the relevant contact's current organization. You can learn a lot about a field and job opportunities through organizations. It's also important to demonstrate interest in the organization because they could very well have an open position when you call! It's critical to research the relevant contact's organization prior to the information interview so you can ask very focused questions that show your contact you've done your homework. Most job seekers don't do this, so their questions tend to be very generic and unimpressive to the relevant contacts. Use resources identified previously to help you research organizations (See "Researching Organizations/Employer Profiles" in Appendix A and "Researching Organizations" in Appendix C). The best resource typically is the organization's Web page, if they have one.

Sample Questions Relating to the Organization

- I noticed from your Web page that XYZ Corporation's primary services are A, B, and C. It was interesting to read how B service is doing well in European markets. To what do you attribute its success?

(*NOTE:* Most job seekers ask the generic question, *What are the products or services that your company offers?* You can see how research adds substance to your questions!)

- I also read that your management philosophy lends itself to a more hands-off approach, allowing employees to become self-sufficient and resourceful. How successful has this philosophy been?

- What is the work atmosphere like here? How is the morale?

- I saw that your leading competitors are A and B corporations. How has your company done over the past five years compared to your competitors? What distinguishes XYZ Corporation from its competitors?

- The Web page reported 125 employees working within your regional branch. What does the organizational structure look like? Where does your division fit into the larger picture?

- It's obvious that your organization is big on customer service. What do you see as the biggest challenge to maintaining this high level of customer service?

Questions Relating to the Work Field (Phase 3)

The third phase of questions moves the focus away from the specific organization and toward the work field or industry in general. Again, the purpose of this phase of questions is twofold—it's helpful to learn more about the field you're pursuing, but you also want to show your relevant contact that you're committed to the field and know something about it. Once again, research is the key. If you've not been keeping up with current trends and events in the field, you should do some research. Go to the library and read some recent articles from journals or other periodicals related to the field. For general workforce trends, use some of the recommended Internet sites and printed resources found under "Career and Workforce Trends" in Appendices A and C. If you have a close personal contact who works in the field, ask her to offer trends in the field from her perspective. The types of questions that will reveal your knowledge of the field and impress your relevant contact are those based on recent trends and issues related to the field.

Sample Questions Relating to the Work Field

- Some of the more prevalent issues and challenges facing our field today appear to be A, B, and C. What do you see as the biggest challenge in our field today?

- What needs to occur to meet that challenge?

- What are your predictions on some of the major changes that will take place in our field over the next twenty years?

- I've been reading about this new XYZ software that's supposed to revolutionize our field in ten to twenty years. What's your perspective on this?

- Are there professional associations to which you belong? Which ones are the best?

- Do you attend any annual conferences or conventions?

Questions Relating to Exploring Career Opportunities (Phase 4)

Up to this point, you've been focusing your attention on your relevant contact, the organization, and issues in the career field. By doing this, you've demonstrated a genuine interest and knowledge in their organization and field. You've also built a positive rapport with your relevant contact and most likely impressed him through your substantive questions and prior research. Now's the time to finally get to the issues and questions centering on *you* and any available career opportunities. Your goal here is to ask for information on the types of career opportunities that may exist in their organization or other organizations in the field and how you should pursue these opportunities.

Sample Questions Relating to Exploring Opportunities

- I just have a few more questions, but I wanted to first thank you for sharing your thoughts and advice today. I must say, the more I hear about your organization, the more I'm impressed. What advice would you give me, with the kind of background that I have, regarding the types of positions that are realistic for me to pursue?

- What's the best way for me to pursue these opportunities?

- What are the skills and personal qualities valued for the positions you mentioned?

- What type of educational background and experience are important to have for these positions?

- How are position openings announced to people outside of the organization?

- It appears that a master's degree is valued in our field. What type of advanced degree would you recommend?

(*NOTE:* There are purposely not as many questions in this fourth phase. You don't want to push too much regarding your status with the company, for it may put the relevant contact on the defensive or make you look a tad desperate. You don't want to destroy the positive rapport you built by coming across as too self-centered at this point in the conversation. You shouldn't expect your relevant contact to do too much for you on the spot. If you did your job and presented a strong impression of yourself, chances are your contact will look into things for you after your conversation. Be patient.)

Questions Relating to Receiving Referrals (Phase 5)

You never want to leave an information interview without asking for referrals to other organizations and contacts in the field. Like in Phase 4, you need to use some judgement regarding how many questions you ask at this point in the interview. If you sense your relevant contact is trying to wrap things up, end the interview immediately. Don't overstay your welcome. Keep track of the time, and don't go over the time you allotted.

Sample Questions Relating to Referrals

- Are there any colleagues or associates who you think would be good for me to talk to?

- Are there other organizations in the field that you would recommend me contacting?

- Have you heard of any organizations that are growing or expanding?

- Do you know anyone in these organizations that I may want to contact?

- Are there publications you would recommend that list vacancies in our field?

- Are there any employment agencies that you know of that would be worthwhile to contact?

Step 5: Arrange the Information Interviews with Your Relevant Contacts

Many of the same issues and decisions you needed to make regarding your correspondence with helper contacts apply here. Here are some issues you must take care of before you get in touch with your relevant contacts. For more details, refer back to the section on helper contacts.

- **Where and When to Contact Your Relevant Contacts**
  With the exception of those relevant contacts who are close friends or family, you should contact your relevant contacts during the day at work.

- **Determine the Type of Initial Correspondence**
  You can call, write, or e-mail your relevant contacts. It depends on your skills and comfort in talking on the phone and your relationship with each relevant contact.

- **Gathering Contact Information**
  Once you know where you're contacting your relevant contacts and whether you're calling or writing, you must gather the appropriate phone numbers and addresses.

- **Choose an Information Interview Format**
  For each relevant contact, you must decide whether you want to conduct your information interview face-to-face or over the phone. You may also conduct information interviews through e-mail, but the experience isn't nearly as effective. I highly recommend that you try to arrange face-to-face information interviews, unless it's feasibly or logistically impossible. There's a much greater potential for building a strong relationship with your relevant contacts face-to-face than over the phone. Your relevant contacts will feel more inclined to help you when they meet with you directly. Also, scheduling a meeting with someone indicates a certain level of

seriousness or importance. Realize, however, that even though you may want to meet face-to-face, your relevant contacts may prefer to correspond with you over the phone. Therefore, try to meet face-to-face, but be flexible. An information interview should *always* be at the convenience of your contact.

Calling Your Relevant Contacts to Arrange an Information Interview

When you decide to call, it's critical that you have your prepared questions in front of you. As stated earlier, your relevant contact may prefer to answer your questions right there on the spot, so be prepared.

Getting Past the Protective Receptionist

Your first objective is to speak directly with your relevant contact. Often, when you call someone at work, a receptionist answers, many of which have been trained to protect certain employees' time by screening calls. When you call and ask to speak to your relevant contact, the receptionist may likely ask, "What's it in reference to?" This is *not* the time to reveal all by responding, "I'm networking to get a job." Say something like, "I was referred to Ms. Contact by Joe Smith, Director of Marketing at XYZ Corporation, regarding a project I'm working on." Hopefully this will be enough to pass you through to your contact. However, the receptionist may still want to know more: "And what does the project entail?" At this point, you should politely say something to the extent of, "It's a little tough to explain, and I'm under a time crunch. Could you please connect me to Ms. Contact?" Be persistent yet polite.

What to Do When You Get Voice Mail

For those relevant contacts that you don't know very well, leaving a message on voice mail can be a comfortable way for you to break the ice. Leave a polite message briefly explaining why you're calling. Don't, however, ask your contact to call you back. Inform him or her that you'll call back sometime later. The next time you call back, you can simply tell the receptionist that you're calling your contact back (which technically you are). This makes it sound as though your contact called you and will hopefully save you from having to play twenty questions again with the receptionist.

What to Say When You Finally Get Through to Your Contact

If you know the relevant contact fairly well, start by asking how they're doing and bring up a common-ground topic, if there is one. Then get into why you're calling. If you don't directly know your relevant contact, introduce yourself and state the name of the person who referred you. You don't want to come on too strongly at first. Saying that you're looking for a job right off the bat may scare the contact off. Below is a sample script to give you an idea of the tone that is recommended for your initial conversation.

Sample Script

Arranging a Face-to-Face Information Interview

Hi, Ms. Jones. My name is Anita Job. I worked with your nephew Joseph at the Town Store. He recommended giving you a call. I'm seriously considering banking as a career and am currently trying to learn more about the industry and the types of opportunities that exist. Joseph told me you work for XYZ Bank and have a lot of experience in the field. I'd love the opportunity to sit down with you for a half hour at your convenience and get your thoughts and advice on banking. Would you be willing to meet with me at some point? Great! When would it be convenient for us to meet? Sounds good. And where's the best place to meet? Your office? Great! Should I just come straight to your office, or will a receptionist have to buzz you? Okay. Ms. Jones, I really appreciate this. I'll see you next Wednesday. Bye.

If you decide to conduct an information interview over the phone rather than in person, your script changes a little. See the following sample script.

Sample Script

Arranging a Phone Information Interview

Hi, Ms. Jones. My name is Anita Job. I worked with your nephew Joseph at the Town Store. He recommended giving you a call. I'm seriously considering banking as a career and am currently trying to learn more about the industry and the types of opportunities that exist. Joseph told me you work for XYZ Bank and have a lot of experience in the field. I'd love the opportunity to talk with you over the phone at your convenience and get your thoughts and advice on banking. Would you be willing to schedule a time to talk? Great! When would it be convenient for you to talk? I won't need more than a half hour of your time. 3:30 on Friday. Sounds good. And what number would be best for me to call? 555-5555. Got it. Ms. Jones, I really appreciate this! I'll talk to you next Friday. Thank you. Bye.

Writing Your Relevant Contacts to Arrange an Information Interview

The other option for arranging information interviews is writing a letter and following it up with a call. The benefit of writing is that you can revise and edit your letter as many times as you want. When you call someone, you only get one chance. The downside is that it takes two correspondences to arrange each meeting. The tone is very similar to the one used in the sample scripts above. Make sure to inform your relevant contact that you'll be calling on a certain date. Review the sample letter below. For more detail on business-letter format, see the sample cover letters in Chapter 7.

E-mailing Your Relevant Contacts to Arrange an Information Interview

If you feel uncomfortable calling your relevant contacts, e-mailing them is not a bad option. You can potentially arrange the information interview without ever talking to the contact. The relevant contact may simply reply to your e-mail through an e-mail of his own, stating the date, time, and location of the meeting. The only concern with using e-mail to arrange information interviews is that it gives the relevant contact an easier "out." Conveying disappointing news to someone through e-mail is much easier than conveying disappointing news over the phone. You can end your e-mail letters one of two ways:

> Please reply to this e-mail and let me know whether or not you are willing to meet with me.

Or:

> I will call you on Thursday, January 20, to see if we can schedule a time to meet.

Other than the possible difference in endings, the e-mail letter should read very similarly to the sample letter previously presented.

Step 6: Conduct the Information Interview

There are obvious differences between conducting face-to-face information interviews and phone information interviews. Face-to-face information interviews contain the added dimension of non-verbal presentation. Therefore, both forms of information interviewing are presented separately.

Conducting Face-to-Face Information Interviews

You should take the following items with you to each information interview:

- A professional binder with a notepad and pen
- Copies of your resume
- Your list of questions that you generated
- Any supporting documents (see Chapter 7)
- Any literature that you have on the company

The first impression is always very important. To help form a good first impression, follow these suggestions:

- Arrive 10 to 15 minutes early. Be on time.

Dear Ms. Jones:

Your nephew Joseph recommended contacting you. I worked with him at the Town Store. I am seriously considering banking as a career. Currently, I am trying to learn more about the industry and the types of opportunities that exist. Joseph told me you work for XYZ Bank and have a lot of experience in the field. I would love the opportunity to sit down with you for a half hour at your convenience and get your thoughts and advice on banking. Would you be willing to meet with me at some point?

I will give you a call on Thursday, January 20, to see if we might be able to schedule a time to meet. I would greatly appreciate it! Thank you for your time and consideration.

Sincerely,

Anita Job

- Come professionally dressed unless you know the relevant contact extremely well or you're meeting at the contact's home. (See Chapter 14 for tips on dressing professionally)
- Offer a firm handshake, make eye contact, and introduce yourself.
- Thank your relevant contact for his time right after you sit down to begin the meeting.

During the main part of the information interview, it's important to present strong nonverbal skills throughout. See Chapter 14 for details on effective nonverbal communication skills. Following are general guidelines to follow during the information interview:

- Follow your list of questions to effectively incorporate the P-O-W-E-R Model of information interviewing (Review Step 4, "Use the P-O-W-E-R Model to Generate a List of Questions to Ask your Relevant Contacts," if you haven't already).
- Maintain good posture.
- Maintain eye contact.
- Take notes as you go.
- Be attentive and enthusiastic.
- Ask follow-up questions from time to time to show you're listening and interested.
- Smile and have a sense of humor.
- Be natural. Be yourself.

Guidance

Following up with individuals you have networked with is very important. You cannot assume that busy people will always remember that you are actively in the job market. It is important, however, to do so in a very thoughtful and non-invasive manner so as to not appear too aggressive or worse—desperate.
—Glaxo Wellcome

Once your questions are used up (from the P-O-W-E-R Model) or time runs out, stand up and thank your relevant contact. Make sure you don't go over your time. Only go over the time you allotted if your contact insists that it's okay to do so. Make sure you have the accurate contact information of your relevant contact and of anyone else that may have helped you or spoken to you. You'll need this information for thank-you letters.

Step 7: Follow Up and Track Results

Immediately after the information interview, organize your notes. Make sure to write down any tasks or follow-up correspondence you agreed on. Use the contacts form from Chapter 8 to help organize your feedback and information. Write a thank-you letter and submit it that same day or the next day at the very latest. Prompt thank-you letters are impressive and create a lasting impression. For more information on thank-you letters, see Chapter 15.

THE WHOLE IN ONE

- Networking is a critical part of the job-search process. Information interviewing is the best method of networking to incorporate into your job search.

- "The 7-Step Plan for Mastering the Information Interview" offers a polished approach to getting the most out of your information interviews.

- Use your personal, professional, and community contacts to generate a strong list of networking contacts. Use your helper contacts to assist you in generating additional relevant contacts.

- Since networking is all about relationships, using the P-O-W-E-R Model will ensure that you build strong relationships with your contacts throughout the information interviews. The P-O-W-E-R Model focuses on the best progression of questions to incorporate.

- A critical step in the networking process is arranging information interviews. You can call, write, or e-mail contacts to arrange your information interviews.

- When conducting information interviews, it's important to be on time, form a strong first impression, maintain effective nonverbal skills, and keep to the allotted time frame.

- After the information interviews, it's critical to organize your notes and promptly send a thank-you letter.

ASSIGNMENT

Complete the last strategy under Goal 4 of your Personal Job Search Trainer.

Part IV

Landing the Perfect Job

Chapter 12

Interview Prep 101: Get Inside the Interviewer's Head

GET THE SCOOP ON . . .

- The Big 4 interviewer concerns
- Sample questions within the Big 4
- Responding to the Big 4 concerns
- The 20-step prep plan
- Identifying your selling points
- Powerful questions to ask the interviewer
- Practice interviewing

THE BIG 4 INTERVIEWER CONCERNS

Interviews for a teaching position are taking place at the local high school. Review the following question and response, and see what you think:

> Interviewer: How did you become interested in teaching?

> Candidate: Well, to be honest, I originally chose teaching because I wanted to coach baseball and have my summers off.

Did the candidate answer the question? Yes. But is that all that the interviewer wanted to know? Behind every question is a bigger concern. *Interviewing* is responding to questions. *Successful interviewing* is responding to underlying concerns. Candidates who respond favorably to the real underlying concerns get job offers. Herein lies the secret to winning interviews.

In the preceding example, the underlying concern is "Is the candidate's heart in teaching?" Let's see how the answer changes when the candidate responds to the underlying concern:

> Interviewer: How did you become interested in teaching?

> Candidate: Well, to be honest, I originally chose teaching because I wanted to coach baseball and have my summers off.

If I knew then what I know now, my answer would have been very different. I had no idea back then the great opportunity teachers have. I had no idea at the time that I'd play a significant role in shaping and developing young people's lives. I didn't realize or appreciate what it meant to be a role model. I had no idea that I would feel so rewarded after seeing a self-defeating, apathetic child turn into a positive, productive adult. At the time, teaching was an afterthought. Now, it's a huge part of who I am.

By responding to the bigger concern, the candidate's passion for teaching was expressed, and the recruiter got the answer she was looking for. To successfully prepare for interviews, you must know the interviewers' underlying concerns and learn how to respond to them.

When you participate in interviews, today's recruiters have four major concerns (the Big 4) about you.

1. Do you want the job?
2. Can you do the job?
3. Will you fit in?
4. Are you self-reliant?

All interview questions fall under one or more of the Big 4 interviewer concerns. If you know how to address these concerns when you answer an interviewer's questions, you'll be able to handle any interviewing situation that comes your way! It's critical, therefore, that you understand these four concerns and develop strategies for responding. Following is a thorough description of the Big 4 interviewer concerns. Under each concern, you'll see the types of questions asked, followed by *prep tasks* which will help you prepare to effectively address each specific concern. These prep tasks can then be consolidated into one master list that will serve as your road map to interview preparation. By the way, the sample questions presented here are the most common questions asked in real interviews. For additional interview questions, see Appendix G.

Big Concern 1: Do You Want the Job?

Recruiters know that employees are more productive when they genuinely like what they do and where they work. It's a simple fact of nature that occurs everywhere. One of the most obvious examples is found in students. Students typically perform better in those subjects they enjoy. They'll spend more time and energy studying for tests and writing papers when they like what they're learning.

This first underlying concern is even more prevalent now than it used to be. With all the job-hopping occuring today, recruiters are concerned that candidates may "take the job on the run" and leave within months of being hired. They need to be convinced that you don't view this job as just another stepping stone to something you *really* want.

Sample Questions Related to Big Concern 1

- Why do you want this job?
- What is appealing to you about this opportunity?
- Why do you want to work for us?
- How did you learn about our company?
- How did you become interested in (your career field)?
- How do you feel about moving to this area of the country?
- How do you see this position being different from your past jobs?
- Where do you see yourself in five years?
- Are you involved in any trade/professional organizations?
- I see from your resume that you were an intern at ABC Corporation. How was that experience?

Responding to Big Concern 1: Do You Want the Job?

The big interviewer concern—Do you want the job?—can be broken down into four main aspects: the job description, the organization, the industry, and the location. No matter which of the previous questions you're asked, you must be able to convince the interviewer that you're genuinely interested in doing the job, working in the company, working in the field, and living in the area.

Prep Task 1: Identify Specific Aspects about the Job Description That Appeal to You the Most.

Closely review the responsibilities and duties of the job description and determine those that are most appealing to you. You also need to pinpoint *why* those particular responsibilities are appealing. It's not enough to tell a recruiter that responsibilities A, B, and C are appealing. Explaining *why* they're appealing to you adds weight to your responses.

Prep Task 2: Research the Organization and Determine Why You Want to Work for Them.

Time and time again, interviewers report that candidates failed in the interview because "they didn't know anything about the company." Most job candidates answer too vaguely when asked about their interest in the company. Saying that the company is appealing to you because it's a "large, growing, well-respected company" isn't concrete enough. Any recruiter worth his or her salt will see right through a vague response like that. You must research the company and talk to contacts in the field to identify specific reasons why you want to work for *that particular company.*

Prep Task 3: Pinpoint Characteristics about the Career Field that Appeal to You.

Interviewers want to know that you're committed to the field. You must be able to express three to four characteristics of the field that excite you. One way to indicate your level of interest is by demonstrating your knowledge of the current trends. Review recent trade and professional publications or talk to your contacts to identify a few interesting current trends or issues related to your field.

Prep Task 4: Determine What You Like about the Job's Location.

Determine how your values are consistent with the job's location. Some examples of geographic values may include being close to family, small town atmosphere, good climate, or conducive to hobbies. Interviewers want to be convinced that the location is at least moderately appealing to you. Even if they think you're perfectly qualified for the job, they may not extend an offer if they think you'll be miserable living in the surrounding area.

Prep Task 5: Review Your Resume for Experiences You Enjoyed.

Many interview questions relate to what's on your resume. One way for recruiters to find out your level of interest is to determine how much you enjoyed similar past experiences listed on your resume. You must review your relevant experiences and identify appealing aspects of each so you're ready to respond during the interview.

Big Concern 2: Can You Do the Job?

This concern is probably the most common and self-explanatory one. If the interviewer wasn't already somewhat convinced that you have the experience, skills, and academic training to effectively perform on the job, you wouldn't have been selected to interview. However, candidates often look a lot better on paper than they do in real life. You must be able to sell your skills and experience in person.

Sample Questions Related to Big Concern 2

- What are your greatest strengths and weaknesses?
- How can you contribute to our organization?
- What makes you the best candidate for this position?
- Why should I hire you?
- Tell me a little bit about yourself.
- Tell me how a friend or someone who knows you well describes you?

> **FYI**
>
> *It's very easy to be misinterpreted during interviews. You know exactly what you mean when you give a response, but the recruiter may be thinking something different. The best way to eliminate misunderstandings is to include explanations and examples of past experiences in your answers.*

- If I were to talk to your former boss, what would she say about you?
- If I were to talk to someone you supervised, what kind of a boss would they say you are?
- I see from your resume that you worked at XYZ Company. What were your key responsibilities there?
- What has been your greatest professional accomplishment?
- How will your experience at ABC Organization help you in this position?
- What parts of this position do you anticipate being most challenging?
- What skills or qualities do you think are important to have in this position?
- How would your education/training benefit you in this position?

Responding to Big Concern 2: Can You Do the Job?

Your main goal here is to identify your selling points. You must identify all your skills, qualities, experiences, and academic training that are most important to the company and position.

Prep Task 6: Select Your Top Skills as They Relate to the Position.
Closely review the responsibilities and duties of the job description and determine the primary skills needed to succeed. From these primary skills, identify the ones you've acquired in the past and be ready to explain how and where you developed them. The more examples you can give the recruiter, the more you'll validate your skills and personalize your response.

Prep Task 7: Establish Hands-On Experiences That Are Most Relevant and Substantive.
Determine which experiences are most relevant to the position and company. Recruiters will often ask you to talk about various experiences listed on your resume. They're interested in hearing about your responsibilities, but they can read them from your resume. They're most interested in what you got out of the experience and how you benefited from it. More specifically, they want to know how that experience could help you perform better on the job they're considering you for.

Prep Task 8: Identify Relevant Education and/or Training.
You need to identify any relevant courses, training programs, majors, minors, specializations, projects, papers, or experiments you have under your belt. Determine the most important aspects of each one and be prepared to talk about how they would benefit you on the job.

Prep Task 9: Determine Your Most Relevant Personal Qualities.
Identify personal qualities that will benefit you on the job. Don't be afraid to tell recruiters that you have a great sense of humor or that you

work well under pressure. If it's a quality of yours that will help you do the job, mention it. If you're having trouble coming up with any personal qualities to talk about, review the job description to help you come up with qualities relevant to the job. Just be sure to give the recruiter examples. It's not enough to tell them that you have a great sense of humor. Tell them how your sense of humor has helped you through tense situations in the past and will help you handle the more stressful aspects of the job for which you're interviewing.

See Appendix F for a listing of common personal qualities to help you find the right terms to describe your qualities.

Prep Task 10: Prepare to Answer Questions Relating to Your Computer and Communication Skills.

In addition to those skills that are most relevant to the job, you must be ready to describe your writing skills, verbal communication skills, and computer skills. These skills are valued across all fields and companies, regardless of position or title. Recruiters know that very few people can do the job without these skills. Be prepared to discuss these skills with recruiters.

Big Concern 3: Will You Fit In?

You may have many interests, skills, and experiences related to the job, but that doesn't prove to the interviewer that you'd fit in well with the organization or the people around you. There's a unique culture that exists in each organization, sometimes referred to as the "corporate culture." You must be able to demonstrate that you're a team player and a proponent of diversity.

Another important aspect of "fit" has to do with morale. Interviewers are looking for candidates who will get along well with their co-workers and contribute to an overall positive morale. They want to hire people with a sense of humor and who are likable, friendly, and positive. All the experience and skills in the world won't help you if you come across as cynical or pessimistic in the interview.

Finally, recruiters want to find candidates who are mature. They want people who can tactfully resolve conflicts and work equally well with co-workers from diverse ethnic and racial backgrounds. Recruiters don't want people they think will get sucked into petty games or interoffice politics.

Sample Questions Related to Big Concern 3
- How would someone who knows you well describe you?
- Tell me about a conflict you previously had with another person and how you dealt with that conflict?

- If you disagreed with something your supervisor asked you to do, what would you do?
- What are the important factors for working well as a team?
- What is your definition of diversity?
- What type of work atmosphere do you prefer?
- What is your management philosophy?
- Describe what *tactful confrontation* means.
- How important is a sense of humor at work?
- What do you like to do in your spare time?
- Tell me a little bit about yourself.
- Who do you admire most and why?
- A co-worker comes in your office, closes the door, and begins to talk negatively about someone else that works here. What would you do?
- How do you handle pressure?

Responding to Big Concern 3: Will You Fit In?

In responding to this concern, you must tell recruiters how you handle conflicts, work in teams, deal with pressure, and appreciate diversity. You must also show that you have a sense of humor and that you work well with a wide variety of people.

Prep Task 11: Prepare to Talk about Your Thoughts and Experiences in Resolving Conflicts.

Resolving conflict is an important factor in most interviews. You must identify what you think is important in conflict resolution. You also need to choose a conflict you previously had that's appropriate to share during an interview. Concentrate on how you resolved that particular conflict and what you would have done differently.

Prep Task 12: Prepare to Talk about Your Thoughts and Experiences Relating to Diversity.

Identify what you think diversity can add to an organization and how you feel about it. Determine those qualities that are important to have in order to get along with people from diverse backgrounds. Identify an experience you had working with someone from a different racial or ethnic background, and be prepared to talk about it during the interview.

Prep Task 13: Prepare to Talk about Your Thoughts and Experiences Relating to Teamwork.

Be ready to express your thoughts on the key factors of building and maintaining a successful team. Again, be prepared to give examples during the interview. Identify an appropriate past experience working on a team, and think about the factors that made that experience positive.

Prep Task 14: Determine Your Management Philosophy and Related Experiences.

Determine the type of relationship that you think should exist between a supervisor and subordinate. Identify a past experience centering on your relationship with a supervisor or subordinate. Analyze that relationship, and be prepared to talk about the positive and negative aspects.

Prep Task 15: Identify Your Work Style Preferences.

Identify the type of work atmosphere you prefer. Do you like a relaxed, informal environment or a serious, fast-paced one? Think about how you work under pressure and manage your time.

Prep Task 16: Prepare to Talk about Your Life Outside of Work.

Identify the activities and hobbies outside of work that you're comfortable talking about. Think of any community service involvement worth mentioning in an interview.

FYI

Interviewers don't want to hire someone they think may "rock the boat" and be a pain to work with. During interviews, recruiters try very hard to determine how you deal with conflict and work with other people. You must be ready to answer questions that relate to this concern.

Big Concern 4: Are You Self-Reliant?

In the fast-paced, ever-changing world of work, recruiters must hire candidates who are self-sufficient. Nobody has the time to take care of other people, and the company won't hire you if they think they'll have to baby you. You must be able to take care of yourself and be self-motivated to continually improve and learn. As problems arise, you must have the ability to figure things out for yourself or be resourceful enough to find the answer elsewhere. Self-confidence, adaptability, and analytical thinking are characteristics that recruiters seek.

Sample Questions Related to Big Concern 4

- What is your approach to handling problems?
- A client calls you with a question, and you don't have the answer. What do you do?
- What is your approach to time management?
- If you disagreed with a co-worker on how to handle a client's concern, what would you do?
- Describe a time when you demonstrated persistence.
- When conflicts with co-workers arise, do you confront them directly or wait it out and let it pass?
- How important is self-confidence in being successful?
- Do you tend to doubt yourself or believe in yourself? Share an example.
- Do you tend to embrace change or avoid it?

- I see on your resume that you have X,Y, and Z computer skills. How did you learn these applications?

Responding to Big Concern 4: Are You Self-Reliant?

You must express to the interviewer that you're self-confident, resourceful, and adaptable and can solve problems on your own.

Prep Task 17: Determine Your Approach to Resolving Problems.
Identify the key steps you take to resolve problems. Think about a good example to bring up in which you demonstrated good problem-solving and analytical skills.

Prep Task 18: Identify Your Organizational and Time-Management Skills.
You must convey to the interviewer that you can organize your work and manage your time. Identify a system or program that you organized or multiple tasks that you juggled that would be worth discussing in the interview.

Prep Task 19: Prepare to Talk about Your Ability to Adapt and Learn New Things.
Determine your willingness and ability to change and grow. Think back to past experiences in which you demonstrated flexibility and a smooth transition to change.

Prep Task 20: Determine Your Degree of Self-Confidence.
Identify past examples where you believed in yourself and trusted your judgement. Recall past experiences where your self-confidence proved beneficial.

The Master List of Prep Tasks: Putting It All Together

Following are all the prep tasks together on one master list. Keep this list handy, and refer to it when you prepare for an interview. For each prep task, think of related examples of past experiences that you can bring up during your interviews.

1. Identify specific aspects about the job description that appeal to you the most.
2. Research the organization, and determine why you want to work for it.
3. Pinpoint characteristics about the career field that appeal to you.
4. Determine what you like about the job's location.
5. Select appealing aspects of each relevant experience on your resume.
6. Select your top skills as they relate to the position.

7. Establish hands-on experiences that are most relevant and substantive.

8. Identify relevant education and/or training.

9. Determine your most relevant personal qualities.

10. Prepare to answer questions relating to your computer and communication skills.

11. Prepare to talk about your thoughts and experience with resolving conflicts.

12. Prepare to talk about your thoughts and experiences relating to diversity.

13. Prepare to talk about your thoughts and experiences relating to teamwork.

14. Determine your management philosophy and related experiences.

15. Identify your work style preferences.

16. Prepare to talk about your life outside of work.

17. Determine your approach to resolving problems.

18. Identify your organizational and time-management skills.

19. Prepare to talk about your ability to adapt and learn new things.

20. Determine your degree of self-confidence.

Guidance

Self-assessment is very important for the job seekers. They must understand themselves and be able to clearly articulate both what they have accomplished and what the driving forces were. Without a strong self-assessment, the interviewee will not be able to provide meaningful and in-depth responses to the interview questions.

—Arthur Anderson

Identify Your Selling Points

Use your results from completing the 20 prep tasks to pinpoint your selling points for each job for which you're interviewing. You may have anywhere from three to ten selling points. Selling points are those experiences, skills, personal qualities, accomplishments, knowledge, and interests that are most relevant to the job and most beneficial to the company. Experiences can include past jobs, specific responsibilities of past jobs, internships, academic projects, volunteer work, or just working closely with an expert in the field. Interests relate to those strong interests or proven commitments you have in the job, company, or career field.

To determine your selling points, closely examine the specific job responsibilities and working relationships that relate to the current opening. Determine the types of skills and personal qualities necessary to do the job, then pinpoint your skills and qualities that are most appropriate. As you're going through this process of identifying selling points, constantly ask yourself, "Which selling points will matter the most to the recruiter of this position?"

During the interview, it's essential that you find a way to express each of your chosen selling points. If, for some reason, you didn't have the opportunity to express all your selling points when you answered the recruiters questions, you can always work them in at the end of the interview. Once you've asked all your questions, bring up the selling points you didn't express in the following way: "Well that's all the questions I have. There's just one more comment I'd like to make. I felt that I didn't do a good job of expressing a few points that I wanted to get across to you today. In addition to the X, Y, and Z skills mentioned earlier, I believe I can offer A and B skills as well. During my volunteer work at . . ." There's always a way to incorporate your selling points!

POWERFUL QUESTIONS TO ASK THE INTERVIEWER

During interviews, you almost always have an opportunity to ask the interviewer some questions. Most of the time, this occurs near the end of the interview after the interviewer is done asking you questions. When appropriate, you can try to incorporate some of your questions into the main part of the interview as long as they're relevant and aren't forced. For example, after answering a question relating to *your* customer service philosophy, you could ask about the *organization's* philosophy regarding customer service. You'll need to use your judgement here regarding how many questions you should interject. If the interview is more formal than conversational, you may want to hold off on your questions until the end.

Guidance

The more you know about the company going into an interview, the better. Not only do you sound intelligent and informed, but it tells the interviewer that you have invested the time to find out about the company.

—Enterprise Rent-A-Car

The Best Questions Are Generated from Research!

The best types of questions are those *generated from research;* they relate to the job, the company, and the relevant career field. Notice that "generated from research" is emphasized here. The most important factor to asking strong, substantive questions is finding concrete, specific information about the company or field and formulating a question around it. Asking generic questions (which the majority of job seekers do) scores no points with recruiters. For example, if you ask the recruiter what primary products or services they offer, you're basically saying to the recruiter, "since I was too lazy to research your company, can you tell me what your company does?"

By asking questions based on research, you give yourself the opportunity to demonstrate your knowledge of and commitment to the job, company, and field. You also show the interviewer that you came prepared and did your homework. Over and over again, recruiters stress the importance of demonstrating knowledge about the company during interviews. Demonstrating knowledge about the company tells recruiters that this isn't just another job you applied for that'll put food on the table; it's something you really *want*.

It's usually best to stay away from initiating questions relating to salary, vacation, and other perks until you're offered the job. However, the interviewer may bring these topics up near the end of the interview. In fact, it's not rare for the interviewer to ask you to reveal your salary range. Therefore, prior to the interview, you must do some research and identify your salary range. It's fine to ask about medical insurance and retirement plans, because they're more standard and less negotiable. See Chapter 15 for more information about what to look for in benefits and how to negotiate salaries.

Sample Questions to Ask the Interviewer

Following are some sample questions related to the job, the organization, and the career field. Notice that they're based from prior research. You'll need to adapt these types of questions to your specific interviewing situation. I don't believe in offering a long list of generic questions to ask the interviewer. If you're asking generic questions, you're not asking the right questions. The questions you ask must come from you and your research. You need to develop a new set of questions each time you interview since each interviewing situation (the job, company, and location) is unique.

Sample Questions Related to the Job

Regarding questions about the job, it's important to show the recruiter that your mind is already "on the job." By asking insightful questions, you indicate a higher level of interest in the position.

- One of the job responsibilities is to serve as a liaison to the public relations office. What do you hope to see accomplished from this relationship?

- The job description stated that experience using database software was a plus. What type of database software do you use, and what are the common types of databases needed to do the job well?

- Another part of the job is to assist in developing the Web page. At my previous job, I was solely responsible for creating and maintaining our Web page. There, I used ABC editor to produce Web pages. Is there an editor that you use? Is there flexibility regarding the type of editor that can be used?

- The person that fills this position will supervise three plant managers. Early on, I would want to meet weekly to build a more solid relationship with the managers. If selected for the position, would there be some flexibility in establishing my own meeting structure?

Sample Questions Related to the Organization

Some of your questions should focus on the organization. The questions about the organization used in the "7-Step Plan for Mastering Information Interviews" in Chapter 11 are questions that can be used during interviews as well. Add those to the following list.

- I noticed from your Web page that your agency is beginning to provide "virtual home care" to elderly patients. How have the patients felt about corresponding with their nurses through a video monitor?

- I also read that teamwork is an everyday reality in your organization. How are teams assigned, and who gets designated as team leaders?

- Your mission states that you want to be the leading supplier of paper products in the world. Who are your top competitors overseas?

- I noticed that all new employees go through an intensive six-week, comprehensive training program. One of the topics covered is diversity training. What does the diversity training entail, and does an appreciation for diversity exist across the organization?

Sample Questions Related to the Career Field

The questions related to the work field used in the "7-Step Plan for Mastering Information Interviews" in Chapter 11 also apply to interviews. Add those to the list below.

- There has been a real push for outcome-based education throughout the public school systems. What type of evaluation system is in place in your school system?

- In a recent article from the *Journal of XYZ,* there appears to be a resurgence of client-centered counseling. Does your agency subscribe to this model?

- From your perspective, how has the infusion of technology affected our field over the past ten years?

- The emergence of online banking has added a new dimension to our field. Currently, how prevalent is online banking in your company? Do you see online banking becoming more prevalent in the future?

PRACTICE MAKES PERFECT

Upon completion of the "Master List of 20 Prep Tasks," you have the information needed to answer the questions (what to say). And from the perfect 10 interview strategies presented in Chapter 14, you'll learn how to effectively present these answers and how to present your best self (how to say it). The only piece that's missing is practice!

Interviewing is not something you do every day. In fact, it's a very unnatural way to communicate. How many times over the past year have you sat down and formally expressed your strengths and accomplishments to someone? We learn very early in life that talking about yourself, let alone bragging, is not good. This is one of the few times in our society where it's okay to talk about yourself in front of a stranger.

Remember that anything new feels unnatural at first. When you first learned how to ride a bike, do you remember how awkward it felt? Then, after hours and hours of practice, it began to feel more natural. After days and weeks of practice, you no longer had to think about riding your bike—you just did it. If you put enough time into practicing interviewing, you'll begin to feel more natural about it.

Videotaped Mock Interviews: The Best Training Around

The best way to practice interviewing is to participate in a videotaped mock (practice) interview. While being videotaped, the mock interviewer (usually a career counselor) asks you a series of questions related to the position and company that you're pursuing. After answering the questions, the career counselor and you sit down and watch yourself in action. It's quite the humbling experience to say the least, but it's the most effective interview training you can get. There aren't many times when you have the opportunity to watch yourself in action.

During the critique session, the career counselor and you can review each question and response as closely and painstakingly as you want. Examine the content of your responses and how you're presenting yourself. Use the perfect 10 interview strategies (in Chapter 14) as a guide to critiquing yourself.

Most college career centers offer videotaped mock interviews to their students—and often to alumni. Check with your alma mater career center to see if you're eligible. If you have a video camera or can get access to one, you can conduct an in-home mock interview. Ask someone you know to act as the interviewer, and develop a list of questions for your interviewer to ask.

Other Ways to Practice

If you don't have access to a video camera, you can still conduct live mock interviews. If you have a tape recorder, you can tape your responses and listen to them later. Ask your mock interviewer to watch for distracting or annoying nonverbal habits. If you feel uncomfortable practicing with another person, you can simply tape record your answers to questions that are written down on a piece of paper. Another way to practice is to answer questions in front of the mirror. It sounds silly, but give it a try. It's a good way to check on your nonverbal communication skills.

No matter what you decide to do, remember that the key is to practice answering questions out loud. You need to practice putting sentences together and begin identifying the right words to use within different responses. Practice helps you determine those prep tasks that you need to more thoroughly go over. For example, if you're having trouble putting together a good response to why you're interested in the field, you may need to research a little more. Practice also helps identify the interview strategies that you need to polish. For example, if your answers are consistently short, you may need to think of more examples to incorporate. The more you practice, the more natural you'll be during the real interview!

THE WHOLE IN ONE

- The most powerful way to prepare for interviews is to get inside the interviewer's head and identify their real concerns.

- Today's interviewers have four underlying concerns: "Do you want the job?"; "Can you do the job?"; "Will you fit in?"; and "Are you self-reliant?" All questions relate to one or more of these big concerns.

- Complete the 20 prep tasks to prepare you for responding to almost every question that comes your way.

- Identifying your selling points prior to each interview and finding a way to present them during the interview are crucial.

- Develop a list of questions based on research that is related to the job, company, and career field for the best questions to ask interviewers.

- There's no substitute for hard work and practice. Interviewing is a skill. The more you practice, the more natural it will feel.

ASSIGNMENT

Complete the "Answer Interview Questions" strategy under Goal 5 of your Personal Job Search Trainer.

Chapter 13

Special Types of Interviews and Tricky Questions

GET THE SCOOP ON . . .

- Behavior-based interviews
- Group interviews
- On-site interviews
- Interviews during a meal
- Phone interviews
- Video interviews
- Formal, structured interviews
- Conversational interviews
- Stress interviews
- Illegal interviews
- Great answers to 5 tricky questions

SPECIAL TYPES OF INTERVIEWS

You will learn very quickly that there are many different kinds of interviews. In an ideal interview, the recruiter asks you questions for about 45 minutes, you ask the recruiter your questions for 15 minutes or so, and the interview ends. Not all interviews are like this, however. You could be interviewed by more than one person at a time, or you could find yourself in an interview that is so hostile and confrontational that you wonder why they bothered to call you in for an interview in the first place.

Don't worry, this doesn't reflect poorly on you. These kinds of interviews (and many other different kinds) are given for a reason. What's important is that you know what recruiters are looking for when they give you a special type of interview and that you respond accordingly.

The Behavior-Based Interview
Behavior-based interviews have become increasingly popular over the past decade. The title "behavior-based" is representative of what this

style is all about—behaviors. The underlying belief of behavior-based interviews is that the best way to predict future performance is to examine past behavior. Therefore, behavior-based interviews use a thorough examination of relevant past experiences to assess your professional competencies and behavioral tendencies.

The easiest way to describe behavior-based interviews is to show you the difference between traditional interview questions and behavior-based questions. Take a look at how the same question is being asked in two different ways.

Traditional style:
How do you handle conflicts with other people?

Behavior-based style:
Describe a conflict that you had with another person and how you dealt with that conflict.

The behavior-based question focuses on the candidate's *past experience* dealing with a real conflict, while the traditional question focuses on the candidate's *general approach* to dealing with conflicts.

The best way to prepare for behavior-based interviews is to identify and reflect on past experiences. Use the 20 prep tasks in Chapter 12 to help you select the types of past experiences you need to identify. For example, Prep Task 12 is "Prepare to talk about your thoughts and experiences relating to diversity." You must identify a couple of experiences where you dealt with or observed certain diversity issues and be prepared to discuss your thoughts, feelings, and beliefs.

You should also closely review *all* past academic, work-related, and volunteer experiences and be prepared to talk in depth about each and every one of them. Dig deep into your past! Get out your old term papers and past projects to refresh your memory regarding prior experiences. There's probably a relevant project or experience from your past that's slipping your mind. Be sure to review the experiences listed on your resume because the behavior-based interviewer will likely ask you to discuss these in more detail.

Following are typical behavior-based interview questions that you're likely to be asked during this type of interview. The underlying issue that the interviewer is assessing is in parentheses.

- Tell me about a time when you felt proud about your work. What did you do that made you feel good about yourself? Why were you able to succeed? (accomplishment, motivation)

- I see that you worked as a volunteer for ABC agency, helping coordinate a large community event. Describe your role and the role of others in coordinating this event. How did you all work

Guidance

Glaxo Wellcome and many other employers use behavioral-based interviewing as part of the selection process. A behavioral-based interview is not one that you can "cheat" on very easily in that you are being asked very direct questions about your past experiences so the best way to prepare is to know yourself and be able to share your insights.

—Glaxo
Wellcome

together to reach the common goal? What did you do well and not so well to help the team function? (teamwork)

- Describe for me a time when you failed or experienced a disappointment. Why was this disappointing to you? How did you react? Describe for me what you did to get through this disappointment. (dealing with adversity)

- Tell me about a difficult situation you had with a previous supervisor. What made this difficult? How did you handle the situation? What things did you do well, and what things could you have done better? (relationship with supervisors, taking ownership of actions)

- Share with me an example when someone criticized you or your work. What parts, if any, of the criticism did you agree with, and what parts didn't you agree with? Describe for me what it was like hearing this criticism. (dealing with criticism)

The Group Interview

You likely will experience an interview where you are interviewed by more than one person at the same time. If you're made aware of a group interview prior to your interview day, it's a good idea to request the names and titles of those who will be interviewing you. This will better prepare you for the questions they ask and the questions you should ask. Following are tips and advice on how to successfully present yourself in a group interview.

- If the facilitator of the group interview doesn't ask everyone to introduce themselves, politely ask them to do so.

- Write down the names and titles of each interviewer. Place their names visually in the same position on your piece of paper as they're sitting in the room. This will help you remember who's who.

- Eye contact is very important and challenging in a group interview. You can really impress your interviewers by maintaining appropriate eye contact with *all* of the interviewers in the room. Here's how you do it: during roughly the first third of your response, maintain eye contact with the person who asked the question. Then gradually make your way around and maintain eye contact with each interviewer. Don't move your eyes and head around too quickly like you're watching someone run by. Stay with each person for 5 to 10 seconds. Then, as you're about to wrap up your answer, bring your eyes back to the person who asked the question.

- During the questions you ask, try to get everyone involved. You can do this by opening up a few questions to everyone or directing at least one question to each interviewer. Due to time constraints, it's usually more realistic to open your questions up to everyone. If one or more of the interviewers don't offer answers, you must use your best judgement on whether or not to ask for their perspective. If you feel as though you built a good rapport with them, you may feel comfortable asking them to offer their perspective. If you sense that they're not generally enthusiastic or positive, it may be too risky singling them out for their views.

- Shake hands firmly while making eye contact with each interviewer at the beginning of the interview and as you're leaving. If an interviewer comes in after the rest of you have sat down, stand up, approach them, shake their hand, and introduce yourself. If you're right in the middle of answering a question, wait until the end of your response to approach them.

- After the interview, promptly send a separate thank-you letter to *each* interviewer. Sending one thank-you letter and having it circulated to all the interviewers can be interpreted as taking a short cut.

The On-Site, Day-Long Interview

When you have on-site interviews, you'll typically have four to seven interviews with different employees spread out over an entire business day. Some may be individual interviews, while others are in a group. It's very helpful to receive an interview agenda. Don't be afraid to call your contact and request one. It shows you're responsible and that you're someone who likes to be prepared. Here are some tips for succeeding during on-site interviews.

- Make sure to get there early. A terrible way to start the day is explaining to everyone why you were late.

- When you have time, take notes throughout the day. Your interviews will be one big blur if you don't take notes along the way. Don't take too many notes *during* each interview. It will get in the way of building a strong rapport with the interviewers. Try to find some time between the interviews or during breaks to jot down important points. Also, make sure you get the names, titles, and mailing addresses for everyone you meet.

- Smile and be friendly to everyone you run into. You never know who has a say in the hiring decision. Be especially nice to the receptionists. The selection committee usually asks receptionists for their impressions of you.

- Keep your energy up! You'll naturally begin to feel a little tired over the course of the day, and you'll likely be asked some of the same questions over and over. While it may be the fifth time you've been asked a particular question, remember that it's the first time that particular interviewer heard your response. Keep your enthusiasm level up each time you respond to the same question.

- Don't think that you have to be original with your questions for each new interviewer. It's okay for you to ask each interviewer the same questions. In fact, it's very helpful for you to receive multiple perspectives on issues. It can tell you how consistent the members are on various issues. Also, you want *all* of the interviewers to know you've done your homework and be impressed with the substantive questions you've prepared.

- Promptly send a thank-you note to everyone who played even the slightest part in your interview day.

The Dining Interview

It's not uncommon to go to lunch or dinner with one or more members of the hiring organization during the on-site interview. Following are some tips to help you get through the meal without spaghetti sauce stains on your jacket.

- Ask the recruiters if they eat here often and what they recommend. It'll take the pressure off you regarding what's appropriate to order.

- Don't order the most expensive item on the menu.

- Order something that won't be hard to eat. Hard-shell crabs, spaghetti, and chicken wings are not highly recommended.

- Order something that's not too filling. Stuffing yourself is not the best way to build a positive image. Plus, you don't want to find yourself in a "food coma" later in the day.

- "Just say no" to alcohol, even if the people interviewing you have a drink. This isn't the time to try to drink somebody under the table. You need to be at your best during an interview. The only exception to this rule is if you're staying overnight on a two-day interview, and you're invited to attend a cocktail gathering of some kind. Just keep it to one drink, and make it last.

- Don't get too personal. Don't get lulled into taking your interviewing cap off too quickly. The other members of the company may feel pretty comfortable and loose with one another, telling jokes and funny stories from the past. Don't get caught up in the moment and begin telling old fraternity or sorority stories. Smile, laugh, and be natural, but stay away from personal stories.

- Offer to help pay for the meal and the tip. Once they decline your offer, thank them for the meal.

Phone Interviews

Many organizations conduct telephone interviews as a way to dwindle down the list of candidates to a smaller number of final candidates. The unique aspect of phone interviews is that you don't see the interviewer and vice versa. This can be good and bad. For those who are more nervous meeting face to face, the phone interview can be a nice gradual way of building rapport. On the downside, it's much more impersonal and, therefore, more difficult to build a strong relationship with the recruiter. Below are tips for succeeding during phone interviews.

- Have some notes handy, but don't rely too heavily on them. Phone interviews, unlike in-person interviews, give you an opportunity to have cheat sheets nearby. However, you can hurt the flow of your conversation if you rely too heavily on them. Have important points written down as reminders, not full-blown sentences. It's similar to a speech. When speakers rely too much on their notes, they're unable to talk naturally to the audience.

- Don't interview in your underwear out by the pool. The sky's the limit regarding what you can wear and where you can conduct your phone interview, but your attire and the atmosphere can have a big impact on your performance. Wear something comfortable but not too comfortable. When you wear shorts and a tee shirt, you feel less professional and more laid back. Also, find a very quiet, intimate place to conduct your phone interview.

- Don't put the interviewer on hold. If you have call waiting, don't pick up the other line. If the neighbor rings the doorbell, ignore it. It's best if someone else is in the house or office with you who can get rid of visitors.

- Have your application materials handy. Make sure you have your list of questions in front of you. Also, keep your resume, reference list, and other supporting documents close by. You never know when you may need them.

- If it's a group phone interview, follow much of the advice offered earlier regarding group interviews. Take down the names and titles of every interviewer. Make sure you know who asked the question before you answer. When you're asking questions, don't leave anyone out.

Video Interviews

Video interviews have been around since the 80s, but they're still pretty rare. In a video interview, you'll be interviewed by someone in a teleconference-type setting. You will see and hear the interviewer on a monitor, and they will see and hear you the same way. Some of the larger college career centers allow students from branch campuses to video interview with employers who are visiting the main campus. If you know that you'll be participating in a video interview, prepare for it as you would for any other interview. You do, however, need to prepare yourself for possible lag time that exists between the verbal communication and the visual communication. You'll often *see* the recruiters talking before you *hear* them, which can take a while to get used to. Also, remember to be as natural as you can. There's a tendency to sit stiffly in your chair during video interviews. Candidates are afraid if they move around, the interviewer won't be able to see them.

The Formal, Stiff Interview

Some interviewers show very little expression in their faces as they methodically proceed through their list of questions. Some act this way because they want to be objective and "professional," while others act this way because that's just the way they are. A natural tendency among candidates is to mirror the interviewer. Candidates tend to act exceptionally formal and serious as a result of their formal and serious interviewer. Don't! The golden rule of interviewing is to *be yourself.* Just because the interviewer isn't real friendly doesn't mean that he's not looking for candidates who are friendly and outgoing. He may even be acting this way to try to rattle you (see stress interviews below). Stay with your plan of presenting your best self!

The Conversational Interview

Other interviewers are much more conversational and less formal. They'll show enthusiasm and engage you in conversation, trying to make you feel more comfortable. Many conversational interviewers genuinely want you to relax so they can assess the real you. So, go ahead and allow yourself to be loose—just don't forget to be professional. Don't get so loose that you forget to sell yourself. It's easy to get carried away and talk in depth about a particular experience that hit a common chord.

The Stress Interview

In high-stress occupations, there'll be an occasional stress interview from time to time. The interviewer will relentlessly grill you and do his best to challenge each and every thing you say. This isn't done to destroy your self-esteem. Recruiters do this to see how you react to stress. Most interviews aren't like this from start to finish. What's more common is a question or two in the interview that causes stress among candidates. Interviewers don't always have to be confrontational either. They might ask you a question that's so bizarre or completely unpredictable that you're caught off guard in order to see how well you think on your feet. See how two different candidates handled the bizarre question below.

> Interviewer: If you were an appliance, what would you be, and why?
>
> Candidate: Excuse me? An appliance? What do you mean? I mean, what does that have to do with accounting? Um, oh boy, I don't know. I never thought about being an appliance.
>
> Interviewer: If you were an appliance, what would you be, and why?
>
> Candidate: An appliance? (pause). Well, I think if I was an appliance, I'd be a toaster. People tend to warm up quickly when they're around me.

Which candidate would you rather work with? The second candidate was able to keep her poise and creatively answer the question. She illustrated her ability to think on her feet. Take your time, think about the question, and deliver your answer in stride!

The Illegal Interview

Illegal questions are not asked frequently. However, from time to time, you may run into a question that's illegal. Many times, the interviewer asks illegal questions out of ignorance. How should you react to illegal or inappropriate questions?

First, you must be aware of the different types of illegal questions. Generally, recruiters are required to ask questions only directly related to the job. It's illegal to ask questions about your height, weight, age, marital status, parenting status, national origin, race or ethnic background, health, social organizations/clubs, and disabilities. It's also illegal to ask if you've ever been arrested or discharged from the military. Below are some of the more common illegal questions:

- Are you married?
- Do you have children?
- Do you plan on having children?
- How old were you when you first started working at XYZ Company?
- Are you a Democrat or Republican?
- Are you a United States citizen?
- How much do you weigh?
- Have you had any medical problems or disabilities that we should know about?

The reality of the situation is that while these questions are illegal, it's very hard to prove something like this in court. To complicate things further, filing suit against the company would, in essence, burn many bridges and could quite possibly ostracize you throughout an entire job field. With this in mind, it's best for you to find a happy medium between defensively refusing to answer illegal questions and happily offering to answer them. It depends on your values and how deeply you feel about certain topics. It also depends on how badly you want that particular job.

Take a look at four different approaches to answering the question, "Do you plan on having children?" Which approach would you feel most comfortable using?

> Interviewer: Do you plan on having children?
>
> Candidate: That is inappropriate to ask! I am offended! What does that have to do with the job?
>
> Interviewer: Do you plan on having children?
>
> Candidate: Yes, thanks for asking. My husband and I plan on having three or four children. We hope to have our first one by next year.
>
> Interviewer: Do you plan on having children?
>
> Candidate: Why do you ask?
>
> Interviewer: Oh, I'm just curious.
>
> Candidate: Well, we're not sure.
>
> Interviewer: Do you plan on having children?
>
> Candidate: I can assure you that any family or personal issues will not affect my performance on the job. I am committed to excelling in this position.

GREAT ANSWERS TO FIVE TRICKY QUESTIONS

Every interview involves questions that are tricky or dangerous to answer. Interviewers have a hidden agenda behind many of these tricky questions. A hidden agenda consists of behind-the-scenes reasons for asking certain questions. For example, the interviewer's hidden agenda or reason for asking the question, "How did you originally become interested in your field," is to assess your level of commitment and interest toward the chosen career field.

The following section identifies five tricky questions. For each question, the interviewer's hidden agenda is revealed, advice on answering the question is provided, and sample answers are offered.

Tricky Question 1: "Tell Me a Little Bit About Yourself."

This question is often presented as the first question of the interview. "Why don't you start off telling me a little bit about yourself?" On the surface, this question seems harmless. However, many job seekers have great difficulty answering this question due to its broad scope and vague nature. What exactly does the interviewer want to know? Should you tell them about the potbellied pig you have for a pet or the half marathon you just completed? Or would the interviewer be more interested in the type of qualities you possess, such as your sense of humor, strong work ethic, and value in community service? The wide-open nature of this question causes problems for many candidates.

The Hidden Agenda

Most interviewers report that they like to start off with this question to get the ball rolling. They want to see what's important to you. If the floor is yours, and you can say just about anything, what do you choose to reveal? You won't choose to talk about something that isn't important to you. Many interviewers like to ask follow-up questions based on the information you present in your response.

The Best Way to Answer

Take advantage of this golden opportunity and reveal some of your selling points related to the job. Introduce a few relevant skills, qualities, or experiences. There are two recommended ways to structure your response. First, you can take the chronological approach, listing some of your relevant experiences in chronological order. See a sample of this first approach below.

> Interviewer: Why don't you start off by telling me a little bit about yourself?
>
> Candidate: Okay. Well, I grew up in a small town in central Pennsylvania. I chose to attend ABC College to major in social work. While at ABC College, I began specializing in working with autistic children during an internship with XYZ Agency, and I haven't looked back since. I've worked with autistic children over the past ten years, developing and implementing strategies and techniques that help to improve their social skills. I'm someone who receives great joy for the smallest improvement seen in one of my children that I'm working with. Over the years, I've developed strong counseling skills, organizational skills, and a passion for my work.

The candidate was able to sell herself through presenting skills, accomplishments, educational training, and her commitment to the field. A second way to answer this question is by listing qualities about yourself. Take a look at this approach below.

> Interviewer: Why don't you start off by telling me a little bit about yourself?
>
> Candidate: Well, people who know me well constantly tell me that I'm a good listener. I've always been interested in other people and their differences. I believe that people are good listeners because they genuinely care about and are interested in other people. Another characteristic of mine is persistence. When I believe in something, I throw myself into it and never quit. Last year, for example, a local dance club, consisting of approximately 30 girls and boys, wanted to participate in a regional competition in New York City. However, it cost $500 to participate. I organized a fundraising campaign that lasted five weeks, spending every free minute I had on the phone fundraising for the kids. I was determined to help give these kids this great opportunity. Finally, I'm someone who loves to learn new things. I'm constantly teaching myself new computer software applications. Recently, I developed a database that tracks results and produces reports for our marketing division. I'm truly someone who embraces change.

FYI

Recruiters want you to answer the question about your weaknesses head-on. Admitting to a weakness and developing a plan to improve it is actually one of the best strengths a person can have! A major characteristic that successful people have in common is a willingness to acknowledge weaknesses and do something about them.

Here, the candidate identified three assets to present during this response. Notice how she qualified these assets through explanations and examples.

Tricky Question 2: "What Is Your Greatest Weakness?"

Your job in an interview is to sell yourself—to highlight your strengths. Naturally, you don't want to introduce one of your big weaknesses! However, recruiters frequently complain about job seekers' attempts to tiptoe around this question. Too many job seekers have taken the advice of numerous job-search experts who tell them to "present a weakness that's really a strength." So for years, job candidates have been using answers that look something like this:

> "I'm a perfectionist. I'm not satisfied until the work that I do reaches a high quality."

Or,

> "I am a workaholic. I love my work so much, I have trouble putting it aside."

The Hidden Agenda

While the responses above could potentially be categorized as weaknesses, recruiters typically don't buy it. You should answer this question directly. Everyone has areas where they need to improve. Recruiters are looking for candidates that aren't afraid of owning up to their weaknesses.

The Best Way to Answer

Being honest doesn't mean being stupid. You don't need to offer a weakness that's going to put you out of the running. For example, if you're pursuing a job in sales, don't tell the recruiter that meeting new people is your main weakness! Try to find a weakness that isn't so directly relevant and important for successfully performing on the job. Below are three helpful steps for answering this question, followed by a sample response.

- Identify a true weakness that's not too relevant to the job.

- Show how it has truly been a weakness.

- Present your plan for overcoming the weakness.

> Interviewer: What is your greatest weakness?
>
> Candidate: I would have to say my greatest weakness is not being able to say no and disappoint people. In the past, I found myself frequently involved in too many things and spread too thin. I was forced to perform tasks quickly and at the last minute. The quality of my work suffered. I still have that tendency to want to say yes to everything, but I have improved substantially. I am saying no much more frequently these days. I feel better about the quality of my work because of it. I've realized that doing less is more. I have also learned how to prioritize and choose only those projects and activities that are most important to me and to the company.

By telling the interviewer how much the weakness has improved, it lessens the negative impact.

Tricky Question 3: "Where Do You See Yourself in Ten Years?"

The number of years varies, but the question remains the same. Whether it's five, ten, fifteen, or twenty years, recruiters are interested in hearing about your long-term goals.

Guidance

Be able to speak to areas where you have not been as successful and what you have done to develop yourself and your skills, as well as, what you have learned form the process.

—Glaxo
Wellcome

The Hidden Agenda

Interviewers want to hire people who have their heart in their field and who won't leave in six months. One way for interviewers to test your level of commitment to the field and the job at hand is through your long-term goals. Recruiters want to determine how well your long-term goals relate to the job and field. A second reason for asking this question is to determine whether you're goal-oriented.

The Best Way to Answer

The best way to answer depends on your situation. If the job you're interviewing for is truly just a stepping stone or a temporary thing, and you don't plan on being in the field very long, you should be careful in how you answer. You must focus more on the skills you see yourself using and less on the field you don't see yourself in. See the following example.

Interviewer: Where do you see yourself in ten years?

Candidate: Well, it's difficult to say. I've always loved sales as a profession and can't see myself in ten years not being in sales in some capacity. Currently, my focus is on obtaining a challenging sales position where the potential for success lies on my shoulders. This position provides exactly what I'm looking for.

Notice how the candidate emphasized his commitment to sales and to obtaining a sales position. He did a good job of selling his commitment to sales and desire for the current opening. If the job you're interviewing for *is* in your long-term field, your answer should be focused more on the field. See the next example.

Interviewer: Where do you see yourself in ten years?

Candidate: I definitely see myself in public relations. In ten years, I hope that I've developed the skills and experience to be considered for a leadership position in public relations, either as a director or associate director. Over the next few years, I want to continually improve my editing and writing skills. This is what I've always loved to do. In addition, I hope to gradually gain a clearer understanding of the logistics of running a PR department.

The candidate was very direct regarding her long-term goal of being in public relations. She also convinced the interviewer that she would be content writing and editing for a while. Sometimes, you can hurt yourself by expressing too much ambition. Recruiters often think that you won't be content enough in the job if you only emphasize the next steps of your career.

Tricky Question 4: "Tell Me about a Conflict That You Had with Someone and How You Dealt with That Conflict?"

This question is tricky because you don't want to talk too much about a negative relationship or ugly situation. The recruiter may begin to wonder about your interpersonal skills. However, everyone has conflicts that come up, so don't be overly concerned about answering the question.

The Hidden Agenda

The hidden agenda in this case is not too hidden. Seeing how you've handled conflicts in the past is a good indication of how you'll handle them in the future. Recruiters want to see your approach to resolving conflicts.

The Best Way to Answer

The first thing to do is identify an appropriate conflict to share. You don't want to bring up an exceptionally personal conflict that makes the recruiter feel awkward. It's better to bring up a conflict that happened at work or at a place other than home. Next, you need to think about the most efficient way to explain the situation. You want to spend as little time as possible talking about the conflict itself. What's most important is talking about how you *resolved* the conflict. Once you determine how you will describe the resolution of the conflict, take time to analyze your behavior. Most candidates end their answer without offering their thoughts on how well they did. Recruiters can take away a lot of good information from your analysis of the conflict. The first sample shows what *not* to do. The candidate focuses way too much time on the conflict itself and not enough time on how it got resolved.

> Interviewer: Tell me about a conflict that you had with someone and how you dealt with that conflict?
>
> Candidate: While working at ABC Corporation, I worked with five other co-workers on developing a new customer-service training program for all employees. Everyone had their tasks to take care of, and we reported on our progress during weekly meetings. Each week, the same thing happened. There were five of us who always did what we were supposed to, meeting all of our weekly goals. But there was one lady, Sally, who never had her work completed. She would make up a long excuse each and every time. One week, it was her child that was sick, and the next week, her dog had to go to the vet. There was always something. Finally, I just looked at her and said that it wasn't fair that we all got our work done, and she never did. I

told her that we had our own problems and issues that came up, but we dealt with them and still completed our work.

This was way too much information on the conflict and not enough on how he resolved it. Also, confronting the person in front of the larger group was not the best way to handle the issue. It's more effective to confront people individually.

Look at the next example. See how the candidate spends more time explaining how he resolved the conflict and less on the conflict itself. Also notice that the candidate took the extra step and analyzed his actions. He admitted to the interviewer that it would've been more effective to approach the lady individually. He proved to the interviewer that he could analyze a specific experience, learn from it, and apply what he learned to future experiences.

Interviewer: Tell me about a conflict that you had with someone and how you dealt with that conflict?

Candidate: While working at ABC Corporation, I worked with five other co-workers on developing a new customer-service training program for all employees. Everyone had their tasks to take care of, and we reported on our progress during weekly meetings. One of the members, Sally, consistently failed to complete her assignments. During one of the meetings, I expressed my disappointment and frustrations with Sally's lack of progress. Sally got very defensive and told me that I was insensitive to her situation. We didn't speak for a while, but from that point on, Sally got her work done on time. I think she needed a little push. Looking back now, I could have handled things better. I should have asked to meet with Sally individually to confront her on this issue. Bringing it up at the meeting made things awkward for everyone. That experience taught me that confronting people individually is a more effective and sensitive way to confront another person.

Tricky Question 5: "Why Should I Hire You?"

This question is similar to the first one, "Tell me a little bit about yourself." The main difference is that it is frequently asked near the end of the interview rather than at the beginning.

This question is pretty broad, thus making it difficult to answer for many candidates. There are potentially 20 to 30 reasons why they should hire you.

The Hidden Agenda

The recruiter often wants to hear, one last time, what you have to offer. The answer to this question can serve as a summary or end-all. It can reassure the recruiter that there wasn't any information left out. It's also another opportunity to determine your abilities related to selling. Can you identify all the sellable features, synthesize the information, and articulate it effectively?

The Best Way to Answer

Some people believe that the best approach to answering this question is to pinpoint one or two of your most relevant selling points that make you stand out from other candidates. If you actually have one or two selling points that you *know* all other candidates don't have, then this advice is fine.

The approach that I recommend is to lay all your cards on the table one last time. The rationale for this approach is that the combination of all your individual selling points makes *you* unique. There's little chance that any other candidate has the same combination of selling points as you do. Therefore, you're personalizing the response.

In doing this, you should realize that you might be somewhat redundant. It's likely that you brought up a number of the selling points earlier in the interview. However, this is the type of information that's worth reiterating. They're your selling points. You want to make crystal clear that the interviewer is well aware of all your selling points. See the following interaction and how the candidate reiterates previous points and combines them with new points.

Interviewer: Why should I hire you?

Candidate: There are many reasons why you should hire me. First, as alluded to earlier, I have the academic training and experience needed for the job. Secondly, due to five years as an editor, my writing skills have reached a high level of quality that will enable me to pump out top-notch press releases in a relatively short period of time. A third reason you should hire me relates to my work ethic. I am a believer that there's no substitute for hard work. I was taught at an early age the meaning of hard work and the meaning of pride in your work. In addition, I am a positive team player. With the emphasis you have on working within teams, it's critical to hire someone who has the interpersonal skills necessary to get along with a wide variety of people. I can't remember the last time I haven't gotten along with someone. I enjoy and

appreciate differences in people and believe that you must respect different styles and ways of doing things. There are usually many different ways to get to the finish line. Finally, and maybe above all, you should hire me because my heart is in this professional opportunity. My heart's not only in the job but also in the company, division, industry, and geographic location. I will give my all in this job because my heart is 100 percent into it!

THE WHOLE IN ONE

- Many special types of interviews exist. It's important that you're aware of these variations so that you can properly prepare for them.

- *Behavioral-based interviews* require you to answer questions through in-depth explanations of past examples.

- During *group interviews,* it's most important to maintain eye contact with every interviewer and keep them all involved.

- The *on-site interviews* usually take up most of a day. Therefore, you must keep your energy up and sell the same answers over and over again during each different interview.

- Ordering the right foods and staying away from alcohol are two important tips to remember when participating in the *dining interview.*

- During *phone interviews,* you must remember not to rely too heavily on a cheat sheet, for you want to speak fluently and come across naturally.

- *Video interviews* are still rare and a bit awkward due to the lag time between actions and words.

- You must continue to be yourself whether the interview is more *formal* or *conversational.*

- Show your poise and think on your feet when *stress* questions occur.

- You should become aware of those questions that are *illegal* and determine a comfortable approach to handling them.

- Certain questions are a bit tricky to answer. You need to identify the interviewer's hidden agenda and decide on the best way to respond.

ASSIGNMENT

Complete the "Types of Interviews" strategy under Goal 5 of your Personal Job Search Trainer.

Chapter 14

Scoring a Perfect 10 on Your Interview Day

GET THE SCOOP ON . . .

- What to wear
- What to bring to the interview
- First impressions
- The 10 best interview strategies
- Interview blunders
- Thank-you letters

THE WARM-UP: GETTING READY ON THE MORNING OF YOUR BIG DAY

It's your big day—the day of your interview. You'll wake up feeling a little different than you do on a normal day. The butterflies start showing up to the party they're having in your stomach, and your palms start feeling a little moist and clammy. These are good things. This shows that you're a human being with natural feelings. To start off on the right foot, you must think about what to wear, what to bring with you, and how to form a strong first impression.

Dressing Up for the Interview: What to Wear

When you dress for an interview, you should have one word in mind—professional. Dress professionally for your interview, and keep it simple. Don't wear something that will cause any type of stir among recruiters and get in the way of your interview. Being hip is not something you should be striving for when you dress for an interview. In fact, if you dress properly, the recruiter should hardly notice what you're wearing because your clothes won't attract attention to themselves. The only thing that they should remember about your appearance is that you looked nice, neat, and professional. Don't go for the dress or suit that *may* knock their socks off! It's also very important to be neat and clean regarding your basic personal hygiene.

You should realize that there are style differences among different career fields, but they shouldn't affect the way you dress for your

FYI

The recent business-casual or dress-down trend makes the question of what to wear more complex to answer. Generally speaking, however, it's still much wiser to go conservative and overdress than to go risky and underdress. No one, to my knowledge, has ever lost a job offer because they overdressed for an interview.

interview. True, creative advertising firms have a very different culture and dress code than that of corporate banks, but you can worry about the everyday dress code *after* you get the job. In the meantime, do yourself a favor and dress professionally for all your interviews, regardless of what kind of company they're with.

Significant differences also exist between men's and women's appropriate attire. Following are tips for men and women regarding dress and general appearance.

Dress Tips for Women

- You're still safer going with a suit with a skirt rather than one with pants. While pants are becoming increasingly more accepted, it's still frowned upon by many recruiters. You'll be taking a risk by going with pants.

- You have more freedom in terms of colors you can choose from, but it depends on the field. For business and corporate positions, some of the more authoritative colors include navy, black, camel, brown, gray, or olive. A deep red is now also accepted by many as a neutral color.

- Shoes should have a small to medium heel and a fresh shine. Typically, open toes are considered too dressy. Your shoe color should be the same as your hemline or darker, never lighter.

- Fingernails should be manicured but not too long. If you paint your nails, use neutral colors.

- Hair shouldn't go below the shoulders. If you have long hair, put it up or back away from your face.

- Keep accessories to a minimum. Don't wear excessive rings, bracelets, necklaces, or earrings. That usually means no more than one per hand, wrist, neck, and ear.

- Hosiery should be worn no matter what. Even if it's the middle of summer and your legs are tan, wear natural color, sheer hose that are the same shade as your shoes or lighter. Your hosiery should never be darker than your shoes.

Dress Tips for Men

- Wear either a single or double-breasted suit, depending on the field, the company, and how it fits you. The jacket's shoulders should be wide enough so that the sleeves hang straight, without bulges when your arms are at your sides. When the suit jacket is buttoned, it should fit comfortably and be long enough to cover the buttocks.

- The recommended suit colors are navy blue and gray. Black is usually too dressy. A solid color is fine, but you can also wear suits

with colored threads and weaves in multiple shades that are subtle enough to look like a solid from a distance. Pick up these colors in the cross weave of your tie.

- Wear shined shoes that are either black or cordovan color. Wingtip or plain shoes are recommended—no loafers or boots. Socks should be the same color as the shoes.

- Trim your fingernails, and have your hair cut. You want to present a neat image.

- If you normally wear earrings, remove them. You'll take a risk by wearing them.

What You Should Bring to the Interview

Don't show up for your interview empty-handed. There's nothing worse than not having something when you really need it, and that goes double for an interview. Here are some items that you should take with you to every interview:

- A professional binder with a notepad

- Two or more pens

- Copies of your resume

- Copies of your reference list

- Your list of questions to ask the interviewer(s)

- Literature on the organization

- A copy of the job description (in case you need to refer to it)

- A time management planner/day planner (demonstrates organizational skills)

- Your portfolio (recommended, yet optional)

- Handkerchief/tissue (in case you sweat or spill something)

- A watch

- Breath mints

- A comb (if it's an on-site, half-day, or whole-day interview)

Develop a Strong First Impression

First impressions are crucial to interviews. A strong first impression can quickly warm the recruiter up to you and make the interview go a lot smoother. Bad first impressions are very hard to overcome and will

leave you fighting an uphill battle during your entire interview. Here are some tips for creating a strong first impression with the recruiter.

- Stand up when the recruiter comes to greet you.

- Extend your hand and offer a firm handshake.

- Look your recruiter right in the eyes.

- Introduce yourself and thank the recruiter for meeting with you: "Ms. Jones, I'm Anita Job. It's a pleasure meeting you. Thank you for meeting with me today."

- Sit down only when the recruiter asks you to or after the recruiter sits down.

- Mention something you like about her office or the company facility.

THE PERFECT 10: THE 10 INTERVIEW STRATEGIES THAT WIN JOBS

Guidance

When I interview a candidate, I want to see self-confidence but not arrogance. Have they set any goals for themselves, short and long term? What motivates them? Are they articulate and good communicators?

—John Hancock

To make your interview the *perfect* job interview, I recommend that you learn 10 interviewing strategies that I call the Perfect 10. The Perfect 10 is a list of the 10 best strategies and tips for excelling during interviews. Following this advice will let you present your best self to the interviewer and increase your chances of getting the job offer you want.

Number 10: Toot Your Own Horn Quietly—Be Confident Yet Humble

There's a thin line between selling yourself and sounding conceited. Your goal is to exude a quiet confidence. Recruiters want to see that you believe in yourself and your skills. However, too much of anything is not good. If you come across too strong, most recruiters will get turned off.

It's important to realize that the industry you're pursuing affects the type of confidence that's expected and tolerated. For example, recruiters looking to hire someone to fill a financial sales position will want to clearly see and hear a high level of confidence demonstrated during the interview. However, a recruiter hiring an elementary school teacher is looking for a less vocal, more intrinsic confidence from the candidate.

Following is an example of crossing the line between confident and arrogant.

Interviewer: Why should I hire you?

Candidate: You should hire me because I am, without a doubt, the best candidate for this job. I have proven communication skills that you'll not find in other candidates. Your clients will want to buy from me. I

have a way with people that makes them want to work with me. Also, I'm extremely hardworking. I'll work until the job is complete. When other salesmen get tired, I'm just getting started. I have more energy than any other candidate out there. Finally, I have the will to win. I hate to lose, so losing is not an option for me. I never say die!

One mistake the candidate made was comparing himself to people he didn't even know. How can you say you're that much better than someone if you don't even know who that someone is? The other mistake he made was being too extreme in his answers. "Losing is not an option" and "I never say die" are two statements that fit into the too extreme category.

Here's the same question, this time with a toned-down response. This response is a good example of the quiet confidence that's recommended.

Interviewer: Why should I hire you?

Candidate: The first reason you should hire me is I have strong communication skills. I have five years of sales experience and have conducted more than 30 workshops and seminars at regional and national conferences. The second reason you should hire me is related to my interpersonal skills. I love to meet new people, which helps me to build a positive rapport with a wide range of people. My clients like to buy things from me because they trust me and enjoy doing business with me. Finally, you should also hire me because of my strong work ethic. I'll work until the job is complete. My relationships with clients are very important to me. Because of this, I'll work around the clock if one of my clients needs me.

This time the candidate was able to come across confident yet humble. This was an illustration of how you can sell yourself without coming across as boasting or bragging.

Number 9: Maintain Good Posture and Use Hand Gestures Appropriately

Actions speak louder than words. The way you sit in your chair can say more about you than you could say during the whole interview. In addition, the way you use your hands can demonstrate nervousness and lack of polish.

The worst thing you can do is lean way back in your chair. Leaning back in your chair is commonly interpreted as lazy, apathetic, cocky, and

disrespectful. Conversely, you don't want to get in the interviewer's face by leaning in too much either. Maintain a straight yet comfortable posture. Don't sit up so straight in your chair that it causes your interviewer to count down to blastoff! Find a comfortable posture that doesn't force you to lean too much in any one direction.

Getting specific: Face the interviewer and align your body squarely toward her. Lay your forearms or wrists (depending how tall you are) comfortably on your lap. Place your feet flat on the floor, shoulder-width apart. If you're more comfortable folding your legs, you can do so as long as it doesn't throw off your posture.

If you're sitting at a table or desk, don't put your arms on the table. It forces you to lean in too much and gives you the appearance of being too relaxed. Also, don't put your binder or other materials on the table right in front of you. You don't want anything in the path of the recruiter.

Use hand gestures only if there's a purpose for using them. If you're emphasizing a point or describing something physical, hand gestures are appropriate. When your hands are flapping uncontrollably due to an excess of nervous energy, you need to make an adjustment. When using your hands, keep them right below your face. If they're too high near your face, they'll be distracting. If they're too low, there's too big of a gap from your eyes to your hands, making it difficult for the interviewer to follow both.

One of the best ways to practice interviewing is to watch yourself in action. Participating in a videotaped mock interview will enable you to see yourself in action and determine whether or not your posture or use of hand gestures needs adjustments.

FYI

Using "like" tends to be most closely associated with the present Generation-Xers. Therefore, younger job seekers have to be extra cautious of using "like" because interviewers will be looking for it more closely than with other candidates.

Number 8: Um. . . Like. . . Um—Watch Your "Ums" and "Likes!"

This is a tough one for a lot of people. Using "um" and "like" has been so deeply embedded into everyday speech that it's difficult to catch unless you're looking for it. The problem is, if you're looking for it, your overall presentation will go downhill. It's difficult to be watching out for the ums and likes while delivering confident, fluent responses.

In our society, the ums are universally more accepted and tolerated than the likes. Using the term "like" in conversation generates a valley-girl, airhead stereotype among many people, and this is certainly not an image you want interviewers to form about you. Read the following two statements out loud and determine the impression you receive from each. Is one more annoying or more potentially damaging than the other is?

Interviewer: How do you manage your time?

Candidate: Um, I tend to, um, use a very detailed day planner. Most days, um, I write down, um, everything I need to do that day. Then I'll even, um, prioritize, um, the various tasks.

Interviewer: How do you manage your time?

Candidate: Like, I tend to, like, use a very detailed day planner. Most days, like, I write down, like, everything I need to do that day. Then I'll even, like, prioritize, like, the various tasks.

The best way to ultimately tone down your ums and likes is to identify where you most frequently use them. Is it at the beginning of each statement? Or is it at the end of each statement while you're thinking of the next statement? Take a look at the following statement, typed verbatim from a taped practice interview.

Interviewer: Where do you see yourself in five years?

Candidate: I guess I see myself, um, (pause), um, working at a large corporation in the public relations department. Specifically, I could see myself, um, (pause), writing press releases and editing company literature.

The ums were used in the middle of the statements. This implies that the candidate starts talking before generating a complete response in his mind. The best way to help eliminate the ums in this case is to get into the habit of pausing after each question, giving yourself an opportunity to formulate a more complete answer before you start talking.

The only time you should worry about this is before the interview. Work on toning down your ums and likes while you're practicing. Once you're in the interview, let it be! The confidence and speech fluency that you'll lose isn't worth the conscious elimination of a few ums or likes.

Number 7: NOT TOO LOUD, N-o-t T-o-o-o-o S-l-o-w—Maintain Good Voice Projection and Speech Rate

Talking TOO LOUDLY THROUGHOUT YOUR INTERVIEW CAN BE ANNOYING! On the other hand, talking very softly may indicate a lack of enthusiasm and self-confidence.

Talking-too-quickly-can-cause-you-to-lose-your-interviewer-and-generate-a-rambling-scatter-brained-image. Conversely, t-a-l-k-i-n-g t-o-o-o-o s-l-o-w-l-y i-s n-o-t g-o-o-d e-i-t-h-e-r-r-r.

You must find that happy medium. First, determine what your natural tendencies are when you talk to people. When you call your friends, do they sarcastically tell you to "turn down your speaker phone"? Or do

you lean on the side of having to speak up all of the time? The same goes for your speech rate. Do you tend to talk so slowly that people constantly finish your sentences? Or do you take it to the other extreme of talking so quickly that your listeners always seem to have a confused look on their faces?

The key is adjustment. You must adjust your natural tendencies to reach a voice projection and speech rate that are more appropriate. At the same time, you don't want to adjust so much that it causes you to come across as being unnatural in the interview. For example, if you talk with a lot of excitement and passion, you may find yourself talking a little too fast and a little too loud. However, if you try to slow down too much, you may fail to express some of your natural enthusiasm.

Just like watching your ums and likes, the time to make conscious adjustments to your tone and speech rate is *before the interview, not during* it. You must practice answering questions with a friend or by yourself and see how it feels to make adjustments. The worst thing that you can do is to be extremely conscious and concerned about your voice projection and speech rate during the interview. You won't be able to concentrate on answering the questions or be loose enough to express yourself naturally. Practice, practice, practice beforehand, and then let it go and be yourself during the interview!

Number 6: Know When to Say When—Provide Enough Detail without Rambling

The length of your responses is important to consider. Since it's impossible to pinpoint the best response length for all answers, it's more beneficial to think of length in terms of detail. How much detail in a response is too much, and how much is not enough? Generally, a good rule of thumb is to answer the question, provide explanations or examples to support and clarify your answer, and then end the response. Many younger candidates tend to give short responses with too little detail. Also, extremely nervous candidates tend to give very short answers in the hope of ending the interviewing experience as quickly as possible. The best way to get a feel for how long and detailed a response should be is to see sample responses with varying lengths and degrees of detail. Review the first sample below.

> Interviewer: I see that you were a volunteer for Special Olympics. What were your responsibilities there?

> Candidate: My main responsibility was organizing the long-jump event. I helped out in other areas as well.

The interviewer doesn't receive enough information regarding the level of responsibility or the types of tasks the candidate performed. All the

candidate really did was verbally restate what was written on her resume. The content of her response didn't hurt the candidate, but it didn't help her sell herself either. Now let's look at the other extreme: too much information!

Interviewer: I see that you were a volunteer for Special Olympics. What were your responsibilities there?

Candidate: I had a great experience volunteering for Special Olympics. My main responsibility was organizing the long-jump event. I first had to make sure the special athletes were registered for the event. Some athletes were not permitted to execute the long jump due to physical ailments. Once they were registered, I had to keep them in their designated order so the appropriate scores were reported. Because it's as much a sociable day as a physical one, it was hard keeping the athletes in order. During the jump, I was responsible for making sure they didn't cross the jump line. If they crossed the jump line, I had to record it and explain to the athletes what they did wrong and that they would have to jump again. If the athletes performed a legal jump, I simply recorded it on my score report. I had to turn in all score reports to the assistant manager. Once I . . .

This was so long we had to cut her off. Most people get bored with too much detail, and interviewers are no exception. You want to explain your points, not belabor them. Now take a look at a response that strikes a good balance between abruptness and rambling.

Interviewer: I see that you were a volunteer for Special Olympics. What were your responsibilities there?

Candidate: I had a great experience volunteering for Special Olympics. My main responsibility was organizing the long-jump event. I was responsible for registering the athletes, keeping them in their appropriate jump order, and recording their distances. In addition to the long-jump event, I assisted the volunteers at the two-mile race. I prepared the runners for the race by keeping them in their designated groups and telling them when it was their turn. Finally, I also helped out in the concession stand, making hot dogs and hamburgers. Overall, the experience was wonderful. It's truly a thrill watching the excitement on the special athletes' faces. I'm looking forward to helping out again next summer.

Number 5: Have a Method to Your Madness—Keep Responses Organized

Remember, interviewers are judging you not only on what you say, but also how you say it. You may have the best answer in your head, but if it's not articulated in a coherent way, you may lose the interviewer. Don't leave anything to the interviewer's imagination or assume that he'll be able to follow you from point A to point C without knowing point B. Make sure the different points you present are understood and retained. When one point runs into another, it's difficult for the interviewer to make sense of it all. And if they didn't clearly hear your points *during* the interview, they'll have a real tough time remembering them *afterwards*. See the following example, illustrating an unorganized response. Along with making it hard for the interviewer to follow, the candidate also presents a poor overall impression of himself.

Interviewer: I see that you were a volunteer for Special Olympics. What were your responsibilities there?

Candidate: Oh yeah, wow, that was a great experience; I mean I really got a lot out of it. It's just so neat to see how excited the special athletes are. I loved helping out. Basically, I helped coordinate the long-jump event. Well, I really did that near the end, and before that, I helped at the concession stand, making hot dogs and hamburgers. The athletes really worked up quite an appetite. So, basically, I did about almost everything. Oh yeah, I also helped to time the runners during the mile and two-mile relay. It was really neat to see how hard the athletes were trying. This one little girl cried at the end of her race. I asked her what was wrong, and she said she didn't do as well as she did last year.

Here are some helpful hints for organizing your responses. First, listen carefully to the question. You want to make sure that you're answering the question that the interviewer has asked. Next, pause after each question. Don't sit there for 20 seconds before responding, but take a few seconds to gather your thoughts. Even when you know the answer before the last word leaves the interviewer's tongue, it's good to pause. Pausing shows that you're not just giving a rehearsed, canned answer (even though you may be). Pausing also indicates that you're under control, poised, and self-confident. As you're thinking about your response, it's helpful to identify the different points you'd like to share. Once you know the points or aspects of your response, you can present them as separate yet connected parts. Pause before each new point, and use transition words to prompt the interviewer that you're moving to a different point. Finally, practicing answering questions in an organized way prior to the interview is, again, the best thing to do. You don't want to be thinking too much during the interview. The example below illustrates a response that is organized and easy to follow. Notice how the candidate answers the question first and saves most of her general reactions for later.

Interviewer: I see that you were a volunteer for Special Olympics. What were your responsibilities there?

Candidate: (Pause) Well, overall I had a great experience volunteering for Special Olympics. My main responsibility was organizing the long-jump event. I was responsible for registering the athletes, keeping them in their appropriate jump order, and recording their distances. In addition to the long-jump event, I assisted the volunteers working at the one- and two-mile races. I prepared the runners for the race by keeping them in their designated groups and telling them when it was their turn. Finally, I also helped out in the concession stand, making hot dogs and hamburgers. Overall, the experience was wonderful. It's truly a thrill watching the excitement on the special athletes' faces. I'm looking forward to helping out again next summer.

Number 4: Keep Your Eyes on the Road—Maintain Eye Contact

The most important nonverbal communication skill, by far, is maintaining eye contact. Good eye contact must be there from the start. When you firmly shake the interviewer's hand and introduce yourself, you must demonstrate good eye contact. Take time right now to visualize in your mind the image of someone who doesn't make eye contact with you when you're shaking hands. What impression do you get of that person? You're probably thinking to yourself that he doesn't have much self-confidence, and that he's shy, insecure, unsociable, and embarrassed. There aren't many positive characteristics associated with poor eye contact.

At the same time, don't go overboard with eye contact. You don't want to stare your interviewer down. Times during the actual interview that are most important to maintain eye contact are when the interviewer is asking the questions and when you are verbally responding. When you're thinking or formulating a response, that's a good time to break from eye contact. In fact, it's unnatural and a bit awkward if you remain looking at the interviewer when you're trying to think of a response. Visualize this scenario in your mind. Isn't it awkward?

You'll have more success maintaining eye contact during those questions and responses that you're more familiar with. When you know an answer well, you don't have to think so much about how you're going to phrase it. It just flows naturally off your tongue. *The biggest obstacle of maintaining eye contact is lack of preparation prior to the interview.* One of the reasons it's so important to complete the 20 Prep Tasks outlined earlier is to be ready to answer the questions. When you're going over the 20 tasks, you're refreshing your memory with key points to bring up during the interview. When these key points are fresh in your mind, you don't have to search so much for them during the interviews. Thinking too much during responses makes it impossible to maintain eye contact. Do most of your thinking *before* the interview, so you can act more naturally during it.

Number 3: Stand Out from the Crowd—Use Past Examples and Explanations to Validate and Personalize Your Responses

One of the biggest complaints among interviewers is that candidates' responses are too vague and impersonal. Short answers blend together from one candidate to the next. You must go beneath the surface with your responses. Don't ramble on forever, but it's necessary to explain your answers. Because the interviewer doesn't know you, there's so much room for misinterpretation. Providing explanations and examples can lower the chance of the interviewer misinterpreting you. Most job seekers tend to be too short with their responses. See the following example.

Interviewer: What are your greatest strengths?

Candidate: Well, I'm a people person, I'm hardworking, and I have good computer skills.

The candidate answered the question, but she was vague. Also, because the strengths were so common, there's a good chance that other candidates said the same thing. One of your major goals of interviewing is to stand out from the crowd—in a positive way. It's difficult to stand out when your answers are vague and common. The best way to stand out and strengthen your responses is by adding explanations and past examples. Providing explanations or past examples can more clearly describe your answers as well as validate and personalize your responses. A *personalized* response is a response that's unique to an individual or person. Refer to the next example below:

Interviewer: What are your greatest strengths?

Candidate: Well, first, I'm a people person. I have always enjoyed getting to know people and listening to their stories. My friends tell me that I'm a great listener. For me, listening comes easy since I am genuinely interested in what people have to say. Next, I see myself as hardworking. I take pride in my work, and, therefore, I tend to throw myself into a project. Recently, I volunteered to help organize a bus trip to New York City for the elderly in my community. I have spent countless hours over the past two weeks making sure all of the arrangements were taken care of. I want it to be a great experience for the elderly folks. Finally, I have strong computer skills. I've never taken a computer class, but I've taught myself how to design and maintain databases and produce desktop presentations. When I worked at ABC Company, I designed a database that maintained all of the sales transactions. From this database, I was able to produce and distribute monthly reports to every sales manager in the region. So, I would have to say that interpersonal skills, work ethic, and computer skills are my three greatest strengths.

The candidate gave the same general answer: people person, hardworking, and good computer skills, but the explanations and examples brought the answer to life! The candidate's claims of being a people person, hardworking, and strong with computers were validated through her examples. Also, the response no longer blended with other candidates' responses because the specific examples and explanations couldn't have come from anyone else.

Number 2: Make Sure "Your Glass Is Half Full"—Always Be Positive!

When you wake up in the morning, do you say, "God, it's a good morning!"? Or do you find yourself saying, "Good God it's morning!"? On your interview day, wake up saying the former! Your responses should always be positive. Don't talk negatively about a person, organization, or anything else. If you had a bad relationship with a former boss or co-worker, you're much better off not bringing it up during the interview. If the interviewer directly asks about your relationship, don't go into detail about your boss. Keep the attention on you and what you could have done to improve the relationship. That shows that you take ownership for your actions and don't push the blame on others. Also, don't bad-mouth an organization. You never know where that recruiter has been or how they feel about certain places. The example below is a prime illustration of how this can hurt you.

Interviewer: Why did you choose to attend Elon College?

Candidate: Well, I didn't want to go to a big university and just be a number. I mean, there are 300 students in a classroom at big universities. The professor doesn't even know who you are or what you look like. Plus, graduate students teach most of the classes at big schools. Elon is just the right size for me.

The candidate thought she was answering the question pretty well. What she didn't realize, however, is that the interviewer got his degree from a big university. He was probably thinking to himself, "I loved my university. She doesn't know what she's talking about." The interviewer now has a negative taste in his mouth toward the candidate. If the candidate would have remained positive, she would have done much better. Let's give her another chance:

Interviewer: Why did you choose to attend Elon College?

Candidate: I chose Elon mostly because the size was just right for me. I really value the opportunity to get to know my professors and interact in the classes. In fact, I have recently completed a research experiment that was co-designed and supervised by a professor in my major. I also wanted a college where the classes were within walking distance from one another.

Notice how the general concept of the candidate's answer was the same as before, but *how she presented* this concept was much more positive. There's not much chance of the interviewer being offended by this response. Always be positive!

Number 1: Don't Sweat It—Keep the Interview in Perspective and Be Yourself!

The big day is here! You have your sweaty palms and butterflies traveling in high gear. The people close to you are all wishing you good luck. This is your future we're talking about, right? It's show time!

It *is* an exciting day, and it doesn't hurt to have sweaty palms and butterflies. A small amount of anxiety is actually helpful in stressful situations. But it's important not to get too excited. When you get overly excited before a big event, it can quickly turn into nervousness. And when you're nervous or uptight, it's hard to perform at your best. When your emotions get the best of you, it's difficult to speak fluently and say things that make sense. Think about when someone pulls out in front of you when you're driving how "fluent" and "articulate" you become. Or think about how "tactfully" you choose your words during a heated argument with a friend or family member.

Be excited, but also keep it in perspective. Focus on the things that you can control, and don't stress over the things that you can't. What's in your control is how well you've prepared and how well you present yourself. The smile you put on your face, the eye contact that you maintain, and the positive attitude you bring with you are all things in your control. The amount of research you've done on the company and your level of preparedness are also things you can control. What's not in your control is whether or not you'll get the job. You could present your very best self and *still* not get the job. There may be an inside candidate or someone with five more years of experience interviewing for the same job. Don't worry about what you can't control.

Don't try to be perfect. You won't be. When you do say something that wasn't quite up to par, don't beat yourself up over it. Remember, in just a few hours, you'll be eating your favorite foods and talking to your favorite people in your life. Everything will be fine!

Believe in fate. If you don't get this job, there's a better one out there for you. If they don't hire you, it's a good indication that the fit wasn't there. You don't want to work for a place that doesn't welcome you with open arms. Remember one of the three P's to success: Persevere through the "No"s. You only need one "YES!"

Finally, above all, *be yourself!* It's the biggest cliché when it comes to interviewing, but it's also the best advice you can get. The more successful you are in building a positive rapport with the interviewer, the better chance you have. You want the interviewer leaving the interview saying to herself, "I like him. He was someone I'd enjoy working with." The interviewer won't feel that way if you were trying to be someone you're not. Be yourself! It's worth repeating. Smile when it's natural to smile, and laugh when it's natural for you to laugh (within reason, of course). Show your enthusiasm when you feel excited. Too many job seekers approach the interview the way they'd approach a formal speech. You're not talking to an audience. You're talking with one person who, by the way, is interested in the same field in which you're interested. Relax, take deep breaths, and let them see the real you!

INTERVIEW BLUNDERS

Following are interview blunders generated from a survey conducted by Robert Half International. These are obviously examples of what NOT to do during your interview.

We've all been interviewed for jobs. And, we've all spent most of those interviews thinking about what not to do. Don't bite your nails. Don't fidget. Don't interrupt. Don't belch. If we did any of the don'ts, we knew we'd instantly disqualify ourselves. But some job applicants go light years beyond this. We surveyed top personnel executives of 100 major American corporations and asked for stories of unusual behavior by job applicants. The lowlights:

1. "... stretched out on the floor to fill out the job application."

2. "She wore a Walkman and said she could listen to me and the music at the same time."

3. "A balding candidate abruptly excused himself. Returned to my office a few minutes later, wearing a hairpiece."

4. "... asked to see interviewer's resume to see if the personnel executive was qualified to judge candidate."

5. "... announced she hadn't had lunch and proceeded to eat a hamburger and french fries in the interviewer's office—wiping the ketchup on her sleeve."

6. "Stated that, if he were hired, he would demonstrate his loyalty by having the corporate logo tattooed on his forearm."

7. "Interrupted to phone his therapist for advice on answering specific interview questions."

8. "When I asked him about his hobbies, he stood up and started tap dancing around my office."

9. "At the end of the interview, while I stood there dumbstruck, went through my purse, took out a brush, brushed his hair, and left."

10. "... pulled out a Polaroid camera and snapped a flash picture of me. Said he collected photos of everyone who interviewed him."

11. "Said he wasn't interested because the position paid too much."

12. "While I was on a long-distance phone call, the applicant took out a copy of Penthouse, and looked through the photos only, stopping longest at the centerfold."

13. "During the interview, an alarm clock went off from the candidate's briefcase. He took it out, shut it off, apologized and said he had to leave for another interview."

14. "A telephone call came in for the job applicant. It was from his wife. His side of the conversation went like this: 'Which company? When do I start? What's the salary?' I said, 'I assume you're not interested in conducting the interview any further.' He promptly responded, 'I am as long as you'll pay me more.' I didn't hire him, but later found out there was no other job offer. It was a scam to get a higher offer."

15. "His attaché (case) opened when he picked it up and the contents spilled, revealing ladies' undergarments and assorted makeup and perfume."

16. "Candidate said he really didn't want to get a job, but the unemployment office needed proof that he was looking for one."

17. ". . . asked who the lovely babe was, pointing to the picture on my desk. When I said it was my wife, he asked if she was home now and wanted my phone number. I called security."

18. "Pointing to a black case he carried into my office, he said that if he was not hired, the bomb would go off. Disbelieving, I began to state why he would never be hired and that I was going to call the police. He then reached down to the case, flipped a switch and ran. No one was injured, but I did need to get a new desk."

AFTER THE FACT . . . THANK-YOU LETTERS

Guidance

One simple thing that relatively few job seekers do that can help create a positive, lasting impression is to send a thank-you letter after an interview. The letter should reiterate your interest in the position and how your skills and experience relate to the job.

—Glaxo
Wellcome

The most important thing that matters regarding thank-you letters is quickly getting them in the hands of the recruiters and professionals. Most professionals only have time for glancing at thank-you letters, thus retaining just bits and pieces of what was on them. But receiving them exceptionally fast sticks in their mind and has the most impact. Recruiters think to themselves, "Wow, that was fast. We just interviewed two days ago." Sending a thank-you note quickly indicates that you're on the ball, responsible, efficient, and productive.

There *are* some interviewers who read thank-you letters more carefully. Therefore, put some thought into the content of your letters. Below are the most important points to include in thank-you letters.

- Thank them for the opportunity and for taking time to interview you.

- Identify two to three appealing aspects of the job that surfaced during the interview, and state that you're now even more interested because of these aspects.

- State the confidence you have regarding the assets you can offer to their organization. Relate these assets to concrete aspects of the job.

- Include any common-ground topics or personal information that the interviewer shared with you (e.g., her son is getting married, or she's going on vacation soon).

A sample thank-you letter is on page 238. Notice how Anita reinforces her interest in the job by targeting a specific aspect of the interview that was compelling. Also, notice how she included a personal note about a

222 Oak Grove
Dallas, TX 55555
December 10, 2000

Ms. Jane Recruiter
Director of Human Resources
XYZ Organization
299 West King Street
Houston, TX 55555

Dear Ms. Recruiter:

Thank you for giving me the opportunity to interview for the
Assistant Manager position last Friday. I appreciate the time you
spent during the interview as well as the tour you provided of your
tremendous facility. I was very impressed with the quality of
services and people that are associated with XYZ Organization.

Our discussion regarding your management model was very
interesting. It was intriguing to learn how successful this management model has been in empowering your employees. I am excited
about the possibility of incorporating such a powerful model into
my management style.

I am confident that the types of management experiences I've had,
combined with my communication and computer skills, will prove to
be assets for your company. Last Friday's interview only reinforced
my desire to join your management team and work for XYZ
Organization.

On a personal note, I hope your nephew's wedding was a big hit
on Saturday! Thanks again.

Sincerely,

Anita Job

wedding they had discussed during the interview. Personal additions help to build a friendly, likable dimension to your image.

THE WHOLE IN ONE

- On your big interview day, you must know what to wear, what to bring, and how to form a good first impression.

- Being conservative with what you wear and the accessories you include is still your best bet.

- Among other things, you should bring copies of your resume, reference list, and a list of questions to ask the interviewer. Place all your materials in a professional binder that contains a notepad and pen.

- To form a good first impression, be on time, smile, shake hands firmly, and make eye contact.

- The "Perfect 10" consists of the ten best strategies and tips to incorporate during the interview. Some of these include delivering responses that are organized, positive, and supported through examples.

- You need to watch your "ums," "likes," and the length of your responses.

- Above all, keep the interview in perspective, and be yourself.

- Reviewing actual interview blunders is a fun way to see what NOT to do during interviews.

- The most critical part of a thank-you letter is getting it in the hands of the interviewers right away! It's good to reiterate your interest and confidence in the job, but most importantly, get it to them quickly. Sending prompt thank-you letters indicates that you're on the ball and responsible.

ASSIGNMENT

Complete the rest of the strategies under Goal 5 (except for the last one) on your Personal Job Search Trainer.

Chapter 15

Evaluating and Negotiating Job Offers

GET THE SCOOP ON . . .

- Learning how to evaluate a job offer
- Benefits packages
- The art of negotiating
- How to deal with and move past rejections

JOB OFFERS AND REJECTIONS

Well, you've done your part. You found a job that's perfect for you, turned in a top-notch resume and cover letter, and did extremely well in your interview. Now it's up to the organization to make a decision. It's important to hope for the best, but anticipate both possible outcomes: receiving an offer or receiving a rejection.

Receiving an Offer

Let's start with the good news. You've earned your position of being the top candidate for the job! Congratulations! This is the fun part. Now all that's left for you to do is review the company's offer and decide whether to accept or decline it. Whatever you do, don't say "yes" right away. Even if you think this is your dream job, take time to review the offer. This is a big decision you're making. Plus, the organization will wonder about you if you start jumping up and down and scream, "Yes! I'll take it!" You don't want to appear desperate or imply that you make rash decisions. Besides, immediately accepting the offer leaves you no room for negotiation.

It's important to become aware of the many parts of a job offer. Once you've reviewed the offer, you'll need to assess it based on your values. Below are the steps you should take in order to make an educated decision on whether to accept, decline, or try to negotiate a better offer.

Step 1: Review the Benefits Package

When you're offered a job, the first question out of everyone's mouth will be, "What are they offering you?" It's doubtful that you'll reply, "A good health-insurance package and retirement plan." Most people think salary when considering job offers. It's crucial to realize that there's much more to an offer than the salary. In fact, a good benefits package adds approximately 30 percent to your salary. Following are important parts of a benefits package that you need to be aware of and seriously review when an offer is made. Note that all of these parts won't be included in *every* package.

Health Insurance

On the top of most people's benefits list is health insurance. Typically, the company pays a certain percentage, and you pay the rest via deductions from your paycheck. Good health-insurance packages contribute 80 to 100 percent of insurance costs. You should realize that this is saving you thousands of dollars per year. If you were to purchase health insurance on your own, it would cost you close to $5,000 per year.

Almost all health-insurance packages cover major medical insurance (major health problems or accidents). From there, read the fine print or ask questions regarding other issues, such as doctor visits and dental coverage. Many health plans work on a co-pay system regarding doctor visits. The insurance covers most of the cost, but you pay a nominal fee of $10 or so per visit. Check out the co-pay fee. Dental coverage varies from plan to plan. Make sure to see if dental coverage is included. Also, if you have a family or a family is in your future, ask about coverage for your spouse and children. Find out about the family plan and its rate.

Retirement Plan

Make sure that the offer includes a retirement plan and that it's transferable. You want to transfer it to the next place you work. The best portable plan to look for is called a *401K Plan*. A 401K plan allows you to put a certain percentage of your gross salary (pre-tax dollars) into an investment fund. Many companies match the percentage you put in or offer a set percentage. On average, people tend to contribute 3 to 10 percent of their gross pay.

Section 125/Cafeteria Plans

The cafeteria plans are flexible plans that allow you to decide where you want your money to go (health insurance, life insurance, dental, child care, etc.). Similar to 401K, you take out a certain amount of your gross pay (before taxes) and put it toward the types of benefits you want. It's more personalized to the needs of the employees. In other words, you can deduct a certain percentage of your gross pay (tax-free) and use it in the way that is best for you. For example, if you're just starting your

FYI

Most job seekers overlook the importance of benefits. They don't realize that a benefits package adds close to 30 percent of their salary! Don't take benefits lightly. This is one time when you need to read the fine print.

career, you may want to put less into life insurance right now and more into your health-care costs in order to get by each month. The cafeteria plan puts *you* in charge of where your benefits money goes, not the company.

Vacation and Sick Days
Find out how many vacation days and sick days you get per year. Many companies offer approximately two weeks paid vacation, plus some paid holidays. Sick days are about the same (10 days per year). A new trend is putting the vacation days, sick days, and holidays together and giving the employee a total number of days off that they can use at their discretion.

Moving Costs
Moving is expensive. If you have to relocate as a result of taking the job, see if the company provides any financial assistance. Most companies offer relocation packages, and they are almost always negotiable.

Tuition Assistance
Continual, lifelong learning is becoming increasingly important. Many companies pay for you to take classes or participate in a training program. This is usually contingent on you earning a minimum grade. Also, determine whether or not the company will pay for you to attend professional conferences.

Company Car
For positions in sales or other jobs requiring a considerable amount of travel, find out if the company provides you with a company car or a car allowance. This can save you a few hundred dollars per month and years of wear and tear on your own car.

Child Care
With more and more unique family units out there and an increase in single parent households, child care is sometimes included as part of the benefits package. Some companies actually have child-care facilities on site, and others offer financial assistance toward the child-care facility of your choice.

Buying Stock in the Company
Some companies allow you to buy stock in their company, but it may vary as to when you're eligible to participate. Determine whether this is an option immediately upon employment or after a certain number of years with the company.

Employee Assistance Programs and Wellness
Employee assistance programs offer counseling to employees with issues such as emotional problems and drug or alcohol addictions. Wellness programs offer activities and workshops to employees on topics that relate to dieting and fitness.

FYI

Trying to sort out all the benefits can be a little confusing. Ask someone you know in the financial field to help you understand the terms of your benefits package. Your contact will be able to help you understand the various insurance and retirement plans.

Step 2: Decide What's Most Important to You in an Offer

The strength of a job offer depends on what's important to you. In addition to reviewing the parts of the offer, you must go through a process of prioritizing your values. Take a look at the following list of values relating to a job offer, and determine how you would rate them. You can also use this list to evaluate offers by answering the questions attached to each value.

■ **Enjoyment and Interest in the Job**
Based on the job description, how appealing are the responsibilities and duties?

■ **Excitement and Challenge**
Will the job be exciting and challenging? Will it be too challenging?

■ **Interest and Respect for the Organization**
Is this the type of organization for which you want to work?

■ **Good Fit**
Do the employees seem like people with whom you'd enjoy working? Do you feel welcomed? Does the organizational culture seem to be a good fit?

■ **Good Career Move**
Does this opportunity nicely position you for future professional opportunities? Does this job move you in the right direction of your long-term goals?

■ **Personal Fulfillment**
Would you feel good about yourself and proud of the position you'd be in? If you would tell a friend or relative where you work and what you do, would you feel proud?

■ **Consistent with Personal Values and Lifestyle**
Will the job allow you to enjoy your personal life? What will the hours be like? Will there be excessive travel? Will you mentally and physically have to take your work home with you?

■ **Geographic Location**
Is the location of the job a place you'd like to be?

■ **Salary and Bonuses**
Does the salary meet your expectations? Are the signing bonus and incentives up to par?

■ **Benefits Package**
How well does the package meet your needs?

Guidance

Candidates seeking employment should prioritize job criteria such as salary, work location, benefits, quality of life, industry, work environment, and type of work, to target an employer of choice and to maximize job satisfaction.
—Bell Atlantic

Step 3: Make Your Decision

In a nutshell, you have three answers you can give the recruiter:

- "Yes, I'll take it!"
- "No, I decline."
- "Yes, but let's negotiate.

If you feel certain that the offer meets most of your important criteria, you can call the recruiter and verbally accept the offer. If you feel certain that the job has too many factors that are inconsistent with your needs, you can decline the offer. However, before completely closing the door on the offer, it's highly recommended that you ask yourself the question, "What would it take to make it an acceptable offer?" Likewise, before calling back and saying yes, ask yourself, "What would it take to make the offer even more appealing?"

Don't shy away from negotiating. As long as you handle it in a positive and professional way, negotiating shows that you believe in yourself and you have a lot to offer. Remember that you were selected as their top candidate. Also, you typically have a greater opportunity to negotiate before you begin working than after.

The Art of Negotiating an Offer

The first question to answer is, "What is the offer lacking" or "What would I like to add?" Again, you must go back to your values and determine what's most important to you. The next question to answer is "What's negotiable?" Generally, the items that are more commonly negotiable include salary, moving expenses, and signing bonuses. Signing bonuses occur more for experienced professionals and in larger corporations. Many items like health insurance, vacation days, tuition reimbursement, and child care are standard to avoid dissention among employees. Also, it gets too complex to alter group rates or plans, such as group health insurance. However, regarding health care, you can negotiate some aspects like *when* the health insurance benefit takes effect. Once you figure out what you want and how you want the offer to improve, you must start building an argument for negotiating.

Building Your Argument

When you're considering whether or not to negotiate, you first have to decide if you have a strong enough case to argue your point. Maybe the company is offering a salary that's well above the average for your position and industry. Maybe the signing bonus or lack thereof is common or appropriate for the industry.

First, research the field and determine the average salary range and signing bonus for your position and industry. Talk to other contacts in the field who may be able to inform you on average salaries and on whether or not signing bonuses are common. Use resources that include salary figures. For example, the National Association of Colleges and Employers (NACE) produces the *Salary Survey* four times per year. The *Salary Survey* includes starting salary offers made to new graduates that received a bachelor's or master's degree. It breaks the salaries down by academic curriculum, functional area, and type of employer. The Bureau of Labor Statistics is another source for finding salary information. Visit their Web page at http://stats.bls.gov:80/datahome.htm to research relevant salaries.

Once you figure out the average salary for your position and industry, determine how that average may increase or decrease depending on your future cost of living. One of the best ways to determine this is by visiting one of the travel/moving sites on the Internet, such as www.homefair.com. Homefair.com includes *The Salary Calculator* that determines the cost-of-living differences among hundreds of U.S. and international cities.

Next, you should identify your strongest assets that you'll bring to the job and the company and include these in with your argument. In addition, determine your moving and relocation costs. If they want you to start quickly, you may have problems selling your house or getting out of your apartment lease. You may need money up front to help you purchase a house or pay for the security deposit of an apartment. If you're moving long distance, the moving costs will be substantial. Determine your moving and relocation costs, and throw those into the negotiating mix.

FYI

A recruiter once told me that they decided to retract their verbal offer due to the unprofessional and abrupt approach that a particular candidate used to negotiate an offer. The candidate used statements such as, "Your offer is insulting," and, "It's ridiculous that we are even having this conversation— aren't I worth more than this?"

Based on the information you gathered, you must determine if you have a case to argue. You may have found that the salary offer is actually better than you thought, due to your research. On the other hand, you may have uncovered the information you need to present a strong argument for more money, a greater signing bonus, or assistance with moving costs.

Making Your Argument: It's Time to Negotiate

Now that you have the information needed to make a sound argument, you can go back to the recruiter and begin the negotiations. Remember that the recruiter will soon be a co-worker, so conduct yourself in a positive and professional manner. Playing serious hardball may not be the best way to begin your new job. Also, realize that nothing's in writing at this point. If you come across exceptionally strong, they can always pull back and retract the offer.

A good way to begin the negotiating call is by reiterating your interest in the position and company. Once you do that, explain the situation and state your argument. Below is an example of a negotiating call.

Candidate: Hi, Jane, it's Anita Job. How are you doing today? Good. Jane, I wanted to get back to you about the job offer. I'm very excited about this opportunity and want to make it work. There are just a few items regarding the offer that I'd like to discuss with you.

The first item is salary. Over the past few days, I've done some research and talked with some of my colleagues in the field. Nationwide, the average salary appears to be a few thousand dollars higher than what you offered. Also, the cost of living for X-city is 7 percent higher than the national average cost of living. Finally, I feel that my ten years of experience and the contacts I've developed will prove to be major assets for your company. Because of this, I believe that a fair starting salary would be $38,000.

Finally, I figured out my moving costs. They come out to be roughly $3,500. I realize you don't give hiring bonuses, but I hope that you provide financial assistance to new employees who must relocate. Jane, I'll feel good about accepting an offer of $38,000 and $3,500 up front for moving expenses.

Having done research adds weight to your argument, as illustrated in this example. Realize that the above example is just one approach to negotiating. You must find the approach and wording that's comfortable and natural for you.

Once the final offer has been made and you're comfortable accepting it, make sure to ask when you'll receive the official offer in writing. YOU MUST GET THE OFFER IN WRITING!

When There Are Multiple Offers and Potential Offers

Having multiple offers is a great "problem" to have! You must first decide which offer is more appealing to you. Then determine if the less appealing offer could be sweetened to a point that would make it your top choice. Once you're ready to negotiate, make sure to include the fact that you have another offer. Having other offers gives you more arguing power, especially when the company really wants you. They don't want a competitor snatching you up.

If you interviewed for a position that you really liked, but the search is still going on, you can ask for an extension from the company that made you an offer. Just realize that you take the risk of being perceived as "waiting for something better." It's a delicate issue that greatly depends on your situation. For example, if you're in a situation where you really need a job, the risk of asking for an extension is greater. If you're not so desperate, and you really want to see whether or not you get an offer from the other company, then the risk isn't so great. When you ask for an extension, be prepared for the possibility of them declining your request. You should decide on what you'd say if they decline your request and require an answer immediately. Also, if you're forced to give an answer by a certain date, contact the other company and explain the situation you're in. Ask them if they can indicate what your chances of getting an offer would be. Again, it doesn't hurt for the other company to know that you have another offer on the table.

It's Ultimately Your Decision

Going to your closest friends, family members, mentors, and career counselors for their support and advice is usually very helpful. Realize, though, that, ultimately, you're the final judge. You'll be the one waking up every day and putting in a full day's work. Also, let your intuition in on the decision. Your gut and heart usually see the answer more clearly than your mind does!

Learning From and Getting Past Rejections

The two most important things to do when you receive a rejection is to learn from it and move on. If the recruiter calls you to tell you that they chose someone else, be polite and professional. Most importantly, ask them if there was something that you could have done differently during the interview. Explain to the recruiter that you'll be interviewing again soon, and it would be very helpful to receive some honest feedback. If the recruiter sends a letter rather than calling, make sure to call and request feedback.

Once you learned from it, move on! It wasn't meant to be. Believe in fate. Live by the old saying, "When the going gets tough, the tough get going." The biggest test of character is what you do when you face adversity. The biggest test of your job search is how you handle rejections.

THE WHOLE IN ONE

- Being forced to evaluate and negotiate job offers is a nice problem to have. You essentially have three options: accept the job offer as it stands, reject the offer, or negotiate the offer.

- The first step is understanding the offer. You must closely review the benefits package, because it usually is worth 30 percent of your salary.

- Assess the offer based on your values or what's most important to you in an offer.

- If you decide to negotiate, you should conduct research to determine how the salary compares to other similar jobs.

- Once you've built up your negotiating argument, present it in a positive and professional way. You don't want to start off on the wrong foot.

- The two most important factors to consider when receiving rejections are to learn from them and quickly get past them. Ask the interviewer for feedback on how you presented yourself. Once you've learned from the experience, forget about it and move on.

ASSIGNMENT

If you haven't already, complete the last strategy under Goal 5 of your Personal Job Search Trainer.

Part V

Succeeding on the Job

Chapter 16

Success on the Job and in Your Career

GET THE SCOOP ON . . .

- Avoiding petty office games
- Confronting your co-workers
- Attitude adjustments that affect your success
- Little extras that are a big hit
- Networking
- Lifelong learning and technical training
- Embracing diversity vs. tolerating it
- Being one job ahead
- Pursuing your big goals sooner than later
- On a personal note . . . May your work enrich your life!

THE 10 CAREER COMMANDMENTS

You did it! You found and landed the perfect job. Now you want to do everything you can to keep the perfect job! Actually, you want to do much more than that. You want to be a big success on the job and, ultimately, in your career. Following are the 10 Career Commandments that will lead you on a path to success and accomplishment. The first five career commandments relate more directly to success on the job, while the last five career commandments relate more generally to success in your overall career. However, since your career consists of the various jobs you have held, success on the job leads to success in your career—the two are interconnected.

The 1st Career Commandment: Thou Shall Respect Thy Co-Worker

There are many mature, positive, first-class people that work in our society. Unfortunately, there are also many insecure, jealous, "small" people out there who search hard for even the slightest flaw in co-workers and then take that flaw to the adult version of "show and tell" with anyone in the office who's willing to listen, especially management.

Be prepared, because sooner or later you'll be tested. The small people will gradually and delicately start checking you out to see if you're interested in playing. They'll make a subtle remark about a co-worker or boss and see how you react. It's tempting to want to play, because you're the new kid on the block and you're hoping to make some friends and be accepted. It's also human nature to be curious.

Nipping it in the bud right away is the best advice I can give you. Don't even go there for a minute. By listening attentively to the small people, even without saying a word, you're encouraging their behavior. You don't have to be hasty about it. Just be so neutrally indifferent that the small people won't want to pick you to be on their team. You're lack of interest will keep you from being drafted.

If the small people don't take the hint, you may have to approach them nicely and confront the issue. Just say that you're new here and you're trying to give everyone the benefit of the doubt by forming your own impressions.

The 2nd Career Commandment: Thou Shall Confront

Two of the biggest working-relationship diseases are avoiding confrontation and not knowing how to properly confront someone. A negative connotation surrounds the term confrontation, so most workers view confrontations as negative and, therefore, usually try hard to avoid them. Avoiding confrontation is not healthy. When people have a concern or an issue regarding the way you're doing something, wouldn't you rather hear it from them rather than allow that concern to build up and turn into resentment? Wouldn't you have more respect for those people if they talked to you about the concern rather than talking to others about it?

Where to Confront

Part of being a mature professional is having the guts to approach a co-worker, supervisor, or supervisee and confront them with issues you have. The next part of being a mature professional deals with *where* you confront them. Always confront co-workers individually, behind closed doors. Too many people bring up issues and concerns directed at a co-worker during staff meetings or other group sessions. Don't hide behind the group to state your concern. All that this does is get everybody feeling awkward and the co-worker who's been singled out feeling embarrassed and angry. Nobody likes to be put on the spot and embarrassed in front of colleagues.

How to Confront

There's an art to positive confrontation. It involves tact and diplomacy. Some people have greater insecurities than others, causing a higher sensitivity to criticism and confrontation. You must respect those varying levels of insecurity and not be naïve enough to think that everyone else should feel the way you do. How many times have you heard people say, "You shouldn't get upset over that!" or "Don't let that bother you"? Did you ever try telling your heart to stop feeling a certain way? Is your mind ever successful in convincing your heart to stop feeling a certain way? Respect the unique feelings of others!

When you confront someone, give him the benefit of the doubt. Tell him that you're seeing things a certain way, and ask him if you may be seeing things unclearly or missing something. View the untactful confrontation example, followed by the tactful confrontation example, to see how a different approach or style can make all the difference.

The Untactful Confrontation

(Joe, Mary's manager, is doing the confronting)

> Mary, I've been meaning to tell you, the way you dealt with that customer's complaint earlier was terrible. You let that guy walk right over you! And he was complaining for about 15 minutes straight! You had other customers rolling their eyes because you couldn't get rid of that jerk.

The Tactful Confrontation

> Mary, I've been wanting to talk to you about our troubled customer who came in earlier today. Do you have a minute? Good. Boy, that guy seemed to be growling at the world. It was a tough situation to handle. We want to let the customer vent and feel as though they've been heard. You did a good job of that. My only concern was how vocal he was and how long he complained. I noticed some of the other customers getting a little frustrated. Did you notice that, too? What do you think we can do about it the next time this happens?

Notice how during the untactful example, the manager, Joe, kept pointing the finger at Mary, implying "you should have done this, and you should have done that." During the tactful example, Joe used the term "we" more often, taking a team approach. Also, the untactful Joe didn't give Mary any benefit of the doubt. He didn't bring her in on the conversation or issue. The tactful Joe asked for Mary's input on how to make the situation better. He also showed much more tact and sympathy by stating that it was a tough situation.

Be Open to Being Confronted—It's a Two-Way Street!

It's important that you're not hypocritical regarding confrontation. If you dish it out, you have to be able to take it, as long as the co-worker confronts you tactfully. Getting defensive when someone confronts you shows weakness. It also deters people from confronting you in the future.

A Slip of the Tongue Can Last a Lifetime

Be cautious of what you say during times when you're angry with co-workers. Choosing inappropriate words or taking an untactful approach to confrontation can ruin relationships. The story below drives this point home.

The Fence

There once was a little boy who had a bad temper. His father gave him a bag of nails and told him that every time he lost his temper, he must hammer a nail into the back of the fence.

The first day, the boy had driven 37 nails into the fence. Over the next few weeks, as he learned to control his anger, the number of nails hammered daily gradually dwindled down. He discovered it was easier to hold his temper than to drive those nails into the fence.

Finally, the day came when the boy didn't lose his temper at all. He told his father about it, and the father suggested that the boy now pull out one nail for each day that he was able to hold his temper.

The days passed and the young boy was finally able to tell his father that all the nails were gone. The father took his son by the hand and led him to the fence. He said, "You have done well, my son, but look at the holes in the fence. The fence will never be the same. When you say things in anger, they leave a scar just like this one. You can put a knife in a man and draw it out. It won't matter how many times you say I'm sorry, the wound is still there. A verbal wound is as bad as a physical one.

—Author unknown

The 3rd Career Commandment: Thou Shall Have a Positive Attitude

Attitude is everything. If you have a positive attitude, you can accomplish many things. The following saying illustrates the impact that your attitude can have on life.

If you think you are beaten, you are;

If you think you dare not, you don't;

If you like to win, but you think you can't,

It is almost certain you won't.

If you think you'll lose, you've lost,

For out of the world we find

Success begins with a person's will;

It's all in the state of mind.

If you think you are outclassed, you are;

You've got to think high to rise.

You've got to be sure of yourself before

You can even win a prize.

Life's battles don't always go

To the stronger or faster man,

But sooner or later, the person who wins

Is the person who thinks, "I can!"

—Author unknown

Building Positive Working Relationships

A positive attitude is the most important factor in building strong working relationships. People like to be around others who are positive. Be quick to compliment co-workers when they do a good job, and be supportive when they need your help. At the same time, be genuine. Don't try to be somebody you're not. People can see through a phony.

New on the Job

When you first begin working at an organization, don't try to make your mark right off the bat. New employees tend to want to prove themselves so fast that they come across as wanting to change the way of the company. Be sensitive to the fact that your co-workers spent years building the company to what it currently is. Don't bulldoze your way in. During meetings, listen and observe more frequently than you offer advice and new ideas. Be patient. Your time will come.

Exude Quiet Confidence

To build respect among co-workers and your supervisor, you must have a confident attitude—just don't come across as being too cocky. It's important to be competitive, but be competitive with yourself and not others. Never initiate conversations about yourself. It makes you appear self-centered and conceited. Ask how others are doing, and show interest in their work. Having confidence in yourself is a great thing, but you don't need to let the world know about it!

The 4th Career Commandment: Thou Shall Go the Extra Mile

Go above and beyond what's expected of you. It's the little extras that separate successful professionals from average professionals. First and

> **Guidance**
>
> *The new hire should take some time and get to know how the organization works. Be observant of others around you and how they act/behave and use your best judgement to adapt into the department.*
> —Research Triangle Institute

foremost, do your job well. Fulfill your responsibilities as outlined in your job description. In addition, volunteer to take on or help out with additional projects. If your supervisor or a senior co-worker is working on an important project, see if you can help out in some way. Determine the gaps or needs of the organization, and offer your time and ideas in meeting those needs.

Seek Out Innovative Ideas in the Field

Read the most current professional journal articles or trade publications, and identify those new ideas that your organization is not taking advantage of. Present these new ideas to your supervisor or team during staff meetings. Attend national and regional conferences and conventions to learn about cutting-edge initiatives. Put together a mini-proposal, incorporating the new strategies and ideas. Present the proposal to your supervisor and other appropriate people. As stated previously, you don't necessarily want to do this during your first week of work. Also, be selective in choosing the more appropriate times and places to present your ideas.

The 5th Career Commandment: Thou Shall Prioritize and Organize

It's a rat race out there. Being busy has taken on a whole new meaning. You don't ask people if they're busy any longer—it's a given. With all of your daily responsibilities, projects, reports, meetings, committee involvement, and putting out unexpected fires, you either prioritize or die. The key to prioritizing your tasks is asking yourself the following two-part question: "What will suffer the most if I don't get it done, and who will notice if it's not done?" For example, let's say that you have to choose between getting a mini-report to a top client who requested it by tomorrow or filing the heaping pile of documents sitting by the file cabinet. If you're smart, you'd temporarily hide the heaping pile in a drawer and work on getting the report to your client. Nobody will notice your heaping pile, but someone important will notice if you don't get the report done.

Know What Your Boss Wants from You

Another important aspect of prioritizing tasks is being extremely clear about what your boss expects of you. If it's not obvious which responsibilities your boss values most, ask her! This is especially important when you first begin working with your boss. Don't just assume you know what's important to your boss. Here are two good questions to ask your boss early on.

- What do you see as the most important responsibilities as related to the company's mission and goals?
- A year from now, what would you like to see accomplished from my area of responsibilities?

Stay Organized

It's essential that you stay organized for two reasons. First, people need information yesterday, so you must be able to quickly find it and access it. Second, your overall professional image is significantly affected by how organized you appear. Today, there's more than just organizing a filing cabinet. You must keep your computer files as organized as your paper files. Frequently, a co-worker or client will ask you for a report or handout that you've produced. You may need to make a few minor changes to it before you send it off to them. If your computer files are organized, you'll be able to quickly find the document, make the changes, and distribute it in a timely fashion. The other major system that you'll need to organize is your e-mail filing system. Some of the e-mails you'll receive from co-workers and clients are important documents to save and store for tracking or documentation purposes. Most e-mail systems include a file-managing system that is easy for you to set up and maintain. Staying organized takes time, but in the long run, you end up saving time and earning more respect among your peers and clients.

The 6th Career Commandment: Thou Shall Network

Remember, close to 80 percent of all jobs are obtained through some form of networking. Since it's projected you'll change jobs seven or more times during your lifetime, it's critical for you to develop and maintain a sizable list of contacts to call on when those career changes occur. Networking is the best way to explore future opportunities and build up your contact base all at once. Through networking, you not only build and maintain contacts in the field, but you can also learn about career trends and opportunities.

Build New Contacts

The bottom line is to get out there and build contacts! Attend regional and national conferences, conventions, and trade shows. Join professional/ trade associations, and become active on their committees. Send in proposals to present at conferences. Presenting at conferences is a great way to become noticed in the field. Co-author or author a journal article or book related to your field.

Don't Burn Bridges—Maintain Current Contacts

In addition to building contacts, you need to maintain the ones you already have. E-mail is a great tool for keeping in touch. In one click of the mouse, you can forward jokes, stories, and quotes to a long list of your contacts. Just make sure you don't offend anyone with certain jokes. You can also attach pictures of your dog and your newborn child to e-mails or send them electronic holiday cards. Periodically, e-mail your contacts individually to see how they're doing and to keep up with their careers.

The 7th Career Commandment: Thou Shall Learn Forever

Continuous, life-long learning is essential for long-term success. Just as you shouldn't be content to stay in your current job forever, you shouldn't be content to just stick with what you know and with the skills you have. Organizations are constantly looking for new and more efficient ways of doing business. It's crucial that you stay current with the field regarding new approaches, techniques, theories, technology, and other innovations.

Embrace Technology

When you talk about life-long learning, you almost always include technology. Like it or not, we're in the "Technology Age" or "Information Age," and it affects everything we do, especially work. There's no turning back, so welcome technology and jump on the virtual train. There are two main categories of technology that you must continually learn about and utilize to survive: field-specific technology and work-general technology.

Field-Specific Technology

Field-specific technology includes equipment, software, or systems that you must be able to use in order to be successful in your field. For example, in the field of accounting, if you don't keep up with the best spreadsheet software on the market, your productivity will suffer and you'll eventually be replaced by someone who's more technologically up to date. Likewise, many advertising professionals must be trained on the best graphic design software in order to create top-quality graphics. Determine the current field-specific technology that's tops in your field, and learn everything you can about it.

Work-General Technology

In addition to any field-specific technology, you need to stay current with the best and newest technology used in everyday business across all career fields. You need to learn how to use new word-processing software for developing, producing, and distributing memos, letters, reports, and many other types of documents. You'll likely need to know how to create, or at least access, a database that stores information related to your work. Also, due to the growing need for accountability and generating outcomes, you may have to use spreadsheet software to compute information and submit quantitative reports.

Scheduling your meetings and organizing your to-do lists has also jumped on the computer bandwagon. Many organizations use an electronic scheduling system that's networked so you can schedule meetings from anywhere in the world. Finally, you must realize that learning all the new ways to correspond via e-mail and access information through the Internet will also be a life-long process.

If what the technology buffs are saying is true, we ain't seen nothin' yet! If you don't embrace technology now, you'll gradually feel like a foreigner who can't speak the language. Don't be an outsider looking in!

The 8th Career Commandment: Thou Shall Embrace Diversity

The workforce will continue to diversify in the 21st century. Asian Americans, Hispanic Americans, and African Americans will continue to enter the workforce at higher rates than white workers do. But diversity in the workplace embodies more than just race and ethnicity. Diversity in the workplace also includes introverts and extroverts, technical and non-technical workers, and dreamers and doers. In addition, the workplace consists of those who are passive and assertive, funny and serious, and sensitive and abrupt. When you think about workplace diversity, think about more than just skin color and gender—think about *all* types of differences among people.

Embracing Diversity vs. Tolerating Diversity

During the past few decades of the 20th century, the American worker has learned the importance of tolerating diversity. Saying the wrong things and demonstrating ignorance costs workers their jobs and sometimes their careers. So tolerating differences among co-workers became a survival technique.

Our diverse workforce in the 21st century emphasizes teamwork as a premium, and organizations and co-workers must take their attitude toward diversity to a higher level. It should no longer be acceptable for you to just tolerate diversity—you must embrace diversity! When you *tolerate* diversity, you *put up with* differences among people. When you *embrace* diversity, you *respect and appreciate* differences among people.

21st-Century Work Teams and Diversity

The strongest teams, whether they're organizational teams or smaller project teams, consist of members that embrace diversity. The weaker teams are those that are still holding onto tolerating diversity. Leaders must emphasize the benefits of having diverse styles and perspectives among team members.

As a team member, you must realize that these different styles compliment each other, not conflict with each other. They enhance the team, not weaken it. A basketball team comprised of five tall centers and no small, quick guards won't be successful. Likewise, a team with all white males and no women or racial minorities will not last very long. A team with all dreamers and visionaries and no doers will result in many great ideas and very few accomplishments. A team with all practical thinkers and no creative thinkers will be unable to see the forest for the trees. Cultural and personality differences among members make teams stronger! You must embrace diversity and encourage your teammates to join you.

Finally, with the workforce becoming more and more global, diversity among organizations' customers and clients will increase. This isn't a trend that's going to go away. Therefore, organizations need a wide diversity of employees to more effectively serve their diverse client base.

The 9th Career Commandment: Thou Shall Stay One Job Ahead

Keep in mind that you're projected to change jobs at least seven times in your lifetime—not necessarily by choice, either. You always have to be thinking one job ahead. Even if you feel content in your current job, you must at least think about possible career moves in the future.

Reflect on Your Interests and Goals

Engage in an ongoing process of self-assessment. Analyze your professional situation to determine the aspects of your job that you enjoy and value most and those you'd rather do away with. Identify those areas of responsibility that you excel in and those that cause you to struggle. Your goal should be to take on new responsibilities or move to new positions that enable you to do more of the things you enjoy doing and less of the things you don't enjoy. Don't become one of the many workers who wait for 5:00 p.m. and weekends. Find the professional situation that is inspiring. As Ernest Newman said, "The great composer does not set to work because he is inspired, but becomes inspired because he is working."

Keep Your Resume Current

Keep your resume updated at all times. You never know when that one contact tries to recruit you for a dream job! Get in the habit of revising your resume as you engage in new responsibilities, take on new projects, or gain new accomplishments. It's easier to describe your experiences and accomplishments when they're fresh in your mind.

Peek at Job Openings—Even When You're Content

Get your hands on the printed or Internet publications listing openings in your field and review those positions for which you'd be qualified. It's healthy to look around and get a feel for the types of jobs that are in demand. Remember, though, that the grass is always greener on the other side of the fence, especially on bad days. If you decide to explore other opportunities, make sure they're worth it. Find out as much as you can about the opportunity from personal contacts or Web page research

FYI

Looking at other job opportunities was once perceived as being disloyal to your company. Today, it's just a smart thing to do. Many workers today love their job but still keep an eye on other career opportunities around them. The two are not mutually exclusive.

before you explore any further. You don't want co-workers or your supervisor to question your commitment to the company unless it's absolutely necessary.

The 10th Career Commandment: Thou Shall Pursue Thy Higher Goals

It's so easy to get caught up in the daily rat race and place your *higher goals* on the back burner. Higher goals could include publishing an article, completing an advanced degree, authoring a book, presenting at a conference, developing a new product, or starting your own business. Most people are so busy in their jobs and personal lives that it becomes extremely challenging to realize any of their higher goals. Below is a sad but common example of what happens to one's higher goals over the years.

The writer that could have been . . .

- Twenty-Something: "I plan on publishing an article once I get settled in my new job."
- Thirty-Something: "Once things slow down, I want to start thinking about publishing an article."
- Forty-Something: "It's so tough to find time to write!"
- Fifty-Something: "Who has time to write articles?"
- Sixty-Something: "I wish I would have made time to publish an article."

There's No Better Time Than the Present!

If you want to realize your big goals and dreams, don't put them off! You may think that you're as busy as you can possibly be and that things will slow down once you're done with that certain project. But guess what? If you do that project well, there'll be many more coming your way. You'll find that you don't get less busy over the years. You'll be given more responsibility, more people to supervise, and more committees to serve on. You'll develop more friends and contacts, and your family will continue to grow. Move your big goals up to the front burner, and start realizing your dreams!

The following exercise is a very clever way to illustrate the importance of bringing your big goals to the forefront.

The Jar of Rocks

(© 1994 Covey Leadership Center, Inc.)

One day, an instructor was lecturing on time management to a group of business students and used an illustration those students will never forget.

As this man stood in front of the group of students, he said, "Okay, time for a quiz." He reached under the table and pulled out a one-gallon, wide-mouthed mason jar and set it on a table in front of him. Then he produced about a dozen fist-sized rocks and carefully placed them, one at a time, into the jar.

When the jar was filled to the top and no more rocks would fit inside, he asked, "Is this jar full?"

Everyone in the class said, "Yes."

Then he said, "Really?" He reached under the table and pulled out a bucket of gravel. Then he dumped some gravel in and shook the jar causing pieces of gravel to work themselves down into the spaces between the big rocks.

Then he asked the group once more, "Is the jar full?" By this time, the class was on to him. "Probably not," one of them answered.

"Good!" the speaker replied.

He reached under the table and brought out a bucket of sand. He started dumping the sand in and it went into all the spaces left between the rocks and the gravel.

Once more he asked the question, "Is this jar full?"

"No!" the class shouted.

Once again, the speaker said, "Good!" Then he grabbed a pitcher of water and began to pour it in until the jar was filled to the brim. Then he looked up at the class and asked, "What is the point of this illustration?"

One eager beaver raised his hand and said, "The point is, no matter how full your schedule is, if you try really hard, you can always fit some more things into it!"

"No," the speaker replied, "that's not the point. The truth this illustration teaches us is this: If you don't put the big rocks in first, you'll never get them in at all."

Source: "First Things First," Stephen R. Covey, A. Roger Merrill, Rebecca Merrill. ©1994 Franklin Covey Co. Reprinted with permission. All rights reserved.

What are the "big rocks" in your life? Make sure to put them in your "big jar" sometime soon. Don't let the gravel and sand in your life keep your big rocks from entering the jar!

MAY YOUR WORK ENRICH YOUR LIFE!

About eight years ago, a young couple came to visit my wife and I regarding a business idea they wanted to get us in on. The young man started off telling a story about his father: "My father worked in the same manufacturing company for forty years, working his butt off day in and day out. He finally retired at the age of 67 but is too old to really enjoy life to the fullest. What kind of a life is that? I know I don't want to wake up one day, when I'm in my late 60s, and realize life has passed me by. I don't want to start living when I'm 67! This business idea will empower us to make enough money so that we can retire in our late 40s, and then start living it up and enjoying life!"

My wife and I couldn't relate. You see, my wife was teaching young children at the time, and I was a career counselor at a large university. We had a very different outlook on our careers than our visitors had. We were living it up and enjoying life every day! Sure, the weekends and holidays were nice, but the time that we spent on the job wasn't so bad either. I look back on that day often and am grateful to be in a profession that I can call my second home. I love coming home each day and spending time with my wife and daughter, but when the next day rolls around, I don't dread going into work. Life is way too precious to only *live it up* on weekends and holidays. You owe it to yourself to find that perfect job that will allow you to live it up each and every day of your life.

May you find that perfect job that will truly enrich your life!

THE WHOLE IN ONE

Knowing and living the 10 Career Commandments will lead you to success on the job and in your career. Following is a summary of the 10 Career Commandments.

- Avoid petty office gossip and games by remaining neutral.

- Confronting co-workers and your supervisor is a good thing to do, as long as you do it tactfully.

- A positive attitude means everything to your career.

- Going the extra mile and doing more than what's expected of you gets you promoted.

- Prioritizing your tasks and organizing the overwhelming amount of information are necessities for the 21st-century worker.

- Networking is a life-long endeavor if you want to experience long-term success.

- Learning for a lifetime and keeping up with the ever-changing technology are two requirements of the contemporary worker.

- For you and your teams to succeed in the 21st century, it's essential to embrace diversity rather than merely tolerate it.

- Even when you're content in your job, you must always explore the future and remain one job ahead.

- If you don't focus on your big goals early on in your career, you may never realize your dreams.

Personal Trainer

Personal Job Search Trainer

Job Seeker: _____

Goal Number 1

Establish My Professional Self-Profile

Strategies and Tasks   **Deadline**

Identify my top SKILLS (that I'm good at)
☐ Complete exercises 2.1 and 2.2 in Chapter 2   _____

Identify my top SKILLS (that I enjoy using)
☐ Complete exercises 2.3 and 2.4 in Chapter 2   _____

Identify my top INTERESTS (in career fields)
☐ Complete exercise 2.5 in Chapter 2   _____

Identify my top PERSONAL QUALITIES
☐ Complete exercise 2.6 in Chapter 2   _____

Identify my top VALUES
☐ Complete exercise 2.7 in Chapter 2   _____

Identify prospective OCCUPATIONS
☐ Complete the self-assessment instruments below
   (See "Self-Assessment" in Appendices A and C):   _____

   _____   _____

Complete my Professional Self-Profile
☐ Fill out the Professional Self-Profile at the end of the
   Personal Job Search Trainer   _____

Goal Number 2

Identify My Perfect Job Target

Strategies and Tasks

Time Frame
(Start Date– End Date)

Read about career fields and occupations of interest
☐ Review the following resources *(See "Exploring Careers" in Appendix A and C):*

_____   _____

_____   _____

Read about organizations of interest
(See "Researching Organizations/Employer Profiles" in Appendix A and "Researching Organizations" in Appendix C):

_____   _____

_____   _____

Talk to contacts working in career fields of interest
☐ Conduct information interviews with my contacts *(See "Mastering Information Interviews" in Chapter 11 and "Information Interview Questions" in Appendix D) :*

_____   _____

_____   _____

Observe contacts working in career fields of interest
☐ Conduct work shadowing with my contacts *(Review work shadowing in Chapter 3):*

_____   _____

_____   _____

Experience career fields of interest
☐ Complete internships or volunteer positions *(See "Internships or Cooperative (Co-op) Education" and "Volunteer Work" in Chapter 3):*

_____   _____

_____   _____

Complete my Perfect Job Target
☐ Fill out the Perfect Job Target at the end of the Personal Job Search Trainer

_____

Goal Number 3

Produce My Self-Marketing Package

Strategies and Tasks   Deadline

Develop and produce all versions of my RESUME
(See Chapters 4, 5, and 6 for information on resumes)

☐ Develop and produce my general, all-inclusive resume   _____

☐ Develop and produce field-specific resumes for the
following career fields of interest: _____

_____   _____

☐ Develop and produce my scanable resume   _____

Develop and produce all versions of my COVER LETTER
(See "Cover Letters and Portfolios" in Chapter 7)

☐ Develop and produce my general Open-Market Cover
Letter and Hidden-Market Cover Letter   _____

☐ Develop and produce field-specific cover letters for the
following career fields of interest: _____

_____   _____

Produce and obtain all REFERENCES documents
(See "References" in Chapter 7)

☐ Develop and produce my list of references.   _____
My references will be the following people:

_____   _____

_____   _____

☐ Obtain letters of recommendation from references   _____

Develop and produce my PORTFOLIO
*(See "The Portfolio: References and Other Supporting
Documents" in Chapter 7)*

☐ Develop and produce my portfolio consisting of the
following documents: _____

_____   _____

_____   _____

☐ Develop and produce a Web-based portfolio   _____

Goal Number 4

Find The Perfect Job

Strategies and Tasks

Time Frame
(Start Date– End Date)

Respond to JOB ADVERTISEMENTS
(See "Strategy 1: Responding to Job Advertisements" in Chapter 9)
☐ Respond to the job advertisements found in the following
resources *(See "Job Openings" in Appendix A and C)*:

_____   _____   _____

POST my resume online
(See "Strategy 2: Posting Your Resume . . ." in Chapter 9)
☐ Post my resume on the following Internet sites *(See "Posting
Your Resume" in Appendix A)*:

_____

Register with EMPLOYMENT SERVICES
(See "Strategy 3: Using Third-Party Employment Services" in Chapter 9)
☐ Register with the following employment services:
(See "Employment Services" in Appendix A and C):

_____

Participate in JOB FAIRS
(See "Strategy 4: Participating in Job Fairs" in Chapter 9)
☐ Participate in the following Job Fairs *(See "Job and Career Fairs"
in Appendix A)*:

_____   _____   _____

Participate in College/Alma Mater Career Programs
(See "The Best Job-Search Strategies in the Open Job Market" Chapter 9)
☐ Participate in the following programs offered by my college/
alma mater career center *(See "College Career Centers" in
Appendix A)*:

_____

Submit resumes to organizations through MASS MAILING
*(See "Contacting Organizations through Mass and Targeted Mailings" in
Chapter 10)*
☐ Mail my resume and general cover letter to a large list of organizations
in my field of interest. Use the following resources to identify organizations *(See "Researching Organizations/Employer Profiles" in Appendix A
and "Researching Organizations" in Appendix C)*:

_____   _____   _____

Engage in NETWORKING AND INFORMATION INTERVIEWING
(See Chapters 10 and 11: networking information interviews)
☐ *Arrange and conduct information interviews with the following
networking contacts (Use the "7-Step Plan for Mastering Information
Interviews" in Chapter 11)*:

_____   _____   _____

Goal Number 5

Win The Interview and Land The Perfect Job

Strategies and Tasks

Time Frame
(Start Date– End Date)

Prepare to ANSWER INTERVIEW QUESTIONS
- [ ] Complete the 20 prep tasks in Chapter 12
  (Also see list of interview questions in Appendix G) _____

Prepare for all TYPES OF INTERVIEWS
- [ ] Review the special types of interviews in Chapter 13 _____

PRACTICE INTERVIEWING
(See "Practice Makes Perfect" in Chapter 12)
- [ ] Practice interviewing using the Perfect 10 Model presented in Chapter 14 _____

COME PREPARED to all interviews
- [ ] Develop a list of questions to ask the interviewer based on researching the organization and field *(See "Powerful Questions to Ask the Interviewer" in Chapter 12)* _____

- [ ] Come professionally dressed and bring the appropriate materials to each interview *(See "Dressing Up for the Interview . . ." and "What You Should Bring . . ." in Chapter 14)* _____

NEGOTIATE offers and accept the perfect job
- [ ] Complete the steps outlined in Chapter 15 for receiving an offer _____

Professional Self-Profile

Job Seeker: _____

Top Values

_____   _____

_____   _____

_____   _____

Top Industries of Interest   **Top Personal Qualities**

Top Skills (Ability)   **Top Skills (Interests)**

Perfect Job Target

Position/Occupation

| First Choice | Second Choice | Third Choice |

Industry/Career Field

| First Choice | Second Choice | Third Choice |

Geographic Location

| First Choice | Second Choice | Third Choice |

Organization

Size: _____

Work Atmosphere: _____
_____

Management Style: _____
_____

Other Characteristics: _____
_____
_____
_____
_____
_____

Appendices

Appendix A

Job Surfing on the Internet

The major Internet sites related to job searching are provided in the following section. The sites are listed within the various parts of a job search. That way, you can quickly find those sites related to your job search needs. For example, if you wanted to post your resume on the Internet, you can go straight to the *Posting Your Resume* section that lists sites for posting your resume. Many larger Internet sites offer multiple services. Therefore, you will see the same site in more than one part. There are so many great, free, career-related Internet sites today for job seekers. I have tried to include as many as I could without overwhelming you. While all the sites listed are worth your visit, I have used two asterisks to indicate sites in each topic that I have found most useful. Have fun job surfing!

CAREER "TOUR GUIDES"

A Good Place to Start

(Links/refers you to countless career-related Internet sites and resources)

CareerSteps.com
http://www.careersteps.com/careersteps/career.htm

** Catapult
http://www.jobweb.org/catapult/catapult.htm

** EmploymentSpot
http://www.employmentspot.com

The Riley Guide
http://www.dbm.com/jobguide

CAREER AND WORKFORCE TRENDS

** America's Career Infonet
http://www.acinet.org/acinet/default.htm

Bureau of Labor Statistics
http://stats.bls.gov/

** CareerMagazine
http://www.careermag.com

Dun & Bradstreet Industry Focus
http://www.dnb.com/industry/hmenu.htm

Occupational Outlook Handbook Online
http://www.bls.gov/ocohome.htm

U.S. News Online
http://www.usnews.com

BEST CAREERS AND JOBS

Based on Job Growth, Salary, Etc.

** America's Career Infonet
http://www.acinet.org/acinet/default.htm

Bureau of Labor Statistics
http://stats.bls.gov/

EmploymentSpot
http://www.employmentspot.com

Occupational Outlook Handbook Online
http://www.bls.gov/ocohome.htm

** U.S. News Online
http://www.usnews.com

"BEST" AND BIGGEST COMPANIES

** Forbes Career Center
http://www.forbes.com/tool/toolbox/monsterboard/

** Fortune Careers
http://cgi.pathfinder.com/fortune/careers/

Fortune 500
http://cgi.pathfinder.com/fortune/fortune500/index.html

** Inc.500
http://www.inc.com/500/

Washington Post—CareerPost
http://www.washingtonpost.com/wl/home.shtml

SELF-ASSESSMENT

AOL.com
http://www.aol.com/webcenters/workplace/
jobs.asp

Bowling Green State University Assessments
http://www.bgsu.edu/offices/careers/process/
step1.html

CareerCity
http://www.careercity.com

** The Career Key
http://www2.ncsu.edu/unity/lockers/users/l/lkj/

CareerPath.com
http://new.careerpath.com/

Careers By Design—Assessment Center
(Cost Involved)
http://careers-by-design.com/
assessments_online.htm

Mapping Your Future
http://www.mapping-your-future.org/planning/

** Self-Directed Search Online (Minimal Cost)
http://www.self-directed-search.com/

Suite 101—Career Planning
http://www.suite101.com/linkcategory.cfm/1018/
2634

What Color Is Your Parachute?
http://www.jobhuntersbible.com

EXPLORING CAREER FIELDS AND OCCUPATIONS

America's Career Infonet
http://www.acinet.org/acinet/default.htm

AOL.com
http://www.aol.com/webcenters/workplace/
jobs.asp

CareerCity
http://www.careercity.com

CareerMagazine
http://www.careermag.com/

CareerPath.com
http://new.careerpath.com/

Career PlanIt
http://www.careerplanit.com

** Experience on Campus
(For College Students)
http://www.experienceonline.com/univ

** JobWeb
http://www.jobweb.org

** Occupational Outlook Handbook Online
http://www.bls.gov/ocohome.htm

The Princeton Review Online
http://www.review.com/index.cfm

VaultReports.com
http://www.vaultreports.com

** WetFeet.com
http://www.wetfeet.com

What Color Is Your Parachute?
http://www.jobhuntersbible.com

SALARY INFORMATION FOR JOBS AND INDUSTRIES

America's Career Infonet
http://www.acinet.org/acinet/default.htm

AOL.com
http://www.aol.com/webcenters/workplace/
jobs.asp

Bureau of Labor Statistics
http://stats.bls.gov/

CareerCity
http://www.careercity.com

Employment Review's Best Jobs.com
http://www.bestjobsusa.com/%7Ecandidate/
salsurvey/2000/index.asp

** Homefair.com
http://homefair.com/index.html

** JobStar California
http://jobstar.org/tools/salary/sal-surv.htm

Occupational Outlook Handbook Online
http://www.bls.gov/ocohome.htm

Wall Street Journal—Careers
http://www.careers.wsj.com

Washington Post—CareerPost
http://www.washingtonpost.com/wl/home.shtml

What Color Is Your Parachute?
http://www.jobhuntersbible.com

Yahoo!Classifieds
http://classifieds.yahoo.com/employment.html

JOB OPENINGS

Action Without Borders
http://www.idealist.org

AOL.com
http://www.aol.com/webcenters/workplace/
jobs.asp

** CareerCity
http://www.careercity.com

Career.com
http://www.career.com/

CareerMagazine
http://www.careermag.com

Career Mosaic
http://www.careermosaic.com

Career Path
http://www.careerpath.com

Career Site.com
http://www.careersite.com/

College Grad Job Hunter
http://www.collegegrad.com

collegerecruiter.com
http://www.collegerecruiter.com

Direct Marketing World
http://www.dmworld.com/jobcenter/jobs.html

Employment Guide's Career Web
http://www.cweb.com

Employment Review's Best Jobs.com
http://www.bestjobsusa.com/%7Ecandidate/
salsurvey/2000/index.asp

Excite
http://www.excite.com (Click on "Careers")

Forbes Career Center
http://www.forbes.com/tool/toolbox/
monsterboard/

Fortune Careers
http://cgi.pathfinder.com/fortune/careers/

HeadHunter.Net
http://www.headhunter.net/

** hotjobs.com
http://hotjobs.com

The Internet Job Source
http://www.statejobs.com

JobDirect.com (For College Students)
http://www.jobdirect.com

jobfind.com
http://www.jobfind.com

job-hunt.org
http://www.job-hunt.org

JobOptions
http://www.joboptions.com

jobs.com (For College Students)
http://www.jobs.com

** Job Source Network
http://www.jobsourcenetwork.com

** JOBTRAK (For College Students)
http://www.jobtrak.com

** JobWeb
http://www.jobweb.org

** Monster.com
http://www.monster.com

NationJob Network
http://www.nationjob.com/new.html

nettemps.com
http://www.nettemps.com

VaultReports.com
http://www.vaultreports.com

Wall Street Journal—Careers
http://www.careers.wsj.com

Washington Post—CareerPost
http://www.washingtonpost.com/wl/home.shtml

WetFeet.com
http://www.wetfeet.com

Yahoo!Classifieds
http://classifieds.yahoo.com/employment.html

POSTING YOUR RESUME

AOL.com
http://www.aol.com/webcenters/workplace/
jobs.asp

CareerCity
http://www.careercity.com

** Career.com
http://www.career.com/

CareerMagazine
http://www.careermag.com

** Career Mosaic
http://www.careermosaic.com

Career Path
http://www.careerpath.com

** Career Site.com
http://www.careersite.com/

collegerecruiter.com
http://www.collegerecruiter.com

Direct Marketing World
http://www.dmworld.com/jobcenter/jobs.html

Employment Guide's Career Web
http://www.cweb.com

Employment Review's Best Jobs.com
http://www.bestjobsusa.com/%7Ecandidate/
    salsurvey/2000/index.asp

Excite
http://www.excite.com (Click on "Careers")

Forbes Career Center
http://www.forbes.com/tool/toolbox/
    monsterboard/

Fortune Careers
http://cgi.pathfinder.com/fortune/careers/

HeadHunter.Net
http://www.headhunter.net/

** hotjobs.comhttp://hotjobs.com

jobfind.com
http://www.jobfind.com

JobOptions
http://www.joboptions.com

jobs.com (For College Students)
http://www.jobs.com

Job Source Network
http://www.jobsourcenetwork.com

** JOBTRAK (For College Students)
http://www.jobtrak.com

** Monster.com
http://www.monster.com

** NationJob Network
http://www.nationjob.com/new.html

nettemps.com
http://www.nettemps.com

RESEARCHING ORGANIZATIONS/ EMPLOYER PROFILES

AOL.com
http://www.aol.com/webcenters/workplace/
    jobs.asp

CareerCity
http://www.careercity.com

** Career.com
http://www.career.com/

CareerMagazine
http://www.careermag.com

Career Mosaic
http://www.careermosaic.com

Career Path
http://www.careerpath.com

Career Site.com
http://www.careersite.com/

College Grad Job Hunter
http://www.collegegrad.com

Employment Guide's Career Web
http://www.cweb.com

Employment Review's Best Jobs.com
http://www.bestjobsusa.com/%7Ecandidate/
    salsurvey/2000/index.asp

excite
http://www.excite.com (Click on "Careers")

Forbes Career Center
http://www.forbes.com/tool/toolbox/monsterboard/

Fortune Careers
http://cgi.pathfinder.com/fortune/careers/

HeadHunter.Net
http://www.headhunter.net/

** Hoovers Online
http://hoovweb.hoovers.com/

The Internet Job Source
http://www.statejobs.com

jobfind.com
http://www.jobfind.com

job-hunt.org
http://www.job-hunt.org

JobOptions
http://www.joboptions.com

jobs.com (For College Students)
http://www.jobs.com

Job Source Network
http://www.jobsourcenetwork.com

** JobWeb
http://www.jobweb.org

Monster.com
http://www.monster.com

NationJob Network
http://www.nationjob.com/new.html

nettemps.com
http://www.nettemps.com

VaultReports.com
http://www.vaultreports.com

Washington Post—CareerPost
http://www.washingtonpost.com/wl/home.shtml

Yahoo!Classifieds
http://classifieds.yahoo.com/employment.html

EMPLOYMENT SERVICES
** Catapult Headhunters, Search Firms, and Temp Agencies
http://www.jobweb.org/catapult/jsrchfrm.htm

** job-hunt.org
http://www.job-hunt.org

Job Source Network
http://www.jobsourcenetwork.com

** National Association of Personnel Services
http://napsweb.org

** National Association of Temporary and Staffing Services
http://www.natss.org

Wall Street Journal—Careers
http://www.careers.wsj.com

Yahoo Employment Section
http://employment.yahoo.com

JOB AND CAREER FAIRS
CareerCity
http://www.careercity.com

** CareerFairs.com
http://www.careerfairs.com

CareerMagazine
http://www.careermag.com

Career Mosaic
http://www.careermosaic.com

** CFG's Map of Fairs
http://www.cfg-inc.com/mapfairs.htm

Employment Review's Best Jobs.com
http://www.bestjobsusa.com/%7Ecandidate/salsurvey/2000/index.asp

jobfind.com
http://www.jobfind.com

jobs.com (For College Students)
http://www.jobs.com

Job Source Network
http://www.jobsourcenetwork.com

** JobWeb
http://www.jobweb.org

COLLEGE CAREER CENTERS
Job Source Network
http://www.jobsourcenetwork.com

JobWeb
http://www.jobweb.org

Field-Specific Job Surfing

The Internet sites in this section are ones relating to a particular career field. Find the career field heading that best matches your interests and search away. Near the end of this appendix are lists of Internet sites related to graduate school and internships. If you are considering going to graduate school or pursuing internships, these sites will be worth your while!

CAREER SITES BY FIELD
From Elon College Career Center Web Page (http://www.elon.edu)

Accounting
American Institute of Certified Public Accountants
http://www.aicpa.org

Arthur Andersen
http://www.arthurandersen.com

Business Job Finder—Accounting
http://www.careers-in-business.com

Deloitte & Touche
http://www.dttus.com

Ernst & Young
http://www.ey.com

KPMG
http://www.us.kpmg.com

PriceWaterhouseCoopers
http://www.pwcglobal.com

Art and Entertainment
Americans for the Arts
http://www.artsusa.org

ArtJob.com
http://www.artjob.com

ArtSource
http://www.ilpi.com/artsource/artsourcehome.html

The Hollywood Mall
http://www.hollywoodmall.com

Telefilm South
http://www.telefilm-south.com

Business
Business Job Finder via Ohio State
http://www.careers-in-business.com

Catapult—Business Sites
http://www.jobweb.org/catapult/emplyer.htm

Elon College MBA Program
http://www.elon.edu/graduate/mba/

Job Safari
http://www.jobsafari.com/index.html

NationJob Network
http://www.nationjob.com/new.html

VaultReports.com
http://www.vaultreports.com

Wall Street Journal Interactive
http://careers.wsj.com

Communications
AJR Newslink
http://ajr.newslink.org/joblink

Avalanche of Jobs for Writers, Editors, and Copywriters
http://www.sunoasis.com

Copy Editor
http://www.copyeditor.com

Editor & Publisher Interactive
http://www.mediainfo.com

JAWS Job Bank
http://www.jaws.org/jobs.shtml

Macmillan Publishers Ltd
http://www.macmillan.com

National Association of Broadcasters
http://www.nab.org

Telefilm South
http://www.telefilm-south.com

TV Jobs
http://www.tvjobs.com

Zap2it.com
http://tv.zap2it.com

Computer Science

DataMasters
http://www.datamasters.com

Developers. Net
http://www.developers.net

Education

Education World
http://www.education-world.com

Elon College M.Ed. Program
http://www.elon.edu/graduate/med/

JobWeb's Database of US School Districts
http://www.jobweb.org/search/schools

Teacher Links via University of Delaware
http://www.udel.edu/CSC/teachers.html

Teachers @ Work—National Educators Employment Network
http://www.teachersatwork.com

Teachers.Net
http://www.teachers.net

Environmental Science

The Environmental Careers Organization
http://www.eco.org

Enviromental Jobs and Careers
http://www.ejobs.org

Sierra Club
http://www.sierraclub.org

The Student Conservation Association, Inc
http://www.sca-inc.org

Government/Political Science

American Political Science Association
http://www.apsanet.org

Federal Jobs
http://www.fedworld.gov/jobs/jobsearch.html

Federal Law Enforcement Career Resources
http://www.concentric.net/~extraord/law.htm

HRS Federal Job Search
http://www.hrsjobs.com

The Internet Job Source
http://www.statejobs.com

Job Source Network
http://www.jobSourceNetwork.com

Official Federal Government Web Sites
http://www.lcweb.loc.gov/global/executive/
  fed.html

USA Jobs
http://www.usajobs.opm.gov

History

Yahoo's History Links
http://dir.yahoo.com/Arts/Humanities/History

Health, Medical, and Physical Education

American Alliance for Health, Physical Education, Recreation and Dance
http://www.aahperd.org

American College of Sports Medicine
http://www.acsm.org

American Physical Therapy Association
http://www.apta.org

America's HealthCareSource
http://www.healthcaresource.com

Elon College Master of Physical Therapy Program
http://www.elon.edu/physther/index.htm

Healthcare Employment Links
http://www.pohly.com/links.shtml

Monster Healthcare Links
http://healthcare.monster.com/links

National Athletics Trainers Association
http://www.nata.org

National Strength and Conditioning Association
http://www.nsca-lift.org

Online Sports Career Center
http://www.onlinesports.com/pages/
  CareerCenter.html

Human and Social Services/Nonprofit

About.com
http://nonprofit.miningco.com/msubjob.htm

Action Without Borders
http://www.idealist.org

Non-Profit Career Network
http://www.nonprofitcareer.com

Peace Corps
http://www.peacecorps.gov

The Riley Guide—Non-profits and Social Sciences
http://www.dbm.com/jobguide/social.html

The Socioweb
http://www.socioweb.com/~markbl/socioweb

Yahoo's Sociology Links
http://dir.yahoo.com/social_science/sociology

International

Asia-Net
http://www.asia-net.com

CareerMosaic International Gateway
http://www.careermosaic.com/cm/gateway

Employment Opportunities in Australia
http://www.employment.com.au

EmploymentSpot
http://www.employmentspot.com

Job Source Network
http://www.jobSourceNetwork.com

JobWeb—International Resources
http://www.jobweb.org/catapult/interntl.htm

Monster.com
http://international.monster.com

Overseas Jobs Express
http://www.overseasjobs.com

Oxford University Language Centre
http://info.ox.ac.uk/departments/langcentre

The Human Languages Page
http://www.june29.com/HLP

Washington Post
http://www.washingtonpost.com/wp-adv/
classifieds/careerpost/front.htm

Math

E-Math
http://www.ams.org

Mathematical Association of America Online
http://www.maa.org

Philosophy

EpistemeLinks.com
http://www.epistemelinks.com

Psychology

American Psychological Association
(The largest scientific and professional organization representing psychology in the US.)
http://www.apa.org

Online Psychology Career Center from Wesleyan University
http://www.socialpsychology.org

Sciences

The American Institute of Biological Sciences
http://www.aibs.org/core/index.html

Chemistry Web Index
http://dir.yahoo.com/science/chemistry

Science Online
http://www.scienceonline.org

OTHER INTERNET SITES CATEGORIZED BY FIELD

Catapult: Employment Services by Field
http://www.jobweb.org/catapult/jfield.htm

Galaxy
http://galaxy.einet.net/galaxy/Business-and-
Commerce.html

GRADUATE SCHOOL SITES

American Library Association
http://www.ala.org

CollegeNet
http://www.collegenet.com

The Elon College Prelaw Program-Links
http://www.elon.edu/pre-law

FastWeb
http://www.fastweb.com

FinAid
http://www.finaid.com

GMAT
http://www.gmat.org

GRADSCHOOLS.COM
http://www.gradschools.com

GRE
http://www.gre.org

JobWeb's Grad School Links
http://www.jobweb.org/catapult/gguides.htm

Law School Admissions Council
http://www.lsac.org

Peterson's Education Center
http://www.petersons.com/graduate/gsector.html

The Princeton Review
http://www.review.com

Student Affairs Virtual Compass
http://www.studentaffairs.com

U.S. News Online
http://www.usnews.com/usnews/edu

Yahoo's College and University Index
http://www.yahoo.com/Education/Higher_
       Education/Colleges_and_Universities

INTERNSHIP SITES

Action Without Borders
http://www.idealist.org

Career PlanIt
http://www.careerplanit.com

Catapult—Internship sites
http://www.jobweb.org/catapult/jintern.htm

College Grad Job Hunter
http://www.collegegrad.com

Cool Works
http://www.coolworks.com/showme

EmploymentSpot
http://www.employmentspot.com

InternshipPrograms.Com
http://www.internshipprograms.com

JOBTRAK
http://www.jobtrak.com

The National Assembly
http://www.nassembly.org/html/search.html

Online Sports Career Center
http://www.onlinesports.com/pages/
       CareerCenter.html

The Washington Center
http://www.twc.edu

Appendix C

Recommended Printed Resources

Recommended printed resources related to job searching are presented in this appendix. Before purchasing any of these resources, see if your public library or local career center has a copy.

CAREER-RELATED CATALOGS

The printed resources recommended are just a small sampling of the large number of career-related resources out on the market. Call and receive one of the three free catalogs that list and describe hundreds of career-related books, CDs, and videos.

Career Success Catalog
Career Communications Inc.
800-346-1848 (toll-free)
Internet: www.CareerBookstore.com

The Job Search Files
Cambridge Job Search
800-744-0100 (toll-free)
Internet: www.cambridgeol.com

The Whole Work Catalog
The New Careers Center: Resources for Career
   Direction
800-634-9024 (toll-free)
Internet: www.wholework.com

CAREER AND WORKFORCE TRENDS

Cam Report
Priam Publications, Inc., East Lansing, MI
Published twenty times a year
Cost: $70 per year
Phone: 517-351-2557
E-mail: mckinl18@pilot.msu.edu
Fax: 517-351-9054

Career Opportunities News
Ferguson Publishing, Chicago, IL
Published six times a year
Cost: 1-year subscriptions: $40; 2-year: $70;
   3-year: $90
Phone: 800-306-9941 (toll-free)
E-mail: customerservice@fergpubco.com

Fax: 800-306-9942 (toll-free)

Journal of Career Planning and Employment SPOTLIGHT
National Association of Colleges and Employers
   (NACE), Bethlehem, PA
SPOTLIGHT published biweekly
Journal published four times a year
Cost: $72 per year for joint Spotlight/Journal
   subscription
Cost of Spotlight: $2.25 each; Cost of Journal:
   $8.50 each
Cost for Members of NACE: FREE
Phone: 610-868-1421
Internet: www.jobweb.org
Fax: 610-868-0208

Workforce Economics Trends
National Alliance of Business, Washington D.C.
Published six times a year
Cost: NA
Phone: 800-787-2848 (toll-free)
E-mail: info@nab.com
Internet: www.nab.com
Fax: 202-289-2869

BEST CAREERS AND JOBS

Best Jobs For the Future
U.S. News & World Report, Washington D.C.
Published annually
Cost: $3.95

Phone: 202-955-2000
E-mail: letters@usnews.com

Jobs Rated Almanac: The Best and Worst Jobs—250 in All—Ranked by More Than a Dozen Vital Factors Including Salary, Stress, Benefits and More
St. Martins Press
Publication: 1999
Cost: $13.56
Phone: 800-201-7575 (Amazon) (toll-free)

BEST AND BIGGEST COMPANIES

500 Largest U.S. Corporations
Fortune Magazine, New York, NY
Publication: 1997
Cost: $14.95
Phone: 800-634-9024 (The Whole Work Catalog)
    (toll-free)
Fax: 303-447-8684

America's Most Admired Companies
Fortune Magazine, New York, NY
Publication: 2000
Cost: USA: $4.95/CAN: $5.95
Phone: 800-621-8000 (toll-free)
E-mail: subsvcs@fortune.customersvc.com

Top 2,500 Employers: The Largest and Fastest-Growing U.S. Companies
Peterson's, Lawrenceville, NJ
Publication: 1999
Cost: $15.16
Phone: 800-338-3282 (toll-free)

SELF-ASSESSMENT

Many of the self-assessment instruments can be purchased and interpreted only by professional career counselors or by individuals who have been certified. Therefore, you should contact a local career counselor from your state employment service, college career center, guidance counseling office, or independent career consulting organization. Ask them if they have one of the instruments listed or others that may be of interest. Also determine the cost of the instrument and overall session with the career counselor.

The Attentional and Interpersonal Style Inventory (Must be certified)
Developed by Robert M. Nideffer, Ph.D.

Determines where you naturally tend to pay attention and identifies your interpersonal style. This information is used to help determine the types of fields and positions that would provide the best fit.

Campbell Interest and Skill Survey (Must Be Certified)
National Computer Systems (NCS), Minnetonka, MN
Phone: 800-627-7271 (toll-free) (ext. 5151)

Identifies your skills and interests and determines how they relate to occupations.

Myers-Briggs Type Indicator (must be certified)
Consulting Psychologists Press, Inc., Palo Alto, CA
Phone: 800-624-1765 (toll-free)

Identifies your natural tendencies or personal preferences across four scales: Introvert/Extravert, Intuitive/Sensing, Thinking/Feeling, and Judging/Perceiving.

Self-Directed Search (Job seekers are eligible)
Psychological Assessment Resources, Inc., Odessa, FL
Phone: 800-331-TEST (8378) (toll-free)
Internet: www.self-directed-search.com (cost: $8.95 for test on the Web)

A self-scoring instrument that identifies your area of interest and how it relates to occupations, academic majors, and leisure activities.

Purchase the "SDS Specimen Set," which includes:

The Assessment Booklet
The Occupations Finder
The Educational Opportunities Finder
The Leisure Activities Finder

You and Your Career Booklet
Cost: $10.00 plus $7.00 shipping and handling

Strong Interest Inventory (Must Be Certified)
Consulting Psychologists Press, Inc., Palo Alto, CA
Phone: 800-624-1765 (toll-free)
    Determines your interests and how these interests relate to occupations.

EXPLORING CAREERS

Great Jobs Series
VGM Career Horizons, Chicago, IL
Cost: $11.95
Phone: 800-346-1848 (Career Success Catalog)
    (toll-free)
Internet: www.careerbookstore.com
    Great Jobs series includes:
        Great Jobs for Accounting Majors
        Great Jobs for Art Majors
        Great Jobs for Business Majors
        Great Jobs for Communications Majors
        Great Jobs for Computer Science Majors
        Great Jobs for Engineering Majors
        Great Jobs for English Majors
        Great Jobs for Foreign Language Majors
        Great Jobs for History Majors
        Great Jobs for Liberal Arts Majors
        Great Jobs for Music Majors
        Great Jobs for Psychology Majors
        Great Jobs for Sociology Majors
        Great Jobs for Theatre Majors

SALARY INFORMATION

Salary Survey
National Association of Colleges and Employers
    (NACE), Bethlehem, PA
Published four times a year
Cost: $220 per year
Phone: 610-868-1421
Internet: www.jobweb.org
Fax: 610-868-0208

JOB OPENINGS

The Chronicle of Higher Education
The Chronicle of Higher Education Inc.,
    Washington D.C.

Published Weekly
Cost: $75 per year
Phone: 800-728-2803 (toll-free)
Internet: www.chronicle.com
    Provides job advertisements at colleges and universities across the nation and internationally.

RESEARCHING ORGANIZATIONS

Adams Jobs Almanac 2000
Adams Media Corporation, Holbrook, MA
Cost: $16.95
Publication: 1999
Phone: 800/872-5627 (toll-free) (in MA: 781-767-
    8100)
E-mail: jobbank@adamsonline.com
Fax: 781-767-2055
    Provides 7,000 company profiles covering the hot industries. 952 pages.

The Almanac of American Employers 2000–2001
Plunkett Research, Ltd., Houston, TX
Publication: 2000
Cost: $179.99 (includes CD-ROM)
Phone: 713-932-0000
Fax: 713-932-7080
    America's 500 largest, fastest-growing employers. 682 pages.

The JobBank Series
Adams Media Corporation, Holbrook, MA
Cost: $16.95
Phone: 800-872-5627 (toll-free) (in MA: 781-767-
    8100)
E-mail: jobbank@adamsonline.com
Fax: 781-767-2055

   The JobBank Series includes:

      The Atlanta JobBank
         (Covers all of Georgia)
      The Austin/San Antonio JobBank
         (Covers metropolitan Austin, San Antonio, and the rest of southern and western Texas)
      The Boston JobBank
         (Covers all of Massachusetts)

The Carolina JobBank
(Covers all of North and South Carolina)

The Chicago Job Bank
(Covers northern and central Illinois)

The Connecticut JobBank
(Covers all of Connecticut)

The Dallas-Fort Worth JobBank
(Covers metropolitan Dallas-Fort Worth and the Panhandle)

The Denver JobBank
(Covers all of Colorado)

The Detroit JobBank
(Covers all of Michigan)

The Florida JobBank
(Covers all of Florida)

The Houston JobBank
(Covers metropolitan Houston)

The Indiana JobBank
(Covers all of Indiana)

The Las Vegas JobBank
(Covers all of Nevada)

The Los Angeles JobBank
(Covers the southern half of California)

The Minneapolis–St. Paul JobBank
(Covers all of Minnesota)

The Missouri JobBank
(Covers all of Missouri, southern Illinois, and Kansas City, Kansas)

The Northern New England JobBank
(Covers all of Maine, New Hampshire, and Vermont)

The New Jersey JobBank
(Covers all of New Jersey)

The New Mexico JobBank
(Covers all of New Mexico and El Paso, Texas)

The Metropolitan New York JobBank
(Covers metropolitan New York City, northern New Jersey, and southwestern Connecticut)

The Upstate New York JobBank
(Covers all of New York state north of New York City)

The Ohio JobBank
(Covers all of Ohio)

The Greater Philadelphia JobBank
(Covers eastern Pennsylvania, southern New Jersey, and all of Delaware)

The Phoenix JobBank
(Covers all of Arizona)

The Pittsburgh JobBank
(Covers western Pennsylvania)

The Portland, OR JobBank
(Covers all of Oregon)

The Salt Lake City JobBank
(Covers all of Utah)

The San Francisco Bay Area JobBank
(Covers the northern half of California)

The Seattle JobBank
(Covers all of Washington state)

The Tennessee JobBank
(Covers all of Tennessee)

The Virginia JobBank
(Covers all of Virginia and West Virginia)

The Metropolitan Washington DC JobBank
(Covers the District of Columbia, all of Maryland, and northern Virginia)

The Wisconsin JobBank
(Covers all of Wisconsin)

Industries covered include:

Accounting and Management Consulting

Advertising, Marketing, and Public Relations

Aerospace

Apparel, Fashion, and Textiles

Architecture, Construction, and Engineering

Arts, Entertainment, Sports, and Recreation

Automotive

Banking/Savings and Loans

Biotechnology, Pharmaceutical, and Scientific R&D

Charities and Social Services

Chemicals/Rubber and Plastics

Communications: Telecommunications and Broadcasting

Computer Hardware, Software, and Services

Educational Services

Electronic/Industrial Electrical Equipment

Environmental and Waste Management Services

Fabricated/Primary Metals and Products

Financial Services
Food and Beverages/Agriculture
Government
Health Care: Services, Equipment, and
   Products
Hotels and Restaurants
Insurance
Manufacturing
Mining/Gas/Petroleum/Energy Related
Paper and Wood Products
Printing and Publishing
Real Estate
Retail
Stone, Glass, Clay, and Concrete Products
Transportation
Utilities
Miscellaneous Wholesaling and many
   others

Peterson's Job Opportunities Series
Peterson's, Lawrenceville, NJ
Cost: $15.16
Phone: 800-338-3282 (toll-free)

Peterson's Job Opportunities Series includes:
   Job Opportunities for Business Majors
   Job Opportunities for Engineering and
      Computer Science Majors
   Job Opportunities for Health and Science
   Majors

Top 2,500 Employers: The Largest and Fastest-Growing U.S. Companies
Peterson's, Lawrenceville, NJ
Publication: 1999
Cost: $15.16
Phone: 800-338-3282 (toll-free)

EMPLOYMENT SERVICES

Directory of Executive Recruiters 2000
Kennedy Publications, Fitzwilliam, NH
Publication: 1999
Cost: $47.95
Phone: 800-531-1026 (toll-free)

The JobBank Series
Adams Media Corporation, Holbrook, MA
Cost: $16.95
Phone: 800-872-5627 (toll-free) (in MA: 781-767-8100)
E-mail: jobbank@adamsonline.com
Fax: 781-767-2055

National Directory of Personnel Services
National Association of Personnel Services,
   Alexandria, VA
Publication: 1999
Cost: $30.00
Phone: 703-684-0180
Fax: 703-684-0071

INTERNSHIPS

Peterson's Internships 2001
Peterson's, Lawrenceville, NJ
Publication: 2000
Cost: $19.96
Phone: 800-338-3282 (toll-free)

Information Interview Questions

Following is a long list of questions that you can ask during information interviews. If you're using information interviews as a way to explore career fields, these questions will work well. However, if you're information interviewing as a networking and job-search strategy, your questions should be generated from research you've done on the company and field. Remember that the strongest questions to ask are those based on research. The questions below can be used, but they should be tied to prior research. Review Chapter 11 to see samples of questions based on research.

QUESTIONS . . .

About Your Contact

- What is your position title? Are there other titles for similar jobs?
- What are your day-to-day duties and responsibilities?
- How did you get to where you are today? Describe your career path.
- Describe a typical work week. How many hours do you work each week?
- Is there much travel associated with your job?
- What do you like and dislike most about your job?
- Is there flexibility regarding hours you work and where you work (out of the home)?
- What are your biggest challenges in this job?
- Which departments or people do you work most closely with?
- How do you see the results of your job?
- Who do you report to?
- Who do you supervise?
- What is your management style?
- What professional organizations are you active in?
- Given your experience and education, what other careers could you pursue?
- What are your long-term career goals?
- What personal characteristics and skills are most essential to perform this job well?

About the Organization

- Describe the culture of the organization.
- What is your company mission?
- What is your company's vision for the future?
- What are the big projects on the plate today for your company?
- What is the company's philosophy regarding customer service?
- What is the company's philosophy regarding diversity?
- Do most of the employees agree with these philosophies and live out these philosophies daily?
- Who are your competitors?
- How do you differ from your competitors?
- How much flexibility do you have in terms of dress, travel requirements, vacation schedule, place of residence, etc.?
- Does your company/organization offer training programs or internships?

About the Career Field/Occupation

- How did you originally get into this field?
- What is the employment outlook for this type of work—now and in the future?
- What are the opportunities for advancement or job mobility?
- How long does it take to climb the ladder to the top of the field? (from position to position)
- Do you have to change companies to move up in this field?
- What is the typical beginning salary range? Range in five years?

- What are some of the major trends or issues in the field today?
- What are the major challenges in the industry?
- Which organizations are considered to be the best in the field?
- Has there been much downsizing in your field?
- What kind of work schedule does this career require?

Advice and Referrals

- What credentials, degrees, licenses, experience, or training are required for entry into this field?
- What educational preparation do you feel would be best?
- What kinds of experiences do you recommend?

- How well suited is my background for this type of work? As you look at my resume, what tips would you give me?
- What trade or professional associations would you recommend me contacting? Would I be eligible to become a member?
- How does your company notify the public of openings?
- What general advice would you give me regarding pursuing opportunities with your organization and others in the field?
- This has been a great experience for me. I would like to meet with other people in the field to receive additional perspectives. Do you have a friend or colleague in the field who may be willing to talk with me?
- Who else would you recommend I contact for more information about this career?

Action Verbs and Skills for Resumes

absorb
accelerate
accompany
accomplish
accumulate
achieve
acquire
act
activate
adapt
add
address
adjust
administer
advise
aid
allocate
allow
amend
amplify
analyze
answer
apply
appoint
appraise
approve
arbitrate
arrange
ascertain
assemble
assess
assign
assist
attain
attend
audit
augment
authorize
award

balance
bill
bring
broaden

budget
build
buy

calculate
carry
catalog
centralize
chair
change
chart
charter
check
clarify
classify
clean
clear
close
coach
code
collaborate
collate
collect
command
communicate
compare
compile
complete
compose
compute
conceive
conceptualize
condense
conduct
confer
consolidate
construct
consult
contract
control
convert
convey
convince
coordinate

copy
correct
correspond
counsel
count
craft
create
cut

deal with
debate
decide
define
delegate
deliver
demonstrate
deposit
describe
design
detail
detect
determine
develop
devise
devote
diagnose
direct
discover
dismantle
dispatch
dispense
display
distribute
divert
document
draft
draw
drive
duplicate

earn
edit
educate
effect

elect
elicit
eliminate
empathize
employ
encourage
enforce
enlarge
enlist
ensure
enter
entertain
equip
establish
estimate
evaluate
exact
examine
execute
exhibit
expand
expedite
experience
experiment
explain
express
extend
extract

facilitate
feed
figure
file
finalize
finance
find
finish
fire
fix
fold
follow
forecast
formalize
formulate
fortify
foster
found
furnish

gather

generate
give
govern
grade
greet
guarantee
guide

handle
head
help
hire
hypothesize

identify
illustrate
imagine
implement
improve
improvise
increase
index
indicate
influence
inform
initiate
innovate
inspect
install
institute
instruct
insure
integrate
interact
interpret
interview
introduce
invent
inventory
invest
investigate
invoice
issue

judge
justify

keyboard
keep

launch
lead
learn
lecture
license
lift
liquidate
list
listen
load
locate
log
lower

maintain
make
manage
manipulate
market
master
measure
mediate
meet
memorize
mentor
merge
minimize
model
moderate
modernize
modify
mold
monitor
motivate

named
negotiate
nominate
note
notify
number

observe
obtain
offer
officiate
open
operate
order

organize
originate
outline
overcome
overhaul
oversee

package
paint
participate
patrol
pay
perceive
perfect
perform
persevere
persuade
photocopy
photograph
pick
pilot
pinpoint
place
plan
post
prepare
prescribe
present
preserve
preside
price
print
problem solve
process
produce
program
promote
prompt
proofread
propose
prove
provide
publicize
publish
purchase

question

raise

rate
read
realize
rearrange
reason
rebuild
recall
receive
recommend
reconcile
record
recruit
rectify
reduce
refer
refine
register
regulate
reinforce
relate
relay
remember
renew
reorganize
repair
repeat
replace
report
represent
request
research
reserve
respond
restore
restructure
retrieve
revamp
review
revise
route
run

schedule
screen
secure
select
sell
send
separate

serve
service
set up
shape
ship
show
simplify
solicit
solve
sort
speak
staff
standardize
start
stimulate
stock
store
straighten
streamline
strengthen
structure
study
succeed
suggest
summarize
supervise
supply
support
systematize

tabulate
tailor
talk
tally
tape
teach
telephone
tell
tend
terminate
test
total
trace
track
train
transact
transfer
translate
transport

treat	undertake	verify
troubleshoot	unify	
tutor	update	
type	upgrade	weigh
	use	win
umpire	utilize	withstand
uncover		work
understand	verbalize	write

Source: Elon College Career Center

Words That Describe Personal Traits

active
adaptable
adept
analytical
assertive
attentive

broad-minded

competent
conscientious
creative

decisive
dedicated
dependable
determined
diplomatic
disciplined
discreet

efficient
empathetic
energetic
enterprising
enthusiastic
experienced
customer-oriented

fair
firm
flexible
forceful

hardworking
honest

innovative
instrumental
intuitive

logical
loyal

mature
methodical

objective
optimistic
organized
outgoing

passionate
patient
personable
persuasive

pleasant
positive
proactive
problem solver
productive

realistic
reliable
resilient
resourceful

self-confident
self-reliant
sense of humor
sensitive
sincere
spontaneous
stable
successful

tactful
team-oriented
tenacious
thoughtful
tolerant
troubleshooter

zealous

Appendix G

The Most Common Interview Questions

Following are common questions asked in real interviews. The questions are placed within the four big interviewer concerns presented in Chapter 12. Review Chapter 12 to receive inside advice on how to respond to the four underlying concerns and related questions.

SAMPLE QUESTIONS RELATED TO THE INTERVIEWER'S BIG CONCERN 1: DO YOU WANT THE JOB?

Why do you want this job?

What is appealing to you about this opportunity?

Why do you want to work for us?

How did you learn about our company?

What do you know about our organization?

How did you become interested in (your career field)?

Why did you choose to attend ABC College?

Why did you decide to major in XYZ?

Describe your most rewarding college experience.

How do you feel about moving to this area of the country?

How do you see this position being different from your past jobs?

What criteria are you using to evaluate the organization for which you hope to work?

Where do you see yourself in five years?

Are you involved in any trade/professional organizations?

I see from your resume that you were an intern at ABC Corporation. How was that experience?

Which of your past jobs/internships was the least interesting? Why?

Which of your past jobs/internships was the most interesting? Why?

What did you like most and least about your last job?

Why have you worked for so many companies in a short period of time?

Describe the ideal job for you.

In what kind of work environment are you most comfortable?

What two or three things are most important to you in your job?

In what part-time/summer jobs have you been most interested? Why?

Tell me your reasons for leaving past jobs.

What do you hope to be earning in five years?

What goals have you set for the near future?

How do you plan to reach your goals?

How does this job fit in with your goals?

What motivates you to put forth your greatest effort?

SAMPLE QUESTIONS RELATED TO THE INTERVIEWER'S BIG CONCERN 2: CAN YOU DO THE JOB?

What are your greatest strengths and weaknesses?

How can you contribute to our organization?

What in your employment history will help you if you were employed with us?

What makes you the best candidate for this position?

Why should I hire you?

Tell me a little bit about yourself.

How do you determine success?

Tell me how a friend or someone who knows you well describes you?

How well do you work under pressure?

If I were to talk to your former boss, what would she say about you?

If I were to talk to someone you supervised, what kind of a boss would they say you are?

I see from your resume that you worked at XYZ Company. What were your key responsibilities there?

What has been your greatest professional accomplishment?

What are some of the things you find difficult to do? Why?

How has your experience at ABC Organization helped you in this position?

What parts of this position do you anticipate being most challenging?

On your previous evaluation, what criticism did your supervisor offer about you?

What skills or qualities do you think are important to have in this position?

How would your education/training benefit you in this position?

What goals have you set for the near future?

How do you plan to reach your goals?

Do you have plans for continued study?

SAMPLE QUESTIONS RELATED TO THE INTERVIEWER'S BIG CONCERN 3: WILL YOU FIT IN?

How would someone who knows you well describe you?

How would you describe your personality?

Tell me about a conflict you previously had with another person and how you dealt with that conflict?

If you disagreed with something your supervisor asked you to do, what would you do?

How would you describe your supervisor's management style?

If I were to talk to your supervisor, what would she say about you?

Have you ever worked in a group? In what capacity?

What are the important factors for working well as a team?

Did you ever have to motivate or encourage someone to do something they didn't want to do? How did you do it?

Would you rather work alone on a task or in a group?

How do you deal with office politics and gossip?

When an issue is raised during a staff meeting, do you tend to jump right in and offer your opinion or sit back and think it through before you talk?

On your previous evaluation, what criticism did your supervisor offer about you? Was it a fair criticism?

If you could change something about your past company, what would it be?

What is your definition of diversity?

What type of work atmosphere do you prefer?

What kinds of people do you dislike the most?

What is your management philosophy?

Describe what tactful confrontation means.

How important is a sense of humor at work?

What do you like to do in your spare time?

What extracurricular activities did you participate in during college?

Tell me a little bit about yourself.

Who do you admire most and why?

Describe your philosophy of life.

A co-worker comes in your office, closes the door, and begins to talk negatively about someone else that works here. What would you do?

What is the most difficult situation you've faced? Why?

How do you handle pressure?

What have you learned from your mistakes?

What is the most important thing our organization can do to help you achieve your objectives?

Do you tend to speak to people before they speak to you?

What was the last book you read or movie you saw? What has been your favorite book or movie over the past year?

SAMPLE QUESTIONS RELATED TO THE INTERVIEWER'S BIG CONCERN 4: ARE YOU SELF-RELIANT?

What is your approach to handling problems?

A client calls you with a question, and you don't have the answer. What do you do?

What is your approach to time management?

If you disagreed with a co-worker on how to handle a client's concern, what would you do?

If you disagreed with something your boss told you to do, what would you do?

Describe a time when you demonstrated persistence.

Describe a recent decision you made.

What have you learned from your past jobs or experiences?

When conflicts with co-workers arise, do you confront them head on or wait it out and let it pass?

How important is self-confidence in being successful?

What have you learned from your mistakes?

How well do you work under pressure?

Do you consider yourself to be a risk taker?

Do you tend to doubt yourself or believe in yourself? Share an example.

Do you tend to embrace change or avoid it?

How do you handle stress?

I see on your resume that you have X, Y, and Z computer skills. How did you learn these applications?

Do you have plans for continued study?

How important is it to set goals? What are your goals?

What is the most difficult situation you've faced? Why?

Describe a time where you showed initiative.

Who is the most analytical person you know and why?

What are some of the things you find difficult to do? Why?

What would you do if you had a decision to make and no procedures existed?

How do you organize and plan for major projects?

NOTES

NOTES

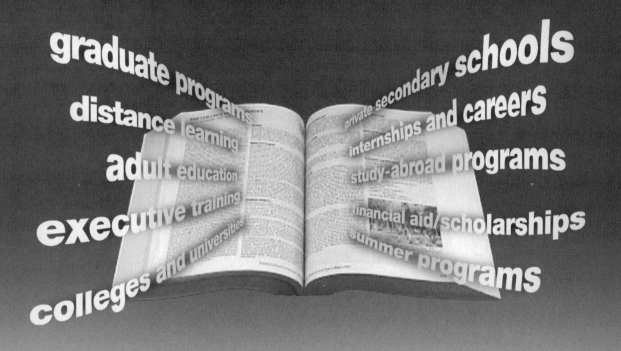